ARABIAN NIGHTS: A SELECTION

TRANSLATED BY SIR RICHARD F. BURTON
ADAPTED BY JACK ZIPES

SIR RICHARD BURTON (1821–90). A flamboyant, multi-faceted character, who was well known as an explorer, swordsman, anthropologist and linguist.

Richard Francis Burton, born in 1821, was educated at Oxford University, but left without taking his degree. In 1842 he joined the Indian army. After leaving India in 1849, he travelled to many destinations, including Mecca, which he visited in disguise; Africa; the Crimea; and Salt Lake City, where he made a study of the Mormons. As a consul he went to Brazil, Damascus (from 1869 to 1871) and Trieste, which is where he died. His extensive writings include over forty volumes of travel, several of folklore and two of poetry, as well as translations from Latin and Portuguese. Sir Richard spoke twenty-five languages and numerous dialects, and is probably best remembered for his versions of Arabian erotic works such as *Arabian Nights* (1885–8), *The Kama Sutra* (1883) and *The Perfumed Garden* (1886; from the French). His frank, detailed and highly valuable notes, combined with his fascination with sexual behaviour and deviance, make his translations both important and readable, but led him to risk prosecution many times under the Obscene Publications Act of 1857, which meant he had often to publish privately. On his death in 1890 his wife, Isabel, destroyed his papers and diaries, including one of his most ambitious projects, a translation of *The Perfumed Garden* from the original Arabic.

Arabian Nights is a wonderful medley of magical tales narrated by the beautiful young Scheherazade, who is telling them to save her own life. Introduced to the West in 1704, these stories remain as fresh, amusing, exotic and enchanting as when they first appeared.

PENGUIN POPULAR CLASSICS

ARABIAN NIGHTS: A SELECTION

TRANSLATED BY
SIR RICHARD F. BURTON
ADAPTED BY
JACK ZIPES

PENGUIN BOOKS

PENGUIN BOOKS

Published by the Penguin Group
Penguin Books Ltd, 27 Wrights Lane, London w8 5tz, England
Penguin Putnam Inc., 375 Hudson Street, New York, New York 10014, USA
Penguin Books Australia Ltd, Ringwood, Victoria, Australia
Penguin Books Canada Ltd, 10 Alcorn Avenue, Toronto, Ontario, Canada m4v 3b2
Penguin Books (NZ) Ltd, Private Bag 102902, NSMC, Auckland, New Zealand

Penguin Books Ltd, Registered Offices: Harmondsworth, Middlesex, England

Published in Penguin Popular Classics 1997
3

Printed in Great Britain by Cox & Wyman Ltd, Reading, Berkshire

Contents

Prologue

In the name of Allah, the Compassionate, who bestows His mercy on all! Praise be to Allah, the Beneficent King, the Creator of the Universe, Lord of the Three Worlds, and grace and blessing be upon Our Lord Mohammed, Prince of the Apostles!

Verily the works and words of our ancestors have become signs and examples to people of our modern age so that they may view what happened to other folk and take heed; so that they may peruse the annals of ancient peoples and read about everything they have experienced and thereby be guided and restrained.

Praise, therefore, be to Him, who has made the histories of the past an admonition for our own time! Their legacy has been passed on to us in the tales called "The Arabian Nights," together with their renowned legends and wonders.

And among these tales, thanks to the Omniscient and Almighty Allah, we have been given

The Story of King Shahryar and His Brother

A long time ago there was a mighty king of the Banu Sasan in the lands of India and China, and when he died, he left only two sons, one in the prime of manhood and the other still a youth, both brave cavaliers. But the elder was an especially superb horseman, and he became the successor to the empire and ruled the kingdom with such justice that he was beloved by all the people of his realm. His name was Shahryar, and he appointed his younger brother, Shah Zaman, king of Samarcan. In the years that followed, each brother was content to remain in his own kingdom, and each ruled with such equity and fairness that their subjects were extremely happy. Everything continued like this for twenty years, but at the end of that time, Shahryar yearned to see his younger brother once more before he died.

So he asked his vizier whether he thought it would be a good idea to visit his brother, but the minister found such an undertaking inadvisable and recommended that he write his brother a letter of invitation and send him gifts under the vizier's charge. Therefore, the king immediately ordered generous gifts to be prepared, such as horses that had saddles lined with gold and jewels, mamelukes, beautiful maidens, high-breasted virgins, and splendid and expensive cloth. He then wrote a letter to Shah Zaman expressing his strong desire to see him, and he ended it with these words: "I, therefore, hope that my beloved brother will honor me with his visit, and I am sending my vizier to make arrangements for the journey. My one and only desire is to see you before I die. If you refuse my request, I shall not survive the blow. May peace be with you!" Then King Shahryar sealed the letter, gave it to the vizier, and urged him to do his utmost to return as soon as possible.

"Your wish is my command," said the vizier, who began making all the preparations without delay. All this work occupied him three days, and on the dawn of the fourth he took leave of his king and journeyed over hills, deserts, and pleasant valleys without stopping night or day. Of course, whenever he entered a realm whose lord was under the rule of King Shahryar, he would be greeted with magnificent gifts and all kinds of fair and rare presents, and he would be obliged to stay there for three days, the customary term for the ritual to honor guests. And when he left on the fourth, he would be honorably escorted for one whole day to speed him on his way.

As soon as the vizier drew near Shah Zaman's court in Samarcan, he sent one of his high officials ahead to announce his arrival. This courier presented himself before the king, kissed the ground, and delivered his message. Thereupon, the king commanded various nobles and lords of his realm to go forth and meet his brother's vizier a good day's journey from his court. After they encountered him, they greeted him respectfully and formed an escort party. When the vizier entered the city, he proceeded straight to the palace, where he kissed the ground and prayed for the king's health and happiness and for victory over his enemies. Then he informed the king that his brother was yearning to see him and presented the letter, which Shah Zaman took from his hand and read. When the king fully comprehended its import, he said, "I cannot refuse the wishes of my brother. However, we shall not depart until we have honored my brother's vizier with three days of hospitality."

Shah Zaman assigned suitable quarters in the palace for the minister, and he ordered tents pitched for the troops and gave them rations of meat, drink, and other necessities. On the fourth day he prepared himself for the trip, gathered together sumptuous presents befitting his elder brother's majesty, and appointed his chief vizier to be viceroy of the land during his absence. Then he ordered his tents, camels, and mules to be brought forth, and he set up camp with their bales and loads, attendants and guards within sight of the city in order to set out early the next morning for his brother's capital.

It so happened, however, that in the middle of the night he suddenly remembered he had forgotten a gift in his palace that he wanted to take to his brother. So he returned alone and entered his private chambers, where he found the queen, his wife, asleep on his own couch, and in her arms she held a black cook with crude features, smeared with kitchen grease and grime. When he saw this, the world turned dark before his eyes, and he said, "If this is what happens while I am still within sight of the city, what will this damned whore do during my long absence at my brother's court?"

So he drew his scimitar, cut the two in four pieces with a single blow, and left them on the couch. Soon thereafter he returned to his camp without letting anyone know what had happened. Then he gave orders for immediate departure and set out on his trip. Nevertheless, he could not help thinking about his wife's betrayal, and he kept saying to himself over and over, "How could she have done this to me? How could she have brought about her own death?" until excessive grief seized him. His color changed to yellow, his body grew weak, and he appeared to be on the verge of death. So the vizier had to shorten the stages of the journey and remain longer at the watering places in order to take care of the king.

Now, when Shah Zaman finally approached his brother's capital, he sent messengers to announce his arrival, and Shahryar came forth to meet him with the viziers, emirs, lords, and nobles of his realm. After saluting him, he was overcome with joy and ordered the city to be decorated in his honor. At the same time, however, Shahryar could not help but see how poor his brother's health was, and he asked him what had happened.

"It's due to the long, hard journey," replied Shah Zaman, "and I'll need some care, for I've suffered from the change of water and air. But Allah be praised for reuniting me with my beloved brother!"

Then the two entered the capital in all honor, and Shahryar lodged his brother in his palace overlooking the garden. After some time had passed, King Shahryar noticed that his brother's condition was still unchanged, and he attributed it to his separation from his country. So he

let him do as he pleased and asked him no questions until
one day when he said, "My brother, I can't help noticing
that you've grown weaker and paler than you were before."

"I'm sick in my heart," he replied, but he would not
tell Shahryar about his wife and all that he had seen.

Thereupon Shahryar summoned doctors and surgeons
and asked them to treat his brother to the best of their
ability, which they did for a whole month, but their
potions had no effect, for he dwelled upon his wife's
treachery. Indeed, he became more and more despon-
dent, and even the use of leeches failed to change his
mood.

One day his elder brother said to him, "I've decided to
go on a hunting expedition. Perhaps you'd feel better if
you joined me."

However, Shah Zaman declined and said, "I am not in
the mood for anything like this, and I beseech you to let
me stay quietly in the palace, for I can't seem to get over
this sickness."

So, King Shah Zaman spent the night in the palace by
himself. The next morning, after his brother had departed, he left his room and sat down at one of the lattice
windows overlooking the garden. There he rested awhile
and became steeped in sad thoughts about his wife's
betrayal, occasionally uttering sighs of grief. Now, as he
was moaning and torturing himself, a secret door to the
garden swung open, and out came twenty slave girls
surrounding his brother's wife, who was marvelously beautiful and moved about with the grace of a gazelle in
search of a cool stream. Shah Zaman drew back from
the window, but he kept the group in sight from a place
where they could not spot him, even though they walked
under the very window where he had stationed himself.
As they advanced into the garden, they came to a jetting
fountain amidst a great basin of water. Then they stripped
off their clothes, and Shah Zaman suddenly realized that
ten of them were women, concubines of the king, and the
other ten were white slaves. After they had all paired off,
the queen was left alone, but she soon cried out in a loud
voice, "Come to me right now, my lord Saeed!" and all
of a sudden a big slobbering blackamoor with rolling eyes
leapt from one of the trees. It was truly a hideous sight.
He rushed up to her and threw his arms around her neck,

while she embraced him just as warmly. Then he mounted her, and winding his legs around hers, as a button loop clasps a button, he tossed her to the ground and enjoyed her. The other slaves did the same with the girls until they had all satisfied their passions, and they did not stop kissing, coupling, and carousing until the day began to wane. When the mamelukes rose from the bosoms of the maidens and the blackamoor slave let go of the queen, the men resumed their disguises, and all except the Negro, who climbed up the tree, left the garden via the secret door and reentered the palace.

Now, after Shah Zaman had witnessed this spectacle, he said to himself, "By Allah, my misfortune is nothing compared to my brother's! Though he may be a greater king among kings than I am, he doesn't even realize that this kind of perfidious behavior is going on in his very own palace, and his wife is in love with the filthiest of filthy slaves. This only proves that all women will make cuckolds out of their husbands when given the chance. Well, then, let the curse of Allah fall upon one and all and upon the fools who need the support of their wives or who place the reins of conduct in their hands!" So, he cast aside his melancholy and no longer had regrets about what he had done. Moreover, he constantly repeated his words to himself to minimize his sorrow and added, "No man in this world is safe from the malice of women!"

When suppertime arrived, the servants brought him the trays, and he ate with a voracious appetite, for he had refrained from eating a long time, no matter how delicious the food. Now he was able once again to give grateful thanks to Almighty Allah for the meal and for restoring his appetite, and he spent a most restful night, savoring the sweet food of sleep. The next day he ate his breakfast with a hearty appetite and began to regain his health and strength and was in excellent condition by the time his brother came back from the hunt ten days later. When Shah Zaman rode out to meet him, King Shahryar looked at him and was astonished by the remarkable change in his brother's appearance, but Shah Zaman did not say or disclose a thing to him. Instead, the two just embraced, exchanged greetings, and rode into the city.

Later when they were seated at their ease in the palace, the servants brought them food, and they ate to their heart's content. After the meal was removed and they had washed their hands, King Shahryar turned to his brother and said, "I am astonished by the change in your condition. I had hoped to take you with me on the hunt, but I realized that your mind was sorely troubled by something, and you looked so pale and sickly. But now— glory be to God!—your natural color has returned to your face, and you're in fine shape. I had believed that your sickness was due to the separation from your family, friends, and country, so I had refrained from bothering you with probing questions. But now I beseech you to explain the cause of your troubles and the reason for your recovery to such good health."

When Shah Zaman heard this, he bowed his head toward the ground, and after a while he raised it and said, "I shall tell you what caused my troubles and bad health, but you must pardon me if I don't tell you the reason for my complete recovery. Indeed, I beg you not to force me to explain everything that has happened."

Shahryar was much surprised by these words and replied, "Let me hear first what caused you to become so sick and pale."

"Well then," began Shah Zaman, "it was like this. When you sent the vizier with your invitation, I made all sorts of preparations for three days and camped before my city to begin the journey early the next day. But that night I remembered that I had left a string of jewels in the palace that I intended to give to you as a gift. I returned for it alone and found my wife on my couch in the arms of a hideous black cook. So I slew the two and came to you. However, I could not help grieving about this affair and regretting what I had done. That's why I lost my health and became weak. But you must excuse me if I refuse to tell you how I managed to regain my health."

Shahryar shook his head, completely astonished, and with the fire of wrath flaming in his heart, he cried, "Indeed, the malice of woman is mighty! My brother, you've escaped many an evil deed by putting your wife to death, and your rage and grief are quite understandable and excusable, especially since you had never suffered anything as terrible as this before. By Allah, had this been me, I would not have been satisfied until I had slain a thousand women and had gone mad! But praise be to Allah, who has eased your tribulations, and now you must tell me how you regained your health so suddenly, and you must explain to me why you are being so secretive."

"Oh brother, again I beg you to excuse me for refusing to talk about this!"

"But I insist."

"I'm afraid that my story may cause you more anger and sorrow than I myself have suffered."

"That's even a better reason for telling me the whole story," said Shahryar, "and in the name of Allah, I command you not to keep anything back from me!"

Thereupon Shah Zaman told him all he had seen from beginning to end, and he concluded his story by saying, "When I saw your misfortune, and your wife's betrayal, my own sorrow seemed slight in comparison, and I became sober and sound again. So, discarding melancholy and despondency, I was able to eat, drink, and sleep, and thus I quickly regained my health and strength. This is the truth and the whole truth."

After King Shahryar heard this tale, he became so furious that it seemed his rage might consume him. However, he quickly recovered his composure and said, "My brother, I don't mean to imply that you have lied to me, but I can't believe your story until I see everything with my own eyes."

"If you want to witness your misfortune," Shah Zaman responded, "rise at once and get ready for another hunting expedition. Then hide yourself with me, and you'll see everything with your own eyes and learn the truth."

"Good," said the king, whereupon he made it known that he was about to travel again, and the troops set up camp outside the city. Shahryar departed with them, and after commanding his slaves not to allow anyone to enter his tent, he summoned his vizier and said, "I want you to sit in my place, and let no one know of my absence until three days have passed."

Then the brothers disguised themselves and returned secretly to the palace, where they spent the rest of the night. At dawn they seated themselves at the window overlooking the garden, and soon the queen and the slaves came out as before and headed for the fountain.

There they stripped, ten men to ten women, and the king's wife cried out, "Where are you, oh Saeed?"

The hideous blackamoor dropped from the tree right away, and rushing into her arms without delay, he exclaimed, "I am Sa'ad al-Din Saood, the auspicious one!"

The lady laughed heartily, and they all began to satisfy their lust and continued to do so for a couple of hours. Then the white slaves rose from the maidens, and the blackamoor left the queen, and they went into the basin. After bathing themselves, they donned their robes and departed as they had done before.

When King Shahryar saw the perfidious behavior of his wife and concubines, he became distraught and cried out, "Only in utter solitude can man be safe from what goes on in this vile world! By Allah, life is nothing but one great wrong! Listen to what I propose, brother, and don't stop me."

"I won't," Shah Zaman responded.

So the king continued, "Let us get up just as we are and depart right away. There are other things more important than our kingdoms. Let us wander over Allah's earth, worshiping the Almighty, until we find someone who has suffered the same misfortune. And if it should turn out that we don't find anyone, then death will be more welcome to us than life."

So the two brothers left through a second secret door to the palace, and they journeyed day and night until they came to a large tree in the middle of a meadow right near a spring of fresh water not far from the seashore. Both drank from the spring and sat down to rest. After an hour had passed, they suddenly heard a mighty roar as though the heavens were falling upon the earth. The sea broke with tidal waves, and a towering black pillar arose from it. Indeed, the pillar of smoke grew and grew until it almost touched the sky. Then it began heading toward the meadow, and the two brothers became very frightened and climbed to the top of the tree, from where they hoped to see what the matter was.

To their amazement, the smoke turned into a jinnee, huge, broad-chested, and burly. His brow was wide, his skin black, and on his head was a crystal chest. He strode to the shore, wading through deep water, and came to the tree in which the two kings were hiding, and sat down beneath it. He then set the chest on its bottom and pulled from it a casket with seven padlocks of steel, which he unlocked with seven keys of steel hanging beside his thigh. Suddenly a young lady appeared from the casket, white-skinned and pleasant, fine and thin, and bright as the full moon or the glistening sun. Taking her by the hand, the jinnee seated her under the tree by his side and gazed at her.

"Oh choicest love of this heart of mine!" he began. "Oh lady of noblest line, whom I snatched away on your wedding night and whom none has loved or enjoyed except myself. Oh, my sweetheart, I must sleep a little while."

He then laid his head upon the lady's thighs, and stretching out his legs, which extended down to the sea, he fell asleep and snored like thunder. Soon the lady raised her head and noticed the two kings perched near the top of the tree. Then she softly lifted the jinnee's head off her lap and placed it upon the ground. Afterwards she stood up and signaled to the kings, "Come down, you two. You have nothing to fear from this ifrit."

They were terribly scared when they realized that she had seen them and answered her in whispers, "By Allah and by your modesty, oh lady, excuse us from coming down!"

"Allah upon you both," she replied, "I want you to come down right away, and if you don't come, I shall wake this jinnee, who will attack you, and you'll die the worst death imaginable!" And she continued making signs to them to come.

So, being afraid, they came down to her, and she rose before them and said, "I want you to mount me and show me how nicely you can sit on my saddle, or else I'll set this ifrit upon you, and he'll slay you in the wink of an eye!"

"Oh lady," they said to her, "we beseech you, by Allah, don't force us to do this. We've given up such things and are in extreme dread of your husband!"

"No more talk. This is the way it must be," she said and swore to them by Him who raised the skies on high without prop or pillar that they would be slain and cast into the sea if they did not perform her will. Consequently, out of fear, King Shahryar said to King Shah Zaman, "Brother, do what she wants you to do."

But Zaman responded, "I won't do anything until you do it first."

And they began quarreling about who was to mount her.

"Why are you two quarreling?" she intervened. "If you do not come forward like men and do the deed I ask you to perform, I'll wake the jinnee!"

Given their fear of the jinnee, they finally did what she asked them to do, one after the other, and after they had dismounted, she said, "Well done!" Next, she took a purse from her pocket and drew out a knotted strand of five hundred and seventy rings and asked, "Do you know what these are?"

"No," they answered.

"These are the signets of five hundred and seventy men," she said, "who have futtered me on the horns of this filthy, stupid ifrit. So, brothers, I also want your royal rings."

After they had taken off their rings and given them to her, she said, "It's true that this jinnee carried me off on my wedding night, put me into a casket, and placed the casket in a chest. After he attached seven strong padlocks to it, he deposited it at the bottom of the deep sea and guarded me so that I would remain chaste and honest, and so that none but himself could have any contact with me. But I have lain under as many men as I've desired, and this wretched jinnee doesn't realize that destiny cannot be averted or hindered by anything and that whatever a woman wants, she will get, no matter how much a man might try to prevent it."

Upon hearing her story, the brothers were left speechless and watched her as she went back to the ifrit, put his head on her lap, and told them softly, "Now get on your way, and put the sight of this malice way behind you!"

So they moved on and said to each other, "May Allah help us and save us from women's malice and cunning! It seems nothing can surpass their power!"

"Just think," said King Shahryar, "how this marvelous lady has managed to deceive a jinnee, who is much more powerful than we are! Indeed, his misfortune is much greater than ours, so it is time to return to our kingdoms.

But I propose that we both never stay married long enough for women to betray us and that we take the proper action to put them in their place!"

Shah Zaman agreed, and they rode back to King Shahryar's encampment, which they reached on the morning of the third day, and after gathering together his viziers, emirs, chamberlains, and high officials, Shahryar gave a robe of honor to his viceroy and issued orders for an immediate return to the city. As soon as he took his seat upon his throne, he sent for his chief minister and declared, "I command you to take my wife and execute her, for she has broken her marriage vows."

So, the minister brought her to the place of execution and carried out the king's orders. Then King Shahryar took his sword in hand and went to the seraglio, where he slew all the concubines and their mamelukes. He also swore a binding oath that whenever he married, he would take his new wife's maidenhead at night and slay her the next morning to make sure of his honor, for he was convinced that there never was or could be one chaste woman upon the face of this earth.

Soon after Shahryar took this oath, his brother, Shah Zaman, asked permission to return home, and he was provided an escort that accompanied him until he reached his own country. Meanwhile Shahryar commanded his vizier to bring him a bride for that night so that he might enjoy her. Accordingly, the vizier produced a most beautiful girl, the daughter of one of the emirs, and the king broke her maidenhead in the evening, and when morning arrived, he commanded his minister to strike off her head. And the vizier did as he was ordered for fear of the sultan. During the next three years the king continued to act accordingly: he married a maiden every night and had her killed the next morning, until his people raised a great outcry against him. Indeed, they cursed him and prayed to Allah that he be utterly destroyed and dethroned. Women began protesting, mothers wept, and parents fled with their daughters until there was not one virgin left in the city.

Nevertheless, the king ordered his chief vizier, the same man who was charged with carrying out the executions, to bring him a virgin as was his wont. When the minister went forth, however, and searched all over, he returned home in sorrow, fearing for his life because the king would be displeased that there were no more virgins left in the city. Now, he had two daughters, Scheherazade and Dunazade. The older one, Scheherazade, had read the books, annals, and legends of former kings, and the stories, lessons, and adventures of famous men. Indeed, it was said that she had collected a thousand history books about ancient peoples and rulers. She had perused the works of the poets and knew them by heart. She had studied philosophy and the sciences, arts, and practical things. And she was pleasant and polite, wise and witty, well read and well bred. Consequently, on that particular day, she said to her father, "Why are you so downcast? You seem to be troubled by something. Remember the words of the poet:

> *"Tell whoever has sorrow*
> *Grief shall never last.*
> *Just as joy has no tomorrow,*
> *Woe is bound not to last."*

When the vizier heard these words from his daughter, he told her from first to last about everything that had happened between him and the king. Thereupon, she said, "By Allah, oh my father, how long shall this slaughter of women last? Shall I tell you what I'm thinking about that would stop all this destruction?"

"Tell me, my daughter," he said.

"I would like you to give me in marriage to King Shahryar. If I should live, I'd become the ransom for the virgin daughters of Moslems and rescue them from his hands and yours."

"Oh Allah!" he cried in his fury. "Have you lost your mind? I won't let you expose yourself to such danger. How can you be so unwise and foolish? I want you to know that unless you have experience in worldly matters, you'll be prey to misfortune!"

"I must do this," she responded. "Come what may!"

Again the vizier became enraged and scolded and reproached her. "In truth, I fear that the same thing that happened to the ox and the donkey will happen to you."

"And just what did happen to them, Father?" she asked.

Whereupon the vizier began.

The Tale of the Ox and the Donkey

There was once a merchant who owned a great deal of money and men, and who had a large number of cattle and camels. He also had a wife and family and dwelt in the country, since he knew a great deal about farming and agriculture. Now Allah Almighty had endowed him with the ability to understand the language of birds and beasts of every kind. However, it was decreed that if he were to divulge the gift to anyone, he would be punished by death. So, out of fear, he kept his unusual gift a secret.

In his barn he had an ox and donkey, each tethered in his own stall next to one another. One day, when the merchant was sitting nearby with his servants and children playing around him, he heard the ox say to the ass, "Greetings, friend. I hope that you continue to enjoy your rest and good care. Everything under you is swept neatly and watered down. Men wait on you and feed you sifted barley, and give you pure spring water to drink. On the other hand, I (unhappy creature!) am led forth in the middle of the night when they set the plow and something called a yoke on my neck. I'm exhausted from cleaving the earth from dawn till dusk. I'm forced to do more than I can and to bear all kinds of mistreatment every night. And at the end of my work they take me back with my sides torn, my neck flayed, my legs aching, and my eyelids sore with tears. Then they shut me up in the barn and throw me beans and hay mixed with dirt and chaff. And I lie in dung and filth, and there is nothing but a foul stench throughout the night. But you are always in a clean place and are always able to relax, except when the master has some business in town, and that's very seldom. Then he just mounts you and rides to the town and returns right away. This is the way things are: I toil and have no rest, while you relax and have leisure time. You sleep while I am sleepless. I starve while you have all you want to eat."

When the ox stopped speaking, the donkey turned toward him and said, "Oh you lost soul! Whoever dubbed you bull-head did not lie, for you are denser than the simplest of simpletons! With all your zeal you foolishly toil for the master, and wear yourself out and kill yourself for the comfort of someone else. At the call of dawn you set out to work and don't return until sundown, and throughout the livelong day you endure all kinds of hardships such as beatings and cursing. Now listen to me, carefully. When you go into the fields and they lay that thing called the yoke on your neck, lie down and don't get up again, even though they hit you with the switch. And if you do have to rise, lie down a second time. And when they bring you home and offer you beans, fall backward and only sniff your food. Don't taste it. Withdraw and content yourself only with the hay and chaff. Pretend you are sick, and continue to do this for two or three days. This way you'll be able to gain some rest from all your hard work."

When the ox heard these words, he knew that the donkey was his friend and thanked him. "This is good advice," he said, and prayed that the ass would be blessed with a fine reward.

The next day, the driver took the ox, set the plow on his neck, and made him work as usual. But the ox took the donkey's advice and shirked the plowing. Consequently, the plowman drubbed him until the ox broke the yoke and made off. But the man caught up to him and tanned him until he thought he would die. Nevertheless, he did nothing but stand still and drop down until evening came. Then the plowman led him home and put him into his stall, but the ox drew back from his manger and neither stamped, nor butted, nor bellowed as he was accustomed to do. Such strange behavior puzzled the plowman. Then he brought the ox beans and husks, but the animal sniffed at them and lay down as far from them as he could and spent the whole night fasting. Next morning the plowman came and saw the manger full of beans, the hay untasted, and the ox lying on his back in a most sorry plight with his legs outstretched and a swollen belly. Of course, he was very worried about him and said to himself, "By Allah, he has certainly become sick, and this is why he wouldn't plow yesterday." Then he went to the merchant and reported, "Master, the ox is sick. He refused his fodder last night, and he hasn't tasted a scrap of it this morning."

Now the merchant understood what all this meant, because he had overheard the talk between the ox and the ass. So he said, "Take that rascal donkey, and set the yoke on his neck. Tie him to the plow and make him do the ox's work."

Accordingly, the plowman took the ass and made him do the ox's work the entire day long. And when the donkey let up out of weakness, the driver made him feel his stick until the animal's ribs were sore and his sides were sunken and his neck flayed by the yoke. When the ass returned home in the evening, he could hardly drag his limbs along. Meanwhile, the ox had spent the day lying at full length and had eaten his fodder with an excellent appetite. He continually heaped blessings on the donkey for his good advice, not knowing how the donkey had suffered and that it was on his account. So, when night set in and the donkey returned to the barn, the ox rose up before him in his honor and said, "May good tidings warm your heart, my friend! Because of you I have rested the entire day, and I have eaten my food in peace and quiet."

But the ass did not reply, because his heart was burning with rage, and he was exhausted from the beating he had gotten. Indeed, he regretted that he had given the ox such good advice and said to himself, "This is the result of your folly in giving good counsel. I was living in joy and happiness until I mixed into somebody else's business. So now I must think of something and trick the ox so that he'll return to his place. Otherwise, I'll die." Then he went wearily to his stall, while the ox continued to thank and bless him.

"And the same thing will happen to you, my daughter," said the vizier. "You will die for not having used your brains. Therefore, I want you to sit still, say nothing, and refrain from exposing yourself to danger. By Allah, I'm offering you the best advice that comes from my affection and great concern for you."

"Father," she answered. "I must marry the king, and you can't stop me."

"I don't want you to do this."

"But I must."

"If you're not silent and do as I say, I'll do to you just what the farmer did to his wife."

"And what did he do?" Scheherazade asked.

After the donkey returned to his stall, the farmer went out on the terrace of his house with his wife and family, for there was a full moon. Now the terrace overlooked the barn, and as the merchant was sitting there with his children playing around him, he soon heard the donkey say to the ox, "Tell me, friend, what do you propose to do tomorrow?"

"To continue to follow your advice, of course," said the ox. "Indeed, it was as good as it could be, and it has given me a good deal of rest. So when they bring me my food, I'll refuse it, blow up my belly, and pretend to be sick."

The ass shook his head and said, "You'd better not do this."

"Why?" the ox asked.

And the donkey answered, "I must warn you that I heard the merchant say to the plowman, 'If the ox doesn't get up from his place to do his work this morning and doesn't eat his fodder today, take him over to the butcher to be slaughtered. Then give his flesh to the poor and make some leather out of his hide.' You see now why I'm afraid for your life. So, take my advice before something terrible happens to you: when they bring you your fodder, eat it. Then get up, bellow, and paw the ground, or else our master will surely have you slain. May peace be with you!"

Thereupon the ox arose, bellowed aloud, and thanked the ass. "Tomorrow, I'll certainly go out into the fields with them," he said, and he ate up all his food and even licked his manger. (All this took place while the merchant was listening to their talk.)

Next morning the merchant and his wife went to the ox's stall and sat down, and the driver came and led the ox out. Upon seeing his owner, the beast whisked his tail, broke wind, and frisked about so merrily that the merchant laughed loudly and kept laughing until he fell over on his back.

"Why are you laughing like this so much?" his wife asked.

"I laughed at a secret, something that I heard and saw, but I can't reveal it to you. If I do, I'll die."

"Well, I insist!" replied his wife. "Tell me why you laughed so loudly and what your secret is! I don't care if you have to die."

"It has something to do with the language of birds and beasts, but I'm forbidden to tell it to you."

"By Allah, you're lying!" she exclaimed. "This is a mere pretext. You were laughing at nobody except me, and now you want to hide something from me. But, by the Lord of the Heavens, if you don't tell me the cause, I won't sleep with you anymore. I'll leave you at once!" And she sat down and cried.

"Why are you weeping?" the merchant responded. "Stop all this jabbering and crying!"

"Tell me why you laughed!"

"Listen, I'm telling you the truth. When Allah granted me the gift of understanding the language of the birds and beasts, I made a vow never to disclose the secret under pain of death."

"No matter," cried she. "Tell me what the ox and donkey were saying, and if you have to die, you have to die."

And she did not stop nagging him until he was worn out and totally distraught. So at last he said, "Summon your father and mother, our kith and kin, and some of our neighbors."

While she went about doing this, he sent for the lawyers and assessors, intending to make his will, reveal his secret to her, and die under the penalty of death, since his love for her was immense. She was his cousin, the daughter of his father's brother, and the mother of his children, and he had lived with her for a hundred and twenty years.

Now, after all the members of the family and the neighbors had gathered, the farmer said to them, "Something strange happened to me some time ago, but if I reveal my secret story to anyone, I am bound to die."

As a result of his remarks, everyone present began

saying to the woman, "May Allah be with you, stop being so shamefully obstinate and realize what the consequences are. Otherwise, your husband and father of your children will die."

"I refuse to change my mind until he tells me his secret," she replied, "even though he may have to die."

So they stopped trying to persuade her, and the farmer got up and withdrew to a small chicken house in order to be by himself and pray before his death. Afterward he was going to return to them, tell his secret, and die. Now, in this chicken house the farmer had some fifty hens under one cock, and while he was getting ready to say his farewell to his people, he heard one of his farm dogs talking to the 'cock, who was flapping his wings, crowing lustily, and jumping from one hen's back to another and treading all in turn.

"Oh Chanticleer!" the dog cried out. "How can you be so mean and shameless! Whoever brought you up should be burned at the stake! Aren't you ashamed of doing such things on a day such as this?"

"And just what is so special about today?" asked the rooster.

"Don't you know that our master is preparing for his death today?" the dog responded. "His wife is determined that he must reveal the secret taught to him by Allah, and the moment he does this he's bound to die. We dogs are all mourning already, but you, you flap your wings, crow as loud as you can, and tread hen after hen. Is this the time for having fun and taking your pleasure? Aren't you ashamed of yourself?"

"By Allah," retorted the cock, "is our master a nitwit? Why doesn't he come to his senses? If he can't manage matters with a single wife, his life is not worth prolonging. Now I have some fifty dame partlets, and I please this one and provoke the other and starve one and stuff another. And through my good governance, they are all well under my control. Our master claims that he is smart and wise, but he has only one wife and hasn't discovered yet how to deal with her."

"Well, what should our master do?" asked the dog.

"He should get up right away," answered the cock, "and take some twigs from that mulberry tree over there and give her a good beating until she cries: 'I repent, oh, my lord! I'll never ask you another question as long as I live!' Then let him beat her nice and hard once more, and after he does this, he will sleep soundly and enjoy life. But this master of ours does not appear to have an iota of good sense or judgment."

When the merchant heard the wise words spoken by the cock to the dog, he arose in haste, cut some mulberry twigs, and hid them in his wife's room. Then he called to her, "Come into your room so that I may tell you the secret and die without anyone looking on."

She entered the room, and he locked the door. All of a sudden he began to beat her back, shoulders, ribs, arms, and legs in a great fury. "Are you going to continue to ask questions about things that don't concern you?" And he kept beating her until she was almost unconscious.

Soon she cried out, "I repent! By Allah, I won't ask you any more questions. I mean it. I repent with all my heart and life!"

Then she kissed his hands and feet, and he led her out of the room, submissive as a wife should be. Her parents and the entire company rejoiced, and sadness and mourning were changed into joy and gladness. Thus the merchant learned family discipline from his cock, and he and his wife lived happily ever after until death.

"And the same thing will happen to you, too, my daughter!" continued the vizier. "Unless you give up pursuing this matter, I'll do what the merchant did to his wife."

But she answered him with firm resolution, "I won't give up, Father, nor shall this tale make me change my mind. So stop your talk and babbling. I won't listen to your words, and if you try to prevent me, I'll go to the king alone and say, 'I asked my father to allow me to marry you, but he refused, since he begrudged you the right to have a maiden like me.'"

"Must it be this way?" her father asked.

"Indeed, it must."

Since the vizier was now weary of contending with his daughter and realized he could not dissuade her from doing what she wanted, he went to King Shahryar, and after blessing him and kissing the ground before him, told him all about his dispute with his daughter and how he now intended to bring her to him that night.

The king was most astonished, since he had made a special exception of the vizier's daughter, and he said to him, "Oh most faithful of counselors, how has this come about? You know that I have sworn by Almighty Allah that after I enter her this night, I shall say to you tomorrow morning: 'Take her and slay her!' And if you don't do this, I'll slay you in her place."

"May Allah guide you to glory and give you long life, your majesty," answered the vizier. "It was she who made this decision. I have told her what is to happen and more, but she won't listen to me, and she insists on spending this coming night with your highness."

So Shahryar rejoiced greatly and said, "So be it. Go get her ready and bring her to me this night."

The vizier returned to his daughter and informed her of the king's command. "By Allah, please don't make your father do this. I'm sure to lose you."

But Scheherazade rejoiced and got everything ready that she needed. Then she said to her younger sister, Dunazade, "Pay attention to what I tell you! After I have entered the king's private chamber, I'll send for you, and when you come and see that he has had his carnal pleasure with me, you're to say to me: 'Oh sister, since you're not sleepy, tell me some new delightful story to entertain us while we are still awake.' And I'll tell you a tale that will be our salvation, if it pleases Allah, for I'm going to tell a tale that will, I hope, divert the king from his bloodthirsty custom."

"I'll do whatever you say," Dunazade replied, "with all my heart."

So when it was night, their father led Scheherazade to the king, who was glad to see her and asked, "Have you brought me what I need?"

"I have," the vizier said.

But when the king took her to his bed, began toying with her, and was about to penetrate her, she wept, and consequently he asked, "What's wrong with you?"

"Your majesty," she replied, "I have a younger sister, and I would like very much to take leave of her tonight before dawn comes."

So he sent at once for Dunazade, and she came and

kissed the ground, and he permitted her to take a seat near the foot of the couch. Then the king arose and did away with his bride's maidenhead, and the three fell asleep. But when midnight arrived, Scheherazade awoke and signaled to her sister, Dunazade, who sat up and said, "May Allah be with you, my sister, please tell us some delightful story to while away the waking hours before dawn."

"I'd be most happy and willing to do this," answered Scheherazade, "if this pious and auspicious king will permit me."

"Permission granted," said the king, who happened to be sleepless and restless and was therefore pleased by the prospect of hearing her story. So Scheherazade rejoiced, and on the first night of many nights to come, she began telling the tales that were to fill the volumes of *The Arabian Nights*.

The Tale of the Merchant and the Jinnee

There was once a very wealthy merchant who had a great deal of business in various cities. Now, one day he mounted his horse and went forth to collect debts that were owed to him in certain towns. The heat was so terrible along the way that he dismounted and sat down beneath a tree. He put his hand into his saddlebags, took out some bread and dry dates, and began to break his fast. When he had finished eating the dates, he threw away the pits with all his might, and suddenly a huge jinnee appeared brandishing a drawn sword. As he approached the merchant, he said, "Stand up so I can slay you just as you've slain my son!"

"How have I slain your son?" asked the merchant.

"When you ate the dates and threw away the pits, they struck my son in the breast as he was walking by, and he died right on the spot."

"By Allah, if I slew your son," the merchant responded, "I slew him by chance. Therefore, I beg your pardon."

"There's nothing you can do," asserted the jinnee. "You must die." Then he seized the merchant, threw him down on the ground, and raised his sword to strike him. But the merchant wept and cried out, "May Allah take pity on me and hear my plea!"

"Cut your words short," the jinnee answered. "You must die."

But the merchant pleaded with him, "Listen to me. There's a great deal of money that's owed to me. I'm very wealthy and have a wife and children and many pledges in hand. So, permit me to go home and take care of all my claims, and I shall come back to you at the beginning of the new year. Allah be my witness that I'll return to you, and then you can do what you want with me."

The jinnee accepted his promise and let him go. So the merchant returned to his city and completed all his transactions. He gave all people their due, and after informing his wife and children what had happened to him, he appointed a guardian and lived with his family for a full year. At the end of that time, he performed the Wuzu ablution to purify himself before death, took his shroud under his arm, said farewell to family, friends, and neighbors, and went forth against his own will. As he left, they began weeping, wailing, and beating their breasts, but he traveled until he arrived at the same garden where he had encountered the jinnee. The day of his arrival was the beginning of the new year, and as he sat weeping over what had happened to him, a very old and honorable sheikh approached, leading a gazelle on a chain. After saluting the merchant and wishing him a long life, he asked, "Why are you sitting all alone in this place? Don't you know that it's the abode of evil spirits?"

The merchant related to him what had happened with the jinnee, and the old man was astounded and said, "By Allah, I've never seen such fidelity, nor have I ever heard such a strange story. If it were engraved for all to see, it would serve as a warning for all those who need to be warned." Then, seating himself near the merchant, he said. "My brother, I won't leave you until I see what is going to happen between you and this ifrit."

And after he sat down and the two were talking, the merchant became extremely anxious, terrified, and depressed. Just then a second sheikh approached them, and with him were two dogs, both black greyhounds. After the second man greeted them with the salaam, he asked them, "Why are you sitting in this place? Don't you know that it is the abode of the demon jinnees?"

So they told him the tale from beginning to end, and they had not been conversing very long before a third sheikh arrived, and with him was a she-mule with a bright bay coat. He saluted them and asked them why they were seated in that place, and they told him the entire story, and he too sat down with them. Just then a dust cloud advanced, and a mighty sand devil appeared amidst the waste. Soon the cloud opened, revealing the jinnee with a drawn sword and eyes shooting fire-sparks of rage, and he stepped forward, grabbed hold of the merchant, and separated him from the rest of the men.

"Stand up so I can slay you just as you slew my son, the soul of my life," the jinnee bellowed.

The merchant wailed and wept, and the three old men began sighing and crying with their companion. Soon the first man, the owner of the gazelle, approached the ifrit and kissed his hand. "Oh jinnee, crown of the kings of the jinn, if I were to tell you a story about me and this gazelle, and if you were to consider it wondrous, would you give me a third of this merchant's blood?"

"If you tell me your tale, oh sheikh, and it is indeed marvelous," the jinnee replied, "I'll give you a third of his blood."

Thereupon the old man began to tell

The First Sheikh's Story

I'll have you know, oh jinnee, that this gazelle is the daughter of my paternal uncle, my own flesh and blood, and I married her when she was a young maid. I lived with her for close to thirty years, but I was not blessed with any offspring. So I took me a concubine, who gave birth to a boy, fair as the full moon with glistening eyes, straight eyebrows, and perfect limbs. Little by little he grew to be a tall young man, and when he was fifteen, it became necessary for me to journey to certain cities with a large amount of goods. But my wife had learned the art of witchcraft, and she turned my son into a calf and his mother into a cow and placed them under the care of the herdsman. So, after a long time had passed and I returned from my journey, I asked for my son and his mother, and she answered me by saying, "Your slave girl is dead, and your son has fled, and I don't know where he's gone."

So my heart grieved for an entire year, and my eyes

did not stop weeping until the time came for the Great Festival of Allah. Then I sent for my herdsman and asked him to choose a fat cow for me. He brought me the one which had been my handmaid, whom this gazelle had bewitched. I tucked up my sleeves, put on an apron, and taking a knife, I began to cut her throat, but she bellowed so loudly and wept such bitter tears that I was astonished. Out of pity, I dropped the knife and said to the herdsman, "Bring me a different cow."

Then my wife cried out, "Slay her! There's none fatter or fairer."

Once more I made a move to sacrifice her, but again the cow bellowed loudly, and I could not bring myself to kill her. Instead, I commanded the herdsman to slay her and flay her. So, he performed the sacrifice and skinned her, but could not find fat or flesh, only hide and bone. I repented when it was much too late, and I gave her to the herdsman and said to him, "Fetch me a fat calf."

So he brought me my bewitched son. When the calf saw me, he broke his tether, ran to me, fawned upon me, and shed tears. Consequently, I took pity on him and said to the herdsman, "Bring me a cow, and let this calf go."

But my wife cried out, "You must kill this calf. It is a holy and blessed day, and nothing is to be slain except what is pure and perfect. And there is nothing among our calves that is fatter or fairer than this one!"

"Look at the cow that I have just had slaughtered at your request and how disappointed we are by the results," I said. "There was no benefit from her at all, and I'm extremely sorry for having killed her. So this time I'm not going to listen to you, and the calf will not be sacrificed."

"By Allah, you have no choice. You must kill him on this holy day, and if you don't kill him, you're no man for me, and I shall not be your wife."

Now, when I heard those hard words, I went up to the calf with knife in hand, unaware of my wife's real purpose. However, when I looked at the calf, I commanded the herdsman to take it away, and he did as I ordered him to do. On the next day as I was sitting in my own house, the herdsman came up to me and said, "Master, I want to tell you something that will make your soul rejoice and enable me to be the bearer of good tidings."

"I'm listening," I said.

"I have a daughter," he began, "and she learned magic in her childhood from an old woman who lived with us. Yesterday, when you gave me the calf, I went into the house with it, and she looked at it and veiled her face. Then she kept laughing and weeping and at last said to me, 'Oh father, has my honor become so cheap that you're now bringing strange men into the house for me?' I asked her, 'Where are these strange men and why are you laughing and crying?' She answered, 'To tell you the truth, the calf that you have with you is the son of our master, the merchant, but his wife bewitched him and his mother. That's why I laughed, and I wept because of his mother, whom the merchant slew unaware that it was she.' Of course, I was most astonished by this revelation, and I could hardly wait until the break of day to come and tell all this to you."

When I heard my herdsman's words, I went with him to his house and was drunk with joy without having the least bit of wine. His daughter welcomed me and kissed my hand, and the calf came right away and fawned all over me as before. "Is it true," I asked the herdsman's daughter, "all that you've said about this calf?"

"Yes, oh master," she said. "He's your son, your very own flesh and blood."

I rejoiced and said to her, "If you can release him from this spell, you can have whatever property and cattle I have."

"Master," she smiled, "I don't desire such goods, and I shall take them only under two conditions: the first, that you marry me to your son, and the second, that you allow me to bewitch your wife and imprison her. Otherwise, I won't be safe from her malice."

Now when I heard these words, I replied, "Not only do I grant you your wish, but you may have all the cattle and the household stuff in your father's charge, and as for my wife, anything you do to her is all right with me."

After I had spoken, she took a cup and filled it with water. Then she recited a spell over it and sprinkled it on the calf, saying, "If Almighty Allah created you as a calf, then remain as you are and don't change. But if you are enchanted, return to your rightful form!"

All of a sudden, the calf trembled and became a man, and I embraced him and said, "By Allah, tell me all that the daughter of my uncle did to you and your mother." And when he told me how everything had happened, I said, "My son, Allah blessed you by enabling someone to restore you to your real form, and you may now receive your rightful due."

Then I married him to the herdsman's daughter, and she transformed my wife into this gazelle by giving her a shape that is by no means loathsome. After this the herdsman's daughter lived with us day and night until she died. Then my son journeyed forth to the cities of Hind and also to the city of this man who has offended you. And I also took this gazelle and wandered with her from town to town seeking news of my son until destiny drove me to this place where I saw the merchant sitting and weeping. Such is my tale!

"This story is indeed strange," said the jinnee, "and thus I shall grant you a third of the merchant's blood."

Thereupon the second old man, who owned two greyhounds, came up and said, "Oh jinnee, if I relate to you what my brothers, these two hounds, did to me, and if you admit that it is more wondrous and marvelous than the tale that you've just heard, will you grant me a third of the merchant's blood as well?"

"I give you my word," said the jinnee, "but only if your adventures are truly more marvelous."

Thereupon the old man began

The Second Sheikh's Story

Let me begin by telling you, oh lord of the kings of the jinn, that these two dogs are my brothers, and I am the third. When our father died and left us a capital of three thousand gold pieces, I opened a shop with my share, and my brothers did the same. However, I had been in business just for a short time when my elder brother sold his stock for a thousand dinars, and after buying equipment and merchandise, he journeyed to foreign lands. He had been gone with his caravan for one whole year when, one day, as I was sitting in my shop, a beggar stood before me asking for alms, and I said to him, "Go try somewhere else!"

In response, the beggar began weeping, "Have I changed so much that you don't recognize me anymore?"

Then I looked at him more closely, and I realized it was my brother. So I stood up and welcomed him, and after seating him in my shop, I asked him what had happened.

"Don't ask me," he replied. "My wealth is all gone, and so is my health."

So I took him to the public bath, dressed him in a suit of my own, and gave him a room in my house. Moreover, after looking over the accounts of my stock in trade and my business profits, I found that my hard work had enabled me to earn one thousand dinars while my principal amounted to two thousand. So I shared the whole thing with him and said, "Just assume that you didn't make a journey abroad but remained at home. There's no reason now for you to be dejected about your bad luck."

He took the share gleefully and opened up his own shop. Things went well for some days, but soon my second brother, that dog over there, also set his heart on traveling. He sold whatever goods and stock in trade that he had, and although we tried to prevent him from leaving, he would not listen to us. He equipped himself for the journey and joined a group of travelers. After an absence of one year, he came back to me just as my elder brother had, and I said to him, "Didn't I try to dissuade you from traveling?"

"Destiny decreed it this way!" he wept and cried out. "Now I am a mere beggar without a penny to my name or a shirt on my back."

So I led him to the bath and dressed him in my own new clothes. Then I went with him to my shop, where I gave him something to eat and drink. Furthermore, I told him, "Brother, I generally draw up the accounts of my shop at the beginning of every year, and I intend to share the surplus with you."

Thus, some time later, when I found a profit of two thousand dinars, I praised the Lord and gave my brother one half and kept the other for myself. Thereupon, he set up his own shop, and we lived peacefully for many days. After a while, however, my brothers began to urge me to travel with them, but I refused and argued, "What did you two gain from all your voyages that would make me want to travel?"

Since I would not listen to them, we each returned to our own shops, where we bought and sold as usual. They kept urging me to travel for a whole year, but I continued to refuse. Finally, after six years had passed, I consented and said, "All right, my brothers, I shall be your companion and am ready to travel. Now, let me see what money you intend to bring with you."

I found, however, that they did not have anything, for they had squandered their funds on rich food, drink, and carnal pleasure. Still, I did not reproach them. Far from it. Instead, I looked over my shop accounts once more, sold what goods and stock in trade were mine, and came out with a profit of six thousand ducats, which I divided into half. After doing this, I went to my brothers and said, "These three thousand gold pieces are for me and you to conduct our trade during our travels. Let's bury the other three thousand in the ground in case anything should happen to us. And if something does, each shall take a thousand to open new shops."

Since they both agreed, I gave each one a thousand gold pieces and kept the same sum for myself. Then we prepared some goods for trading and hired a ship to carry our merchandise and proceeded on our voyage. After a month at sea, we reached a city, where we sold our goods, and for every piece of gold that we had invested we gained ten. And when we were about to resume our voyage, we found a maiden on the seashore clad in worn and ragged clothes. She kissed my hand and said, "Oh master, are you a man of charity and kindness? If so, I am prepared to repay you for your aid."

"You may find me benevolent and a man of good works," I said. "But I don't want any return for my deeds."

Then she said, "Please have me as your wife, oh master, and take me to your city, for I'm giving myself to you. Be kind, for I am one of those on whom charity and good works will not be lost. I can make you a fitting return for them, and you will not be shamed by my condition."

When I heard her words, my heart went out to her as though Allah had willed it. Therefore, I took her, clothed her, gave her a comfortable place in the vessel, and treated her with honor. So we continued our voyage, and I became more and more attached to her so that I could not bear to be separated from her day or night. Indeed, I paid more attention to her than to my brothers, with the result that they grew apart from me and became jealous of my wealth and the large amount of merchandise that I had acquired. So they planned to murder me and seize my wealth, and Satan made this seem right in their eyes.

They waited one night and found me sleeping by my wife's side, whereupon they carried us up to the deck of the ship and threw us overboard. My wife awoke startled from her sleep, and immediately she changed into a jinnee, whereupon she lifted me up, carried me to an island, and disappeared for a short time. When she returned in the morning, she said, "Here I am, your faithful slave, who has duly repaid you for your kindness, for I have saved you from death in the deep waters. I am a jinniyah, and when I first saw you, my heart went out to you by the will of the Lord, for I am a believer in Allah. So I went to you in the condition you saw me, and you married me. But I'm angry at your brothers, and I must certainly slay them."

When I heard her story, I was surprised and thanked her for all she had done. "But," I said, "when it comes to slaying my brothers, you must not do this."

Then I told her the tale of our lives from the beginning to the end, and on hearing it, she said, "Tonight I shall fly like a bird over their ship and sink it, causing them to die."

"By Allah," I responded, "don't do this! Remember the proverb: Whoever helps an evildoer should let the evildoer do his own evil deeds."

"Nothing can help them," the jinniyah replied. "By Allah, I must slay them."

I humbled myself before her and begged that she pardon them, whereupon she picked me up and flew away with me until she set me down on the terrace of my own house. Then I took what I had hidden in the ground, bought new merchandise, greeted various people, and reopened the doors of my shop. When night came, I went home, and there I saw these two hounds tied up. Upon seeing me, they arose, whined, and fawned upon me, and before I knew what was happening, my wife said, "These two dogs are your brothers!"

"Who has done this to them?" I asked.

"I sent a message to my sister, and it was she who transformed them into dogs. And they will not be released from their present shape until ten years have passed."

You find me now, oh jinnee, on my way to my wife's sister, because the time has come to release my brothers from their condition. I stopped at this place when I saw this young man, who told me all that had occurred to him, and I decided not to leave here until I saw what would happen between you and him. Such is my tale!

"This is certainly a remarkable story," said the jinnee. "Therefore, I'll give you a third of this man's blood."

Now the third sheikh, the master of the she-mule, approached the jinnee and said, "If I can tell you a tale more wondrous than these two, will you grant me the remainder of the merchant's blood?"

"You have my word!" the jinnee answered.

Then the old man began

The Third Sheikh's Story

I'll have you know, oh jinnee, that this mule was my wife. Now, it so happened that I had to leave home for one year, and when I returned from my journey, it was night, and I found my wife lying with a black slave on my couch. They were talking, laughing, kissing, and playing the close-buttock game. When she saw me, she stood up and rushed over to me with a jug of water. As she ran toward me, she muttered spells over the water and sprinkled me with it. "Change your shape," she exclaimed, "and become a dog!"

All of a sudden, I was a dog, and she drove me out of the house. I ran through the doorway and did not stop running until I came to a butcher's stall, where I rested and began to eat what bones were there. When the butcher saw me, he grabbed me and carried me into his house, but as soon as his daughter caught sight of me, she veiled her face and cried out, "What are you doing? Why are you bringing men to me?"

"Where's the man?" he father asked.

"This dog is a man, and his wife has enchanted him," she replied. "If you want, I can release him from the spell."

When her father heard her words, he said, "May Allah be with you, my daughter, release him."

So she took a jug of water, and after uttering words over it, she sprinkled a few drops on me and said, "Leave that shape and return to your former one."

And I returned to my natural shape. Then I kissed her hand and said, "I wish you'd transform my wife the same way you just changed me."

Thereupon she gave me some water and said, "As soon as you see her asleep, sprinkle this liquid on her and say the words you heard me utter. Then she'll become whatever you desire."

I returned to my house and found my wife fast asleep, and as I sprinkled the water on her, I said, "Leave that shape and change into a mule."

Within seconds she became a mule, and you are looking at her now, oh jinnee, with your own eyes!

Then the jinnee turned toward her and asked, "Is this true?"

And she nodded her head and replied by signs, "Indeed, it's the truth, for such is my tale."

The jinnee was very pleased by the old man's extraordinary story, and he gave him a third of the merchant's blood. Shaking with delight, he told the three sheikhs, "Thanks to you and your storytelling, the merchant is yours! You've saved him, and I now release him from his punishment."

Thereupon, the jinnee disappeared, while the merchant embraced the old men and thanked them. Then the sheikhs wished him happiness and continued their journeys, each one heading toward the city of his destination.

And Scheherazade noticed that dawn was approaching and stopped telling her tale. Thereupon Dunazade said, "Oh sister, your tale was most wonderful, pleasant, and delightful!"

"It is nothing compared to what I could tell you tomorrow night if the king would spare my life and let me live."

"By Allah," the king thought to himself, "I won't slay her until I hear some more of her wondrous tales."

So they continued to rest in mutual embrace until daylight finally arrived. After this the king got up to perform his official duties, but he did not call upon the vizier to perform the execution. Instead, he went to his assembly hall and began holding court. He judged, appointed, and deposed, forbidding this and permitting that, the rest of the day. After the divan was adjourned, King Shahryar returned to the palace. That night he had his will of Scheherazade, as was his wont, and afterward, as they were relaxing, Dunazade came to her sister and asked her to tell another tale.

"With the king's permission," she said.

And Shahryar replied, "You have my permission."

So Scheherazade resumed her storytelling.

The Fisherman and the Jinnee

There was once a poor old fisherman who had a wife and three children to support. When he went to work, he customarily cast his net four times a day, and no more than that. Now, one day he went to the seashore about noon and set his basket on the ground. After rolling up his shirt and plunging into the water, he cast his net and waited until it settled to the bottom. Then he gathered the cords together and tried to haul in the net. However, he found it too heavy, and no matter how hard he pulled, he could not bring the net up. So he carried the ends ashore, drove a stake into the ground, and tied the net to it. Afterward he stripped, dived into the water, and kept working until he had brought the net up. Filled with joy, he put on his clothes again and went to the net, in which he found a dead jackass that had torn the meshes. In his grief, he exclaimed, "By Allah, this is a strange way to earn a living!" Then he said to himself, "Up and at it! I'm sure that this must be some sort of blessing."

Once the fisherman got the dead ass free of the cords, he wrung out the net and spread it on the shore. Then he plunged into the sea, cast the net again, and cried out, "In Allah's name!" When he began pulling the net, it grew heavy and settled down more firmly than the first time. Now he thought that there were fish in it and tied the net to the stake again. He took off his clothes, dived into the water, and pushed and pulled until he got the net on dry land. Then he found a large clay pitcher filled with sand and mud and was very disappointed.

After throwing away the pitcher, he wrung his net, cleaned it, and cast it into the sea for a third time. Once it had sunk, he pulled at it and found potsherds and broken glass in it. Raising his eyes toward heaven, he cried out, "By Allah, don't You know that I cast my net only four times a day? The third is done, and thus far, You have granted me nothing. So, I beseech You, this time give me my daily bread."

Then he cast his net again and waited for it to sink and settle. When he tried to haul it in, he found that it had become entangled at the bottom. "By Allah!" he exclaimed as he stripped again and dived down into the sea. After freeing the net, he dragged it to land and found a copper jar in the shape of a cucumber. It was evidently filled with something. The mouth was sealed by a lead cap and stamped with the signet of our Lord Solomon, son of David. Seeing this, the fisherman rejoiced and said, "If I sell it in the brass bazaar, I should be able to get ten golden dinars for it." When he shook it, he found that it was heavy and remarked, "If only I knew what was inside! Well, I've got to open it, and then I'll store it in my bag and sell it at the brass market." Taking out his knife, he worked at the lead until he had loosened it from the jar. Then he laid the top on the ground and shook the jar, but he was astonished to find nothing in it. After a while, however, some smoke burst from the jar and soared like a spiral toward the heavens. Once the smoke reached its full height, the thick vapor condensed and became a huge jinnee, whose head touched the clouds while his feet were on the ground. His head was as large as a dome; his hands like pitchforks; his legs as long as masts; and his mouth as big as a cave. His teeth were like large stones; his nostrils, jars; his eyes, two lamps; and his look was fierce and threatening. Now, when the fisherman saw the ifrit, his entire body quivered; his teeth chattered; his spit dried up, and he was so terrified that he could not move or run away.

The ifrit gazed at him and cried, "There is no god but *the* God, and Solomon is the prophet of God." Immediately afterward, he added, "Oh Apostle of Allah, don't slay me. Never again will I slander you, or commit a sin against your laws."

"Oh jinnee," said the fisherman, "did you say, 'Solomon, the Apostle of Allah'? Solomon has been dead for some eighteen hundred years, and we are now approach-

ing the end of the world! What happened to you? Tell me
about yourself. How did you get into that jar?"

Now, when the evil spirit heard the words of the fisherman, he said, "There is no god but *the* God. Be of good
cheer, fisherman!"

"Why should I be of good cheer?" asked the fisherman.

"Because you shall have to die this very hour."

"May heaven abandon you because of your good tidings!" replied the fisherman. "Why should you kill me?
What have I done to deserve death? After all, it was I
who freed you from the jar, saved you from the depths of
the sea, and brought you up to dry land!"

"Ask me only how you will die, and how I shall slaughter you," the jinnee declared.

"What's my crime?" exclaimed the fisherman. "Why
such retribution?"

"Hear my story, oh fisherman," answered the jinnee.

"Tell it to me," said the fisherman, "and be brief, for
my heart is in my mouth."

"I'll have you know that I am one among the heretical
jinn, and I sinned against Solomon. Consequently, the
prophet sent his minister, Asaf son of Barkhiya, to seize
me, and this vizier had me bound and brought me against
my will to stand before the prophet as a suppliant. When
Solomon saw me, he demanded that I embrace the true
faith and obey his commands. But I refused, and he had
me imprisoned in the jar, which was sealed by lead and
stamped by his signet. After Solomon gave orders to a
jinnee, I was carried off and cast into the middle of the
ocean. I lived in the jar for a hundred years, during
which time I said in my heart, 'I'll reward whoever releases me with great riches.' But a full century went by,
and when no one set me free, I began the second and
said, 'I'll open the hidden treasures of the earth for
whoever releases me.' But still no one set me free, and
four hundred years went by. Then I said, 'I'll grant three
wishes to whoever releases me.' Yet no one set me free.
Thereupon I became extremely furious and said, 'From
this time on I promise to slay whoever releases me, and
the only choice I'll give him will be the kind of death he'll
die.' And now, since you've released me, I'll give you
your choice of death."

Upon hearing the ifrit's words, the fisherman exclaimed,

"Oh Allah, why couldn't I have freed him before this! Spare my life, jinnee, and Allah will spare yours."

"Nothing can help you," replied the jinnee. "You must die! I'll only grant you your choice of death. So tell me how you want to die."

"I'd prefer that you pardon me for having freed you."

But the jinnee was resolute and said, "It's precisely because you've released me that I must slay you."

"Oh Chief of the Ifrits," said the fisherman, "I do you a good deed, and you return my good deed with evil."

"No more of this talk," the jinnee answered. "I must kill you."

Now the fisherman paused and thought to himself, "This is a jinnee, and I am a man whom Allah has blessed with cunning. So I must use my brains just as he has sought to make use of his malice." Then he said to the jinnee, "So you're really determined to kill me?"

"Indeed I am."

"But if I ask you a certain question, will you swear on the name engraved on the ring of Solomon that you will give me a truthful answer?"

The ifrit replied, "Yes." But hearing the holy name disturbed him, and he began to tremble. "Ask, but be brief."

"How did you fit into this bottle, which is not even large enough to hold your hand or even your foot? And how did it become large enough to contain you?"

"What?" exclaimed the jinnee. "You don't believe that all of me was in there?"

"No, I don't," responded the fisherman. "I'll never believe it until I see you inside with my own eyes."

And Scheherazade noticed that dawn was approaching and stopped telling her story. Then, when the next night arrived, her sister said to her, "Please finish the tale for us, since we're not sleepy."

The king nodded his approval, and so she resumed.

After the fisherman said to the ifrit that he would never believe him until he saw him inside the jar with his own eyes, the jinnee immediately shook and became a vapor, which condensed and gradually entered the jar until all of it was well inside. Right then and there the fisherman quickly took the lead cap with the seal, stopped the mouth of the jar, and cried out to the ifrit, "Ask me for a favor, and I'll grant you your choice of death! By Allah, I'll throw you into the sea right here, and I'll build a lodge on this spot. And I'll warn whoever comes not to fish here because a jinnee dwells in the waters, a jinnee who graciously rewards the person who saves him with a choice of death!"

Now, when the jinnee heard the fisherman's words and saw himself in limbo, he tried to escape, but he was prevented by Solomon's seal. So he knew that the fisherman had outwitted him, and he became submissive. "I was only jesting with you," he said in a humble manner.

"You're lying!" replied the fisherman. "You're the vilest, meanest, and filthiest of jinnees!" And he moved toward the sea with the ifrit crying out, "No! No!" and him responding with "Yes! Yes!"

Then the evil spirit softened his voice, sweetened his speech, and abased himself. "What are you going to do with me, fisherman?" he asked.

"I'm going to throw you back into the sea," he answered, "Where you were housed for eighteen hundred years. And I'm going to leave you there until Judgment Day. Didn't I say to you, spare me, and Allah will spare you, and don't slay me or Allah will slay you? But you spurned my pleas and intended only to treat me ungraciously. So now Allah has thrown you into my hands, for I am more cunning than you!"

"If you open the bottle, I'll make you a wealthy man," the jinnee replied.

"You're lying, you cursed jinnee," exclaimed the fisherman. "You and I are in exactly the same situation as King Yunan was with the Sage Duban."

"And who were King Yunan and the Sage Duban? What happened to them?" asked the jinnee.

Thereupon the fisherman began to tell

The Tale of King Yunan and
the Sage Duban

A long time ago there lived a king called Yunan, who reigned over the city of Fars in the land of Persia. He was a wealthy and powerful ruler, who had massive armies and was allied with all nations of men. However, his body was afflicted with a leprosy that the doctors were unable to heal. He drank potions, swallowed pills, and used salves, but nothing would help. Finally, a mighty healer of men came to his city, the Sage Duban, who was extremely old and well versed in the works of the Greeks, Persians, Romans, Arabs, and Syrians. Moreover, he was skilled in astronomy and knew everything in theory and practice that could heal or harm a body. Indeed, he was familiar with the virtues of every plant, grass, and herb in the world and how they could benefit or damage a person, and he understood philosophy, medical science, and other branches of the tree of knowledge. Now, this physician had been in the city for only a few days when he heard about the king's malady and how he had been suffering from leprosy and how all the doctors and wise men had failed to heal him. As a result, he sat up the entire night and thought about the king's condition. When dawn broke, he put on his most becoming outfit and went to see King Yunan. After he kissed the ground before him, he wished the king long life and prosperity and introduced himself. "Your majesty, news has reached me that none of your physicians have been able to stop your sickness. However, you will see that I can cure you, and I shall have no need of potions or ointments."

When King Yunan heard these words, he responded with great surprise, "How are you going to do this? By Allah, if you heal me, I will make you and your grandchildren rich, and I will give you sumptuous gifts. Whatever you wish will be yours, and you will be my friend and boon companion." Then the king had him dressed in a robe of honor and asked him graciously, "Is it really possible for you to cure me without drugs and potions?"

"Yes!" he answered. "I'll heal you without the pains and drawbacks of medicine."

The king was astonished and said, "When will all this take place, and how soon? Let it be soon."

"As you wish," he replied. "The cure will begin tomorrow."

Upon saying this, the sage departed and rented a house in the city in order to store his books, scrolls, medicines, and aromatic roots in a better way. Then he set to work by choosing the most effective drugs and balsams. Afterward he carved a polo stick with a hollow inside and a wide end with which to hit a ball. All this was made with consummate art. On the next day when both the stick and ball were ready for use, he went to the king, and after kissing the ground, he asked the king to ride out onto the parade ground to play polo. He was accompanied by his emirs, chamberlains, viziers, and lords of the realm, and before he was seated, the Sage Duban went up to him, handed him the stick, and said, "Take this stick and grip it as I do. Good! Now lean over your horse and drive the ball with all your might until your palm is moist and your body perspires. Then the medicine will penetrate through your palm and will permeate your body. After you have finished playing and you feel the effects of the medicine, return to your palace and wash yourself in the Hammam bath. Then lie down to sleep, and you will be healed. Now, peace be with you!"

Thereupon King Yunan took the stick from the sage and grasped it firmly. After mounting his steed, he drove the ball before him and galloped after it until he reached it, and he did not stop hitting the ball until his hand became moist and his skin perspired so that he imbibed the medicine from the wood. Then the Sage Duban knew that the drugs had penetrated his body, and he told the king that it was time to return to the palace and enter the bath without delay. So King Yunan returned immediately and ordered them to prepare the bath for him. The carpet spreaders rushed about, and the slaves hurried and prepared a change of clothes for the king, who entered the bath and made the total ablution long and thorough. Then he put on his clothes within the Hammam and rode from there to his palace, where he lay down and slept.

Meanwhile, the Sage Duban returned home and slept as usual. When morning dawned, he went back to the palace and asked for an audience with the king. The king ordered him to be admitted, and after the Sage Duban sang a solemn song in honor of the king, the king rose to his feet quickly and embraced him. After giving him a seat by his side, the king had him clothed in a sumptuous robe, for it so happened that after the king had left the Hammam bath, he had looked at his body and had not been able to find a single trace of leprosy. Indeed, his skin had become as clean as pure silver, and he had rejoiced. Now the food trays carrying the most delicious viands were brought, and the physician ate with the king and remained with him all that day. Then at nightfall the king gave the Sage Duban two thousand gold pieces besides the usual robe of honor and other gifts galore. Finally, he sent him home on his own steed.

After the sage had departed, King Yunan again expressed his amazement at the doctor's art and said, "This man cured my body without the aid of ointments. Surely, this shows how great and consummate his skills are! I feel obliged to honor such a man with rewards and distinction and make him my friend and companion until the end of my days."

So King Yunan spent the night in joy and happiness because his body had been healed and had overcome such a pernicious malady. The next day the king left his seraglio and sat on his throne. The lords of estate stood around him, and the emirs and viziers sat on his right and on his left as was their custom. Then the king asked for the Sage Duban, who came in and kissed the ground before him. After the king rose to greet him and seated him by his side, he ate with him and wished him long life. Moreover, he gave him clothes and gifts and did not stop conversing with him until night approached. Then, as a kind of salary, the king gave him five robes of honor and a thousand dinars, whereupon the doctor returned to his own house full of gratitude to the king.

When the next morning dawned, the king went to his audience hall, and his lords, nobles, chamberlains, and ministers surrounded him just as the white encompasses the black of the eye. Now the king had a vizier among the nobility, unpleasant in appearance, sordid, ungenerous, full of envy and ill will. When this minister saw the king place the physician near him and give him all those gifts, he was jealous of him and planned to do him harm. So the minister went before the king and, kissing the ground between his hands, said, "Your majesty, I have some serious advice for you, and though you may not like it, I would be amiss in my duties as your minister if I did not speak my piece."

The king was troubled by the words of the minister and said, "What is this advice of yours?"

"Oh glorious monarch," he responded, "the wise men of former times have a saying which runs like this: whoever does not regard the end will not have Fortune as his friend. And indeed, I have recently seen the king heading in the wrong direction, for he has been bestowing lavish presents on his enemy, on one whose intention is to bring an end to your rule. You have favored this man and honored him unduly by making him an intimate friend. Consequently, I fear for the king's life."

The king, whose face changed color, was greatly disturbed and asked, "Whom do you suspect?"

"Oh king," the minister said, "if you are asleep, wake up! I am pointing at the physician Duban."

"You should be ashamed of yourself!" the king cried out. "He is a true friend, and I've favored him above all other men because he cured me of my leprosy, which had baffled all the physicians of my land. Indeed, there is no one like him to be found in these times—no, no one in the entire world from the far east to the far west! And this is the man whom you are accusing! Why, this very day I granted him a monthly salary and allowance of one thousand gold pieces, and were I to share my realm with him, it would be inconsequential. Therefore, I must assume that you are speaking about him out of mere envy and jealousy just as one spoke about King Sinbad."

And Scheherazade noticed that dawn was approaching and stopped her story. Then Dunazade said, "Oh my sister, your tale is delightful. How sweet and graceful!"

"This is nothing compared with what I could tell you tomorrow night if the king would spare my life," she replied.

Then the king said to himself, "By Allah, I won't slay her until I hear the rest of her tale, for it is truly wondrous."

So they rested that night in mutual embrace until dawn. Then the king went to his audience hall, and the vizier and the troops entered. The reception chamber was thronged, and the king judged, appointed, deposed, permitted, and prohibited during the rest of the day until the court was adjourned, whereupon King Shahryar returned to his pal-ace. Later that night, Dunazade said to Scheherazade, "If you're not sleepy, will you please finish the story for us?"

"With the king's permission," she replied.

"You have my permission," said Shahryad.

And Scheherazade resumed:

If you recall, oh mighty monarch, King Yunan had said to his minister, "Oh vizier, the evil spirit of envy has contaminated you because of this physician, and you are trying to urge me to put him to death, after which I would sorely repent just as King Sinbad repented the killing of his falcon."

"Pardon me, your majesty, what was that about?" asked the vizier.

In reply the king began

The Tale of King Sinbad and His Falcon

There was once a king of Persia who enjoyed all the sporting life, especially hunting. He had raised a falcon which he carried all night on his fist, and he had a little gold cup made for it that was draped around its neck so it could drink at will. Of course, whenever he went hunting, he took this bird with him.

Now, one day as the king was sitting quietly in his palace, the high falconer of his household appeared before him and said, "Your majesty, this is just the right day for hunting."

So the king gave orders accordingly and set out with the falcon on his fist. They went merrily on their way until they found a ravine, where they laid their nets for the chase. Just then a gazelle came within sight, and the king cried, "I'll kill any man who allows that gazelle over there to jump over his head and get away!"

They closed in on the gazelle with the nets, driving it near the king's post. Then it squatted on its hindquarters and crossed its forehead over its breast, as if about to kiss the earth before the king. So unusual was this behavior that the king bowed his brow in acknowledgment to the gazelle, allowing the beast time to jump quickly over his head and disappear from sight. Thereupon, the king turned toward his troops and saw them pointing at him. "Oh vizier," he asked, "what are my men saying?"

"They say," the minister replied, "that you had proclaimed you would kill any man who allowed the gazelle to jump over his head."

"Well, by the life of my head, I shall pursue that gazelle until I bring it back!"

So he set off on his horse, galloping after the gazelle's trail, and he did not stop tracking the beast until he reached the foothills of a mountain chain where the quarry had made for a cave. Then the king set the falcon loose, and when the bird caught up with it, she swooped down, and drove her talons into its eyes, bewildering and blinding it. When he saw this, the king came up, drew his mace, and struck a blow that killed the beast. After that he dismounted, cut the antelope's throat, flayed the body, and hung it on the pommel of his saddle.

Now the time for siesta had arrived, and the surrounding land was parched and dry. There was no water to be found anywhere, and the king and his horse were thirsty. So he went searching until he found a tree moist with water on its boughs, as if butter were melting from its branches. Thereupon the king, who wore leather gauntlets to protect him against poison, took the cup from the hawk's neck, and after filling it with water, he set it before the bird, who suddenly struck it with her claws so that the liquid poured out. The king filled it a second time with the drops from the branches, thinking his falcon was thirsty, but the bird struck the cup again with her claws and knocked it over. Now the king became mad at the falcon and filled the cup a third time but offered it to his horse. Once more, the bird upset it with a flick of her wings.

"By Allah," said the king, "you miserable flying creature! You're keeping all of us from drinking."

So he struck the falcon with his sword and cut off her wing, but the bird raised her head and said by signs, "Look at what's hanging on the tree!"

The king lifted his eyes and caught sight of a brood of vipers, whose poison drops he had mistaken for water. Thereupon he repented for having lopped off the falcon's wing, and after mounting his horse, he moved on with the dead gazelle until he arrived at his camp. After throwing the quarry to the cook, he said, "Take it and broil it." Then he sat down on his chair to relax, but the falcon, still on his wrist, gasped and died. There was nothing left for the king to do but to cry in sorrow and remorse for having slain the falcon which had saved his life.

"Such was the sad story about King Sinbad, and I'm certain that if I were to do as you desire, I would regret it. In fact, I'd be in the same situation as the man who killed his parrot."

"And what happened to him?" the vizier asked.

In reply, the king began to tell

The Tale of the Husband and the Parrot

There was once a merchant who had married a perfectly beautiful wife, who was lovely and graceful. He was, however, so madly jealous of her that he would not leave her to conduct his business. At last an occasion arose that compelled him to travel. So he went to a bird market and bought a parrot for one hundred gold pieces. Then he placed the parrot in his house and expected it to act as a duenna and report to him everything that happened during his absence, for the bird was cunning and never forgot what it saw and heard.

Now the merchant's fair wife had fallen in love with a young Turk, who visited her during her husband's absence, and she treated him to a feast during the day and lay with him during the night. Soon the merchant completed his business, returned home, and began at once to question the parrot about the conduct of his wife while he was in foreign countries.

"Your wife has a male friend, who spent every night with her during your absence," the parrot declared.

Thereupon the husband went to his wife in a violent rage and gave her the beating of her life. Afterward, suspecting that one of the slave girls had been tattling to the master, the woman called them together and made them swear to tell her the truth. Indeed, they all swore that they had kept her secret, and they revealed to her that the parrot was the one who had squealed, insisting that they had heard it with their own ears.

As a result the woman ordered one of the girls to set a hand mill under the cage and to grind with it. Another girl was commanded to sprinkle water through the cage roof, and a third to run around flashing a mirror of bright steel throughout the night. Next morning when the husband returned home after being entertained by one of his friends, he ordered that the parrot be brought before him and asked what had taken place while he was away.

"Pardon me, oh master," said the bird, "I could neither hear nor see anything because of the thunder and lightning that lasted throughout the murky night."

Since it happened to be the height of summer, the master was astounded and cried, "But we're now in July, and there aren't any storms or rain."

"By Allah," replied the parrot, "I saw everything with my own eyes."

Thereupon the merchant, not suspecting his wife's plot, became extremely angry, for he now believed that he had wrongly accused his wife. So he reached out, pulled the parrot from its cage, and dashed it upon the ground with such force that he killed it on the spot.

Some days later one of the slave girls confessed to him the whole truth. But he would still not believe it until he saw the young Turk, his wife's lover, come out of her chamber. Consequently, he drew his sword and slew him by a blow on the back of the neck, and he killed his wife in the same way. Thus, the two of them, laden with mortal sin, went straight to hell. Despite the fact that the merchant now knew the parrot had told the truth, and despite the fact that he honored the bird with his mourning, his grief could not bring it back to life.

Upon hearing the words of King Yunan, the minister responded, "Your majesty, do you honestly think that I'm plotting against the Sage Duban? I'm only giving you my opinion and some advice. If you accept my advice, I think you'll be saved. Otherwise, you'll be destroyed just like that young prince who was treacherously betrayed by a certain vizier."

"And how did that come about?" asked the king.

In reply, the minister began

The Tale of the Prince and the Ogress

There was once a prince who was extremely fond of hunting, and consequently, his father commanded one of his viziers to accompany the prince wherever he went. One day the young prince went hunting and was accompanied by his father's minister. As they jogged on together, they caught sight of a big wild beast.

"Let's catch that noble beast!" cried the vizier to the prince.

So the prince followed it and soon disappeared from everyone's sight. Meanwhile, the beast got away from him in the woods, where he lost his way and could not decide which way to turn. All of a sudden a maiden appeared out of nowhere with tears streaming down her cheeks.

"Who are you?" the prince asked.

"I'm the daughter of a king among the kings of Hind," she responded, "and I was traveling with a caravan in the desert when drowsiness overcame me and I unwittingly fell from my horse. So now I'm cut off from my attendants and am quite bewildered."

After hearing these words, the prince took pity on her and helped her onto his horse. She sat on the horse's crupper, and they rode together until they came to an old ruin, where the maiden said to him, "Oh master, please stop. I must obey a call of nature."

After setting her down at the ruin, the prince waited and waited, but she took so long that he thought that she was wasting too much time. So, he followed her trail and was surprised to discover that she was a wicked ogress and had gone to tell her brood that she was going to bring them a fine fat youth for dinner.

They responded by crying out, "Bring him to us quickly, Mother, so we can fill our bellies!"

When the prince overheard their talk, it was clear that he would die, and his muscles quivered in fear. As he turned away to take flight, the ogress came out of the ruin and saw him trembling.

"Why are you so afraid?" she asked.

"I've encountered an enemy, whom I dread with all my might," he replied.

"Didn't you say that you are the son of a king?" asked the ogress.

"Indeed, I am," he said.

"Then why don't you give him some money?" she said. "That would satisfy him."

"He won't be satisfied with my money, only with my life," he stated. "And I'm petrified of him and fear for my life."

"If you're so distressed as you say," she said, "ask help from Allah, who will surely protect you from any harm or evil that threatens you."

Then the prince raised his eyes toward heaven and cried out, "May Allah help me in my need! Grant me victory over my foe. Protect me with all your might. Praise be to Allah!"

After hearing his prayer, the ogress decided to let him live, and the prince returned to his father and told him how the vizier had failed to protect him. Consequently, the king summoned the minister to him and slew him on the spot.

"Likewise, King Yunan, if you continue to trust this physician, you will die the worst kind of death. This man whom you have made your intimate companion and whom you treat with such great respect will work your destruction. Didn't you see how he healed your disease from the outside by something you grasped in your hand? Most assuredly he'll destroy you in the very same manner that he healed you!"

"You have spoken the truth," replied King Yunan. "It may be that this sage has indeed come as a spy with the intention of killing me, for certainly if he cured me by something held in my hand, he can kill me by something given me to smell. Well, minister, tell me what I should do with him."

"Have him summoned to you this very instant," replied the vizier, "and when he comes, have his head cut off, and you will be rid of him and his wickedness. Trick him before he tricks you."

"You have again spoken wisely, oh vizier," said the king, and he sent a servant to call the sage, who came in a joyful mood, for he did not know what was in store for him. When Duban entered, he gave thanks to the king for the generous gifts he had received and wished him well.

"Do you know why I have summoned you?" the king responded curtly.

"Only Allah Most Highest knows all there is to know!" the sage declared.

But the king retorted, "I have summoned you to take your life and to make sure that you are utterly destroyed."

Duban the Sage was puzzled and astonished by this strange statement, and he asked, "Oh king, why do you want to slay me? What harm have I done you?"

"Men tell me that you are a spy who has been sent to kill me," said the king, "and therefore I'm going to kill you before you kill me." Then he called his executioner and said, "Strike off the head of this traitor and deliver us from his evil practices."

"Spare me," said the sage, "and Allah will spare you. If you slay me, Allah will slay you."

And he repeated the very same words that I said to you, oh jinnee, and yet you wouldn't let me go because you were so bent on killing me. Likewise, King Yunan's only response was, "I shall not be safe without slaying you. You must understand that since you healed me by

something that I held in my hand, I can't be safe from
your killing me by something you might give to me to
smell or other such things."

"So this is your reward!" remarked the sage. "You
repay good only with evil."

"Nothing can help you," declared the king. "You must
die and without delay."

Now when the physician was sure that the king would
slay him without waiting, he wept and regretted the good
that he had done for the king. The executioner stepped
forward, bound Sage Duban's eyes, and drew out his
sword. Then he turned to the king and said, "With your
permission."

But the sage wept and cried, "Spare me, and Allah will
spare you. If you slay me, Allah will slay you! Is this the
reward that I deserve? It seems to me that you're giving
me nothing but crocodile boon."

"What do you mean by crocodile boon? Tell me!" the
king demanded.

"It's impossible for me to tell you anything in this
state," countered the sage. "May Allah bless you if you
spare me."

And he wept profusely until one of the king's favorites
stood up and said, "Oh king, grant me the blood of this
physician, for we have never seen him sin against you or
do anything except heal you from a disease which baffled
every doctor and scientist in your kingdom."

"You don't understand why I am putting this physician
to death," announced the king. "Listen carefully! If I
spare him, I shall be sentencing myself to certain death,
for someone who healed me of such a malady by something held in my hand can slay me by something held to
my nose. And I'm afraid that he may kill me for some
price. Indeed, he might be a spy whose sole purpose in
coming here was to plot my destruction. So nothing can
help him: die he must, and only then shall I be sure of
my own life."

"Spare me, and Allah shall spare you," Duban cried
again. "If you slay me, Allah will slay you."

But it was in vain, and when the doctor knew for
certain that the king would kill him, he said, "Oh king, if
nothing will help me, grant me a small delay so that I
may go to my house, take care of my obligations, and tell

my people and neighbors where to bury me and distribute my books of medicine. Besides, among my books I have a most rare one that I would like you to keep as a treasure in your vaults."

"And what is in the book?" the king asked.

"Things beyond your imagination, and the most amazing secret is that if you turn three pages right after you cut off my head and read three lines of the page on your left, my head will speak and answer every question that you deign to ask it."

The king was most astonished, and, laughing with delight at the novelty, he said, "Do you really want me to believe that when I cut off your head, it will speak to me?"

"Yes, your majesty!"

"This is indeed a strange matter!" said the king, and he decided instantly to send him closely guarded to his house, where Duban settled all his obligations. The next day he went to the king's audience hall, where emirs, viziers, chamberlains, nabobs, nobles, and lords of estate were gathered together, making the chamber as colorful as a garden of flowers. The doctor went up to the king carrying an old worn book and a little metal can full of powder like the one that is used to protect the eyes. Then he sat down and said, "Give me a tray."

So they brought him one, and he poured the powder onto it, smoothed it down, and said, "Oh king, take this book, but do not open it until my head falls. Then place my head on this tray, press it down on the powder, and the blood will immediately stop flowing. That is the time to open the book."

Thereupon the king took the book and made a sign to the executioner, who arose and struck off the sage's head. Afterward he placed it on the middle of the tray and pressed it down on the powder. When the blood stopped flowing, Duban's eyes glistened again, and he said, "Now open the book, oh king!"

The king opened the book, and found the pages stuck together. So he put his finger to his mouth to moisten it, and he was then easily able to turn over the first six pages, but he found nothing written on them. So he cried out, "Doctor, there's nothing written here!"

"Turn the pages some more," Duban replied.

The king continued to turn the pages, but the book was poisoned, and before long the venom penetrated his system so that the king had strong convulsions and cried out, "The poison has done its work!"

And now the Sage Duban's head replied, "Fortune repays an ungrateful tyrant's oppressive ways with the just punishment he duly deserves!"

No sooner had the head stopped speaking than the king rolled over dead.

"Now I would like you to know, oh jinnee, that if King Yunan had spared the Sage Duban, Allah would have spared him, but he refused to do so, and thus Allah slew him. So, you see, ifrit, if you had spared me, Allah would have saved you."

And Scheherazade noticed that dawn was approaching, and she stopped telling her story.

"Oh my sister," said Dunazade, "how delightful, sweet, and graceful your tale is."

"That is nothing compared to what I could tell you this coming night if the king were to spare me and I could live."

"By Allah," the king said to himself, "I won't slay her until I hear the rest of the story, for it is truly wondrous."

They rested that night in mutual embrace until dawn finally came. Then the king went to his audience hall, where the viziers and troops came. So the king judged, appointed, deposed, commanded, and prohibited the rest of the day. When the court was adjourned, the king returned to the palace, and later that night Dunazade said to her sister, "Please finish the story for us."

And Scheherazade replied, "I shall, if the king gives his permission."

"Permission granted," said the king.

So Scheherazade resumed her tale.

Then the fisherman said to the ifrit, "If you had spared me, I would have spared you. But you wouldn't be content unless I died. So now I'll let you die by keeping you jailed up in this jar, and I'll hurl you into the sea."

Then the jinnee roared and cried out, "By Allah, fisherman, don't do this! Spare me, and pardon my past deeds. If I've been tyrannical, then you should be generous, for it is said that when good is done to him who has done evil, the evildoer will stop doing evil deeds. So do not deal with me as Umamah dealt with Atikah."

"And what was their story?" asked the fisherman.

"This is not the time for storytelling with me in this prison," said the jinnee. "But if you set me free, I'll tell you the tale."

"Enough talk," responded the fisherman. "Nothing can help you. I'm going to throw you back into the sea, and there's no way you'll ever be able to get out the bottle. When I humbled myself before you and wept, you sought only to slay me. I had done you absolutely no harm, and yet you repaid my kindness with evil. So now that I know just how evil you are, I shall warn whoever may fish you from the sea to toss you back again, and you'll remain under these waters until the end of time, when your own end will come."

"Set me free!" the jinnee cried. "This is a noble occasion for generosity, and I'll pledge never to do you any harm. In fact, I'll help you get whatever you need so you'll never be poor again."

The fisherman paused a moment and then finally accepted his promise on the condition that the jinnee would not harm him but would enter into his service. After making the jinnee swear a solemn oath by Almighty Allah, he opened the top, and the pillar of smoke rose up until it was completely out of the bottle. Then it thickened and became once more the hideous ifrit, who immediately kicked the bottle and sent it flying into the sea.

Upon seeing how badly the bottle was treated, the fisherman thought his turn would certainly come next, and he piddled in his pants. "This does not augur well for me," he said to himself, but he took heart and cried out, "Oh jinnee, keep your promise, for you will be judged later on how well you have kept your promises! You've made a vow to me and have sworn an oath not to deceive me. If you do, Allah will take His revenge, for He is a jealous God, who gives respite to the sinner but does not let him escape. So, let me remind you what the Sage Duban said to King Yunan, 'Spare me, and Allah will spare you!' "

The ifrit burst into laughter and stalked away, saying to the fisherman, "Follow me."

The man walked after him at a safe distance to make sure he might have a chance to escape, and they went around the suburbs of the city and entered some woods. After marching through the woods, they came to a vast wilderness, and in the middle of it stood a mountain lake. The jinnee waded into the middle of it and cried again, "Follow me!"

After the fisherman did this, the ifrit told him to cast his net and catch some fish. The fisherman looked into the water and was astonished to see all sorts of different-colored fish—white, red, blue, and yellow. When he cast his net and hauled it in, however, he saw that he had caught four fish, each with a different color. He rejoiced a great deal, and even more when the jinnee said to him, "Carry these to the sultan and offer them to him as a gift. In return he'll give you enough to make you a wealthy man. Now, you must pardon me, for I know of no other way of serving you. As you know, I have lain in the sea eighteen hundred years and have not seen the face of the world until just recently. Just remember not to fish here more than once a day." Then the ifrit wished the fisherman Godspeed and said, "May Allah grant that we meet once again." Thereupon the jinnee struck the earth with one foot and the ground parted and swallowed him up.

After his astonishment subsided, the fisherman took the fish and headed for the city. As soon as he reached home, he filled a clay bowl with water and threw the fish into it. Then he carried the bowl with the wriggling fish to the king's palace, as the ifrit had told him to do, and offered them to the king, who was amazed by the sight, for never in his life had he seen such marvelous fish as these.

"Give these fish to the slave girl who does our cooking," he said to his vizier, who carried the fish to the girl and told her to fry them.

After he had carried out his chore, the vizier returned to the king, who commanded him to give the fisherman four hundred dinars. After the fisherman received them, he ran home stumbling, falling, and jumping up, for he thought the whole thing was a dream. In reality, however, he bought everything his family wanted and was extremely joyful and happy to be with his wife once again.

In the meantime the sultan's cook cleaned the fish and set them in the frying pan. Then she basted them with oil until one side was dressed. When she turned them over, however, the kitchen wall split open, and there appeared a beautiful and graceful lady with an oval face and black eyelashes. She wore a silk dress lined in blue. Large earrings adorned her ears, a pair of bracelets her wrists, while rings with priceless gems were on her fingers. In one of her hands she held a long rod of rattan cane, which she thrust into the frying pan, and she said, "Oh fish! Oh fish! Are you keeping your pledge?"

When the cook saw this apparition, she gasped and fainted. The young lady repeated her words two more times, and at last the fish raised their heads from the pan and spoke in an articulate way, "Yes! Yes!"

After this the young lady upset the frying pan and went away the same way she had entered. The kitchen wall closed behind her, and when the cook recovered from her faint, she saw the four fish charred black as charcoal, and they cried out, "His staff broke in his first bout."

Once again the maiden fainted and fell to the ground. While she was in this condition, the vizier came for the fish, and when he saw her lying on the ground, completely dazed, he shoved her with his foot and said, "Bring the fish for the sultan!"

After recovering from her daze, she informed the vizier what had happened, and after getting over his astonishment, he sent for the fisherman. When the fisherman arrived, the vizier said to him, "I want you to fetch four more fish like those that you brought before."

Accordingly, the man returned to the lake and cast his net. When it settled, there were suddenly four fish in it just like the first. He carried them straight to the vizier, who took them to the cook and said, "Get up now and fry these fish in front of me so I can see what's going on here."

The maiden arose, cleaned the fish, and put them into the frying pan over the fire. After a few minutes the wall split into two, and the young lady appeared as before. In her hand was the wand, which she thrust into the frying pan again, and she said, "Oh fish! Oh fish! Are you keeping your pledge?"

Suddenly the fish lifted their heads and repeated, "Yes! Yes!"

* * *

And Scheherazade noticed that dawn was approaching and stopped telling her story. When the next night arrived, however, she received the king's permission to continue her tale and said,

When the fish spoke and the young lady upset the frying pan with her wand and left by the way she had come, the vizier cried out, "We must tell the king about this."

So he went and told the king what had happened, and the king responded by saying, "I must see this with my own eyes." The first thing he did was to send for the fisherman, whom he commanded to bring four other fish like the first. After the fisherman returned with the fish, the king rewarded him with four hundred gold pieces and turned to the vizier. "I want you to get up and fry the fish before me!" he commanded.

"To hear is to obey," the minister replied. He had the frying pan brought to him, cleaned the fish, and set the pan with the fish in it over the fire. Suddenly the wall split in two, and out burst a black slave like a huge rock carrying a green branch in his hand.

"Oh fish! Oh fish!" he cried in loud and terrible tones. "Are you keeping your old pledge?"

In turn the fish lifted their heads from the frying pan and said, "Yes! Yes! We're true to our word!"

Then the huge blackamoor approached the frying pan and upset it with the branch and left by the way he had come. After he had vanished from their sight, the king inspected the fish and found them all charred black as charcoal. Utterly bewildered, he said to the vizier, "This is truly a matter that should be made known to everyone, and as for the fish, there's certainly something marvelous connected to them."

So he summoned the fisherman and said to him, "You'd better fear for your life, fisherman, if you lie to me! Where did you catch these fish?"

"From a lake lying in a valley behind that mountain which you can see from your city," he replied.

"How many days' march is it from here?" the king asked.

"Your majesty, it's only a half hour from here."

The king was puzzled by this reply, but he quickly ordered his troops to get ready for an excursion. The fisherman had to lead the way as guide, and under his breath he began cursing the jinnee. They walked until they had climbed the mountain and descended into a great desert which they had never seen before in their lives. When they reached the valley set between four mountains and saw the lake with the red, white, yellow, and blue fish, they were even more astounded. The king stood fixed to the spot in amazement and asked everyone present, "Has any one of you ever seen this lake before?"

They all responded by saying that they had never seen the lake before, and they also questioned the oldest inhabitants they met, men well stricken in years, but each and every one of them responded that he had never seen such a lake in that place.

"By Allah," said the king, "I shall neither return to my capital nor sit upon the throne of my forebears until I learn the truth about this lake and these strange fish." He then ordered his men to dismount and set up camp all around the mountain. Then he summoned his vizier, a minister with a great deal of experience, sagacious, perceptive, and well versed in such affairs. "I've something in mind that I want to tell you about," the king said. "My heart tells me to travel forth tonight all alone and to search out the mystery of this lake and its fish. I want you to take my seat at the tent door and say to the emirs, viziers, nabobs, and chamberlains that the sultan is sick and has ordered you not to let anyone enter his tent. Be careful that you don't let anyone know my plans."

Since the vizier did not oppose his plan, the sultan changed his clothes, slung his sword over his shoulder, and left by a path which led up one of the mountains. He marched the entire night until dawn arrived, and he continued walking even then until the heat became too much for him. After resting for a while, he resumed his march and continued through the second night until dawn, when he suddenly noticed a black point in the far distance and said to himself, "Perhaps someone there will be able to tell me about the mystery of the lake and its fish!"

As he drew near the dark object, he realized that it was a palace built of dark stone plated with iron. One side of the gate was open, while the other was shut. The king's spirits rose high as he stood before the gate and rapped lightly. Hearing no answer, he knocked a few more times, yet nobody came. "Most likely it's empty," he said to himself. So he mustered up his courage and walked through the main gate into the large hall, where he cried out, "Holla, anyone here? I'm a stranger and traveler in need of food!" He repeated his cry two more times, but there was still no reply. So he made up his mind to explore the place, and he boldly strode through the vestibule into the very middle of the palace, but he did not find anyone.

The palace was furnished with silken materials that had gold stars on them, and there were hangings over the doorways. In the middle of the palace was a spacious court with four open salons set off on the sides. A canopy shaded the court, and in the center was a flowing fountain with four lion statues made of gold, spouting water from their mouths that was as clear as pearls. Birds were flying freely all around the place, and there was a net of golden wire set over the palace that prevented them from flying off. In short, there was everything imaginable in this palace except human beings.

The king was amazed by all this, but he felt sad that he had found no one who could reveal to him the mystery of the lake, the fish, the mountains, and the palace itself. When he sat down near the fountain to ponder the situation, however, he soon heard a mournful sigh that seemed to come from a grieving heart. The sultan sprang to his feet and followed the sound until he encountered a curtain draped over the entrance to a chamber. After raising it, he saw a young man sitting upon a couch about three feet above the ground. He was a handsome man and well-proportioned. His forehead was as white as a flower, and his cheeks were rosy. The king rejoiced and greeted him, while the young man, who was wearing a crown studded with gems, remained seated in his caftan of silken stuff lined with Egyptian gold. His face was sad with the traces of sorrow as he returned the royal greeting and said, "My lord, your dignity demands that I rise to greet you, but I can only beg your pardon for failing to do so."

"You have my pardon," the king said. "Please regard

me as your guest who has come here on a special mission. I would appreciate your telling me the secret of this lake and its fish and about this palace and your loneliness and why you are grieving."

When the young man heard these words, he began to weep so much that his bosom became drenched with tears. The king was astounded by such an outburst and asked him, "What's causing all these tears, young man?"

"Why shouldn't I weep when I am in the condition that I'm in?" responded the youth, who put out his hand and raised the skirt of his garment. Immediately the king realized that the youth's lower half was stone down to his feet, while his upper half was human and alive. Upon seeing this, the king was full of compassion and cried out, "Alas, young man, my heart goes out to you! In truth, you heap sorrow upon my sorrow. I had only wanted to ask you about the mystery of the fish. But now I am concerned to hear your story as well. Do not put me off, young man. I want you to tell me your entire tale right now."

"Lend me your ears, your sight, and your insight," he replied.

"All are at your service!" the king stated.

"My situation is highly extraordinary," the youth said, "and so is that of the fish. And if my tale could be engraved somewhere for all to see, it could serve as a wonderful warning."

"Why is that?" asked the king.

And the young man began to tell

The Tale of the Enchanted Prince

I'll have you know, my lord, that my sire was king of this city, and his name was Mahmud, lord of the Black Islands and ruler of what are now these four mountains. He reigned threescore and ten years, after which he died, and I was appointed sultan in his place. I took my cousin as my wife, the daughter of my paternal uncle, and she loved me with such abounding love that whenever I was absent she did not eat or drink until she saw me again. She had been living with me for five years when, on a certain day, she went to the Hammam bath and stayed there a long time. After asking the cook to get everything ready for our supper, I went into the palace and lay down on the bed where I was accustomed to sleep. Then I requested two maidens to fan my face, one sitting by my head and the other at my feet. But I was restless because my wife was absent, and I could not sleep. Though my eyes were closed, my mind and thoughts were wide awake. Soon I heard the slave girl at my head say to the one who was at my feet, "How I pity our poor master! His youth is being wasted, and it is all on account of our mistress, that cursed whore, who's betraying him!"

"Yes, you're right. May Allah curse all faithless women. Our talented master deserves something better than this harlot who sleeps with someone else every night."

"Is our master dumb and foolish?" asked the slave girl who sat by my head. "Why doesn't he question her?"

"Shame on you!" the other replied. "Our master doesn't know what she's doing, nor does he have a choice. She drugs his drink every night before he goes to bed. So he sleeps deeply and doesn't have an inkling about where she goes and what she does. But we know that after giving him the drugged wine, she puts on her richest clothes and perfumes. Then she goes away until the break of day, when she comes back to him and burns a pastille under his nose so he can awake from his deathlike sleep."

When I heard the slave girl's words, I was livid with rage, and I thought night would never fall. Soon, however, my wife returned from the bath, and we had dinner together. Afterward, as was our custom, we sat half an hour together and got ready to drink some wine. When she called for the particular wine I used to drink before sleeping and handed me the cup, I pretended to drink it but actually poured the contents into my bosom. Soon I lay down and let her think that I was asleep. Suddenly she cried out, "Sleep out the night, and never wake again. By Allah, I loathe you and your whole body. My soul is disgusted from living with you, and I can't wait for the day when Allah will snatch away your life!"

Then she rose and put on her most beautiful dress and

dowsed herself with perfume. Moreover, she slung my sword over her shoulder, opened the gates of the palace, and went on her evil way. So I got up and followed her as she threaded her way through the streets until she came to the city gate, where she said some words that I could not understand. All of a sudden the padlocks dropped by themselves as if broken, and the doors of the gate opened. She went through (and I after her without her noticing anything) and walked until she came to the garbage heaps and a reed fence built around a round-roofed hut of mud bricks. After she entered the door, I climbed onto the roof and managed to look inside without being seen. There I saw my wife approach a Negro slave with his upper lip like the cover of a pot, and his lower like an open pot—lips which could sweep up sand from the gravel floor of the cot. To boot, he was a leper and a paralytic, lying upon some sugar-cane trash and wrapped in an old blanket and dirty rags. She kissed the ground before him, and he raised his head so as to see her and said, "Woe to you! Why are you so late? Some of my black brethren were here with me for a while, and they drank their wine and had their young ladies. But I could not drink because you were absent."

"Oh my lord," she said, "my heart's love, don't you realize that I'm married to my cousin, whose very looks I loathe, and I hate myself when I am in his company? And if I were not afraid for your sake, I would not let a single sun rise before turning his city into a heap of rubble, and the ravens would croak, the owls hoot, and the jackals and wolves would run amok and loot. Indeed, I would have all the stones of the city removed to the back of the Caucasus."

"You're lying, damn you!" the slave responded. "Now I'm going to swear an oath by the valor and honor of blackamoor men (and don't think that our manliness is like the poor manliness of white men) that from this day forth, if you stay away from me until this hour, I will reject your company, nor will I glue my body to your body and strum and belly-bump. Do you think you can play fast and loose with us, you cracked pot, just so we can satisfy your dirty lust? You stink! Bitch! Vilest of the vile whites!"

When I heard his words and saw what was going on

between these two wretches, the world became dark all around me, and my soul no longer knew where it was. Meanwhile my wife stood up weeping humbly before the slave and said, "Oh my beloved, oh light of my eyes!" And she did not stop weeping and abasing herself until he deigned to accept her pleas. Then she was quite glad, stood up, took off her outer garments, and said, "Oh master, what do you have here for your slave to eat?"

"Take off the cover of the pot," he grumbled, "and you'll find some boiled bones of rats we dined on. Pick at them and then go to that slop pot, where you'll find the rest of some beer that you may drink."

So she ate, drank, and washed her hands. Afterward she went and lay down by the side of the slave on the cane trash, and after stripping herself stark naked, she crept in with him under his dirty cover and rags. When I saw my wife do this deed, I completely lost my head and climbed down from the roof. After I entered the hut, I grabbed the sword which she had with her and I was determined to slay them both. First I struck at the slave's neck and thought that death now beckoned him.

And Scheherazade noticed that dawn was approaching, and she stopped telling her story. When the next night arrived, however, she received the king's permission to continue her tale and said,

After striking the slave, I had thought that I had slain him, for he uttered a loud hissing groan, but I had only cut the skin and flesh of the gullet and two arteries! When these sounds awoke my wife, I sheathed the sword and rushed to the city. Then I entered the palace, lay down on my bed, and slept until morning. Later, when my wife aroused me, I saw that she had cut off her hair and had put on mourning garments.

"Oh, son of my uncle," she said, "don't blame me for what I'm doing. I have just learned that my mother is dead, and my father has been killed in a holy war. Moreover, one of my brothers has lost his life from a snake sting, and another has died by falling off a cliff. There is nothing I can or should do but weep and lament."

When I heard her words, I held back my reproaches

and only said, "Do what you think best. I certainly will not hinder you."

So she continued to grieve and mourn for one whole year, and when the full year had passed, she said to me, "I'd like to build a tomb with a cupola in your palace that I will set aside only for my mourning, and I'll call it the House of Lamentations."

"Do what you think best," I said again.

Then she built for herself a cenotaph in which she could mourn, and she also placed a dome on top of it under which there was a tomb like a Santon's sepulcher. It was to this place that she carried the slave and housed him, but he was exceedingly weak because of his wound and unable to make love to her. He could only drink wine, and from the day of his injury he could not speak a word, but he continued to live because his appointed hour for death had not yet arrived. Every day, morning and evening, my wife went to him and wept over him. She gave him wine and strong soups and kept doing this for one more year. I tolerated all this patiently and paid no heed to her. However, one day I went into her chamber without her noticing it, and I found her weeping, slapping her face, and crying, "Why are you so absent, my heart's delight? Speak to me, my life. Talk with me, my love!"

When she had stopped weeping, I said to her, "Cousin, let this mourning suffice, for there's nothing to gain from pouring forth tears!"

"Don't try to stop me," she answered, "or I'll do something violent to myself!"

So I kept my peace and let her go her own way. Indeed, she continued to indulge her affliction for yet another year. At the end of the third year I became tired of all this mourning, and one day, when I was annoyed and angry because of some frustrating matter, I happened to enter the cenotaph and heard her say, "Oh my lord, I never hear you say a single word to me! Why don't you answer me?"

All this caused me to become enraged, and I cried out, "That's enough! How long is this sorrow to last?"

When she heard my words, she sprang to her feet crying, "Shame on you, you cur! This is all your fault! You have wounded my heart's darling and have caused me a great deal of woe. Not only that, you've wasted his youth so that he has had to lay in bed these past three years more dead than alive!"

In my wrath I cried, "Oh you dirtiest of harlots and filthiest of whores, futtered by Negro slaves hired to have a go at you! Yes, indeed it was I who did this good deed," and snatching my sword, I drew it and tried to cut her down.

But she laughed at my words and ridiculed me by saying, "To heel, hound that you are! Alas for the past that cannot return to life, nor is it possible to bring the dead back to life. But Allah has indeed placed the person in my hands who did the deed that burns my heart with a fire which doesn't die and a flame which cannot be quenched!" Then she stood up, and pronouncing some unintelligible words, she said, "By virtue of my magic powers, you are to become half stone and half man!"

As a result, oh king, I have become what you see before you, unable to rise or to sit, neither dead nor alive. Moreover, she enchanted the city with all its streets and yards, and she used her magic to turn the four islands into four mountains around the lake about which you've been asking me. And the citizens, who were of four different faiths, Moslem, Nazarene, Jew, and Magian, she transformed into fish. The Moslems are the white, the Magians red, the Christians blue, and the Jews yellow. And every day she tortures me and gives me a hundred lashes, each of which draws floods of blood and cuts the skin of my shoulders to strips. Finally, she covers my upper half with a haircloth and throws these robes over them.

Upon saying all this, the young man began shedding tears, and the sultan turned toward him and said, "Prince, although you've relieved me of one concern, you've added another. Tell me, my friend, where is she? Where is the mausoleum in which the wounded slave is lying?"

"The slave is lying under that dome over there," the young man said, "and she's sitting in the chamber across from that door. Every day at sunrise, she comes to me and strips me. Then she gives me a hundred lashes with the leather whip. I weep and shriek, but there is no power in my legs to get away from her. After she finishes

tormenting me, she visits the slave and brings him wine
and boiled meat. You can see for yourself, she'll be here
tomorrow early in the morning."

"By Allah," the king declared, "I'm going to do you a
favor, young man, and the world will take note of it. It
will be such a bold deed that it will be chronicled long
after I am dead."

Then the king sat down by the side of the young prince
and talked till nightfall, when he lay down and fell asleep.
But as soon as dawn approached, he arose, put on his
shirt, drew out his sword, and rushed to the place where
the slave was lying. He followed the light of the candles
and lamps and the smell of the incenses and unguents
that led him to the slave. With one stroke of his sword he
killed him on the spot, after which he carried him out
and threw him into a well that was in the palace. Soon
thereafter he returned to the spot where the slave had
lain and put on his garments. Finally, he lay down with
his sword close by his side. After an hour or so the
accursed witch arrived and went first to her husband,
whom she stripped and flogged cruelly with a whip, while
he cried out, "Ah! That's enough! Take pity on me,
cousin!"

But she replied, "Did you take pity on me and spare
the life of my true love, on whom I doted?" Then she
drew the haircloth over his raw and bleeding skin and
threw the robe over his entire body and went to the slave
with a goblet of wine and a bowl of meat broth in her
hands. She entered the dome weeping and wailing, "Oh
my lord, say something to me! Oh my master, talk awhile
with me!"

The king lowered his voice and, twisting his tongue,
spoke the way that blackamoors speak. "Hear now, hear
now, only Allah is all powerful and all glorious!"

Now when she heard these words, she shouted for joy
and fainted. Upon recovering her senses, she asked, "My
lord, can it be true that you've regained the power of
speech?"

"You curse of my soul," the king replied in a small and
faint voice, "do you deserve my talking to you?"

"Why shouldn't you?" she asked.

"Because you torment your husband the entire day,"
he responded, "and he keeps calling on heaven for aid so

that I can't sleep from morning until evening. And he prays and curses us so much that I'm greatly disturbed. If things were different, I would have regained my health long ago, and it is this situation that prevents me from answering you."

"With your permission," she said, "I'll release him from the spell."

"Release him, and let's have some rest," the king declared.

"As you wish," the woman said, and she went to the palace, where she took a metal bowl, filled it with water, and said certain words over it that made the contents bubble and boil. Then she sprinkled some of the water over her husband, saying, "By virtue of the dread words that I have spoken, return to the form that is your own."

Suddenly, the young man shook and trembled, and finally he rose to his feet, and rejoicing at his salvation, he cried aloud, "I testify that there is no god but *the* God, and in truth, Mohammed is His Apostle, whom Allah blesses and keeps."

Then she said to him, "Go away and never return. If you do, I'll surely slay you!"

So he departed, and she returned to the dome and said, "My lord, come out so I can look at you and your godliness!"

The king replied in faint low words, "Why? What have you accomplished? You've gotten rid of the branch but not the root of my troubles!"

"Oh my darling," she asked, "what is the root?"

"Shame on you, curse of my soul!" he answered. "The people of this city and of the four islands lift their head every night in the lake in which you have turned them to fish, and they cry to heaven and call down its anger on me and you. And this is the reason why my body cannot return to health. Go at once and set them free. Then come to me and take my hand and raise me up, for I've already regained a little strength."

When she heard the king's words, still supposing him to be the slave, she cried out in joy, "Oh my master, your every word is my command!" So she sprang to her feet full of joy and ran down to the lake, where she took some of its water in the palm of her hand.

* * *

And Scheherazade noticed that dawn was approaching, and she stopped telling her story. When the next night arrived, however, she received the king's permission to continue, and she said,

Now the sorceress took the lake water and said some unintelligible words over it. Suddenly the fish lifted their heads and stood up like men. The spell on the people of the city had been removed. What was the lake became once again a crowded capital: the bazaars were thronged with folk who bought and sold; everyone became busy once again and began doing what they had normally done; and the four mountains became islands as they were before. Then the wicked sorceress returned to the king (still thinking he was the Negro) and said to him, "Oh my love, give me your honored hands so that I can help you stand up."

"Come nearer to me," said the king in a faint tone.

When she came close enough to embrace him, he grabbed his sword and struck her through the breast so that the point showed gleaming through her back. Then he struck her a second time and cut her in two, casting her to the ground in two halves. After doing this, he departed and found the young man, now freed from the spell, awaiting him. The king told him about his release, and the prince kissed his hand with abundant thanks.

"Do you want to continue to dwell in this city or come with me to my capital?" the king asked.

"Your majesty, do you know how far it is between your country and this city?"

"Two and a half days," said the king.

But the other replied, "You must be dreaming, my lord! It would take a good year for a sturdy walker to reach your country. You wouldn't have made it here in two and a half days if it weren't for the fact that my city had been enchanted. And now, my king, I shall never part from you. No, not even for the twinkling of an eye."

The king rejoiced at his words and said, "Thanks be to Allah, who has brought us together. From this hour on, you are my son and my only son, for until now I have not been blessed with offspring."

Thereupon they embraced and rejoiced. When they returned to the prince's palace, the prince informed his lords and nobles that he was about to visit holy places as a pilgrim, and he ordered them to get everything ready for the occasion. The preparations lasted ten days, after which time he set out with the sultan, whose heart yearned for his city, which he had not seen for a good year. They journeyed with an escort of mamelukes carrying all sorts of precious gifts and rare items, and it took them twelve months before they approached the sultan's capital. Messengers were sent in advance to announce their arrival, and the vizier and the entire army came out with great joy to meet their king, for they had given up hope of ever seeing him again. The troops kissed the ground before him and were glad to see him safe and sound. After he entered his palace and took his seat upon his throne and the minister came before him, the king told him what had happened to the young prince, and the vizier congratulated him on his narrow escape. After restoring order throughout the land, the king gave many generous gifts to his people and said to the vizier, "Bring me the fisherman who gave us the fish!"

So he sent for the fisherman, who had actually been responsible for bringing about the liberation of the prince's city, and when he came to the palace, the sultan bestowed on him a robe of honor, and asked him how he was doing and whether he had children. The fisherman told him that he had two daughters and a son. So the king sent for them and took one daughter for his wife and gave the other to the young prince, while he made the son his head treasurer. Furthermore, he appointed the vizier to be sultan of the city in the Black Islands that had once belonged to the young prince and sent him there with an escort of fifty armed slaves together with robes of honor for all the lords and nobles of that city. The vizier kissed his hands and went on his way, while the sultan and the prince dwelled at home in all the solace and the delight of life. Finally, the fisherman became the richest man of his age, and his daughters lived with the kings until death brought an end to their lives.

No sooner had Scheherazade concluded her tale than she said, "And yet, oh king, this tale is no more wondrous than the remarkable story of the ebony horse."

The Ebony Horse

Once upon a time there was a great and powerful king of Persia named Sabur, whose wealth and wisdom surpassed all other monarchs in his day and age. Moreover, he was generous, kind, and beneficent. He comforted those whose spirits were broken, and he treated those who fled to him for refuge with honor. He loved the poor and was hospitable to strangers, and he always sought to defend the oppressed against their oppressors.

King Sabur had three daughters as beautiful as flower gardens in full bloom and a son as handsome as the moon. And it was his custom to celebrate two holidays during the year, the Nau-Roz or New Year, and Mihgan or the Autumnal Equinox. On both occasions he threw open his palace, gave alms to the people, made proclamations of safety and security, and promoted his chamberlains and viceroys. The people of his realm came to him, saluted him, and celebrated these holy days with joy, and they also brought him gifts, servants, and eunuchs.

Now, King Sabur loved science and geometry, and on one holiday, as he sat on his throne, three wise men entered his palace and approached him. They were cunning inventors and masters of all sorts of crafts. Indeed, they could make things so unusual and rare that it was impossible to discern how they were invented. These men were versed in the knowledge of the occult and knew all about the mysteries of the world. Each one was from a different country and spoke a foreign language. The first was a Hindi or Indian, the second a Roumi or Greek, and the third a Farsi or Persian.

When the Indian stepped forward, he prostrated himself before the king, wished him a joyous holiday, and placed before him a gift befitting his dignity: it was a man of gold set with precious gems and jewels and holding a golden trumpet in his hand.

When Sabur saw this, he said, "Tell me, sage, what can this figure do?"

And the Indian answered, "My lord, if this figure is placed at the gate of your city, he will be a most powerful protector, for whenever an enemy tries to enter, the figure will blow this trumpet against him, and he will be seized with palsy and drop down dead."

The king was extremely astonished by this gift and declared, "By Allah, if you are telling the truth, I'll grant you anything you wish or desire."

Then the Greek stepped forward, and after prostrating himself before the king, he gave him a silver basin with a golden peacock and twenty-four golden chicks in the middle of it. Sabur looked at the basin and then inquired, "Tell me, sage, what can this peacock do?"

"My lord," he answered, "whenever an hour of the day or night elapses, it pecks one of its young, cries out, and flaps its wings every hour on the hour. Then, when the end of the mouth arrives, it will open its mouth, and you will see the crescent inside it."

And the king said, "If you're telling the truth, I'll grant anything you wish or desire."

Then the Persian sage stepped forward, and after prostrating himself before the king, he presented him with a horse made of the darkest ebony wood with a gold and jeweled inlay and with saddle, stirrups, and bridle suitable for the majesty of the king. When Sabur saw the horse, he was extremely astounded and admired the beauty of its form and style. So he asked, "What can this wooden horse do? Tell me its virtue and whether it can move."

"My lord," the Persian answered, "if one mounts this horse, it will carry him wherever he wants. It can ride through the air and cover the space of a year in a single day."

The king was amazed by these wonders, especially since they came all on the same day, and he turned to the Persian sage and said, "By Allah, if you are telling the truth, I'll certainly grant you whatever you desire."

Then he entertained the sages for three days so he

could try out their gifts. During that time each one demonstrated what his invention could do: the man of gold blew his trumpet; the peacock pecked its chicks; and the Persian sage mounted the ebony horse, which soared with him high in the air and descended again. When King Sabur saw all this, he was amazed and overcome with joy. Then he said to the three sages, "I'm now convinced of the truth of your words, and it behooves me to keep my promise. So, you may now ask for whatever you want, and I shall grant your wishes."

Well, news about the beauty of the king's three daughters had reached these sages, and thus they asked, "If the king is content with us and our gifts and allows us to make a request, we beg that he give us his three daughters in marriage so that we may become his sons-in-law."

"Your wish is granted," the king said and ordered the kazi to come right away so that he could marry his daughters to these sages.

Now it so happened that the princesses were behind a curtain and witnessed this entire scene. The youngest saw that her husband-to-be was at least a hundred years old. He had white hair, a drooping forehead, mangy eyebrows, cropped ears, a dyed mustache and beard, red eyes, bleached and hollow cheeks, a flabby nose, overlapping teeth, loose lips like camel's kidneys, and a face like a cobbler's apron. In short, he was a terror, a horror, a monster. Indeed, he was the most frightful sight of his time. In contrast, the girl was the fairest and most graceful of her time, more elegant than the finest gazelle, more tender than the gentlest breeze, and certainly more beautiful than the brightest full moon. She was made for love and walked with a graceful sway that captivated all those who saw her. In short, she was more beautiful and sweeter than her two sisters, who were splendid specimens themselves. So when she saw her suitor, she went to her room and strewed dust on her head, tore her clothes, slapped her face, and wept.

Now, her brother, Prince Kamar al-Akmar, had just returned from a journey, and when he heard her weeping like that he entered her chamber (for he loved her with more affection than his other sisters) and said, "What's wrong with you? What's happened to you? Tell me everything, and don't hide a thing."

"My brother," she responded, "I have nothing to hide. Our father has decided to do something atrocious, and I intend to leave the palace. And I'll do this even if he doesn't consent, for the Lord will provide for me."

"What's the meaning of this talk?" her brother responded. "What's caused all this trouble and disturbed your heart?"

And the princess answered, "Our father has promised me in marriage to a wicked magician who has brought him a horse of black wood as a gift. This magician has bewitched our father with his craft and sorcery, but as for me, I don't want to have anything to do with him, and I wish I had never been born because of him!"

After her brother comforted her, he went to his father and said, "Who is this wizard that you're going to wed to my youngest sister? What's so wonderful about his present that you don't care if your daughter is deeply distressed? Do you think what you're doing is right?"

Now the Persian was standing nearby and heard the prince's words, which filled him with rage. Meanwhile the king replied, "My son, if you saw this horse, you'd be amazed." Then he ordered the slaves to bring the horse before him, and they did as he commanded. When the prince saw the horse, he was pleased, and being an accomplished cavalier, he mounted it right away and struck its sides with the stirrups. However, it did not move, and the king said to the sage, "Go and show him how it moves so that he may help you obtain your wish."

Of course, the Persian was still holding a grudge against the prince because the young man was opposed to his marriage with the princess. So he showed him the button on the right side of the horse that would make the horse take off and said, "Push this," and went away. Thereupon the prince pushed the button, and the horse soared with him high in the air as if it were a bird, and it kept on flying until it disappeared from everyone's sight. The king was extremely upset by this and said to the Persian, "See to it that you get him to descend."

"Oh lord," the Persian responded, "there's nothing I can do. You'll won't see him again until Resurrection Day, for he was too ignorant and too proud to ask me about the button for descending, and I forgot to tell him where it is."

When the king heard this, he became extremely angry and had the sage whipped and thrown in jail, while he himself discarded his crown, slapped his face, and pounded his breast. Moreover, he closed the doors of his palace, and he was joined by his wife, his daughters, and the rest of the people of the city in weeping and mourning for the prince. Thus, their joy was turned into sorrow and their happiness into sadness.

In the meantime, the horse kept soaring with the prince until it drew near the sun. As a result, the prince gave himself up for lost and repented for having mounted the horse. "Truly," he said, "the sage tricked me because of my youngest sister. By Allah, it seems I'm lost, but there must be a button for landing if there is one for taking off." Now, he was a smart and clever man, so he began to feel all the parts of the horse, but he saw nothing except buttons like cock's heads on the right and left shoulders of the horse. "That's all there is, it seems," he said to himself, "just these two buttons." Then he pushed the one on the right, and the horse increased its speed and flew higher. So he stopped and pushed the button on the left, and immediately the steed's upward motion slowed until it began to descend little by little toward the face of the earth.

And Scheherazade noticed that dawn was approaching, and she stopped telling her story. When the next night arrived, however, she received the king's permission to continue her tale and said,

When the prince saw what was happening and realized that he had learned to control the horse, he was filled with joy and thanked Almighty Allah, who had delivered him from certain death. Then he began to turn the horse's head wherever he wanted to go, and he made it soar and descend at his will until he attained complete mastery over it. Finally he made it descend, and this descent took the entire day, because the horse had carried him far from the earth. As he descended, he amused himself by viewing the different cities and countries that he had never seen before. Among them was a very beautiful city amidst a verdant countryside rich in trees and streams with gazelles gliding over the plains. Upon seeing this city he began musing to himself, "I wish I knew the name of that city and in what country it was!" And he began to circle and observe it.

By this time, the day had begun to decline, and it was near sunset. So he said to himself, "Certainly there's no better place to spend the night than in this fine city. I might as well stay here, and early tomorrow morning I'll return to my kith and kin and my kingdom. Then I'll tell my father and my family what happened and what I've seen." Now he began looking for a place where he might safely land, and where no one might catch sight of him. Soon he glimpsed a tall palace in the middle of the city. It was surrounded by a large wall with lofty towers and battlements and was guarded by forty black slaves clad in complete mail and armed with spears and swords and bows and arrows. "That's a good spot," he said, and he pushed the descent button, which made the horse fly down like a weary bird, and he landed gently on the terrace roof of the palace.

After the prince dismounted and gave his praise to Allah, he inspected the horse and said, "Whoever invented and built you so perfectly was a clever craftsman, and if the Almighty grants me a long life and reunites me with my father and family safe and sound, I'll certainly bestow on him all kinds of gifts and treat him with the utmost generosity." By this time, night had come, and he sat on the roof until he was certain that everyone in the palace was asleep. Indeed, he was extremely hungry and thirsty, for he had not eaten or drunk anything since he had been separated from his father. So he said to himself, "I'm sure that there's plenty to eat and drink in this palace."

So he left the horse above and went down into the palace in search of something to eat. Soon he came to a staircase, and after he went down to the bottom, he found himself in a court paved with white marble and alabaster, which shone in the light of the moon. He was astounded by the place and the fine architecture, but there was not a single sign of a living soul, and he was surprised and perplexed. After he looked to the right and the left, he could not decide which way to go and said to himself, "Perhaps it would be better if I returned to where I left my horse and spent the night by its side. Then, as soon as day dawns, I'll mount it and ride away."

*   *   *

And Scheherazade noticed that dawn was approaching, and she stopped telling her story. When the next night arrived, however, she received the king's permission to continue her tale and said,

As he was talking to himself, he spotted a light inside the palace, and after heading in that direction, he found that it came from a candle that stood in front of a door to the harem. Next to the candle was a huge eunuch, who was asleep. He looked like one of the ifrits of Solomon or a tribesman of the jinn, as long and as broad as a tree. As he lay on the floor, the pommel of his sword gleamed in the flame of the candle, and at his head was a bag of leather hanging from a granite column. When the prince saw the eunuch, he was frightened and said, "May Allah help me! Oh Holy One, just as you saved me in the sky, please let me escape safe and sound from this adventure!"

After saying this he reached for the leather bag, and after grabbing hold of it, he carried it to the side, opened it, and found some very good food. Thereupon, he ate his fill and refreshed himself. Afterward he returned the bag to its place and drew the eunuch's sword from its sheath while the slave kept sleeping.

Then the prince continued exploring the harem until he came to a second door with a curtain drawn before it. So, he lifted the curtain, and upon entering the room, he saw a couch of whitest ivory lined with pearls, jacinths, and jewels and four slave girls sleeping around it. He went up to the couch to see what was on it and found a young lady lying asleep. She looked like the full moon rising over the eastern horizon with her brow decorated by white flowers, her hair shining, her cheeks crimson and dotted by dainty moles. Indeed, he was amazed by her stunning beauty as she lay there, and he no longer was afraid of dying. So he went up to her, and trembling in every nerve and shuddering with pleasure, he kissed her on the right cheek, whereupon she awoke right away and opened her eyes. Seeing the prince standing before her, she said, "Who are you, and where have you come from?"

"I'm your slave and lover," he said.

"And who brought you here?" she asked.

"My Lord and my destiny," he replied.

"Then," said Shams al-Nahar, for that was her name, "perhaps you're the one who asked my father yesterday for my hand in marriage and was rejected by him because he thought you were atrocious. By Allah, if that's the case, my sire lied through his teeth when he said this, for you're quite handsome."

Now the son of the king of Hind had wanted to marry her, and her father had rejected him because he was indeed ugly and uncouth, and the princess thought the prince was the rejected suitor. So, when she saw how handsome and elegant he was (for he was clearly more radiant than the moon), she was ignited by the flaming fire of love, and they began to converse and talk. Suddenly, her waiting women awoke, and upon seeing the prince with their mistress, they said to her, "My lady, who is this man?"

"I don't know," she said. "I found him sitting by me when I woke up. Perhaps he's the prince who sought my hand in marriage from my father."

"By Allah," they cried out, "this man is not the one who sought your hand in marriage, for the other was hideous, and this one is handsome. Indeed, the other man is not even fit to be his servant."

Then the slave girls ran out to the eunuch, and after they waked him from his slumber, he jumped up in alarm.

"How is it that you're supposed to be on guard in the palace," they said, "and yet men come into our chamber when we are asleep?"

When the black heard this, he quickly grabbed for his sword but could not find it, and he was seized by fear. Totally confused by what was happening, he rushed to his mistress, and upon seeing the prince sitting and talking to her, he said, "My lord, are you a man or a jinnee?"

"Woe to you, you unluckiest of slaves!" the prince replied. "How dare you compare a son of the royal Chosroës with one of those pagan devils!" And he became like a raging lion, took the eunuch's sword in his hand, and said, "I am the king's son-in-law, and he's

married me to his daughter and commanded me to go
and see her."

When the eunuch heard these words, he replied, "My
lord, if you are indeed the man you say you are, she's
only fit for you, and you are worthier of her than anyone
else."

Thereupon the eunuch ran to the king, shrieking aloud,
tearing his garments, and tossing dust on his head. When
the king heard this outcry, he said, "What's happened to
you? Speak quickly, and be brief, for you've sent chills
up my spine!"

"Oh king," answered the eunuch, "go and rescue your
daughter, for a devil of the jinn, who's taken on the guise
of a king's son, has got possession of her. Get up at
once!"

When the king heard this, he would have liked to kill
the eunuch for being so careless and letting a demon get
hold of his daughter. Instead, he stood up and rushed to
his daughter's chamber, where he found her slave women
awaiting him.

"What's happened to my daughter?" he asked.

"Your majesty," they answered, "slumber overcame
us, and when we awoke, we found a young man sitting
on her couch in conversation with her. He looks like the
full moon, and we've never seen a man as handsome as
he is. So we asked him to explain everything, and he told
us that you had given him your daughter in marriage.
That's all we know, nor are we sure whether he's a man
or jinnee. Whatever he is, he is certainly modest and
well-bred and has done nothing disgraceful."

Now when the king heard these words, his wrath cooled,
and he raised the curtain little by little, and as he looked
in, he saw his daughter talking with a handsome prince
whose face glistened like the moon. Yet he felt he must
protect his daughter's honor and could not control his
feelings. So he brushed the curtain aside, rushed in, and
drew his sword like a furious ghoul.

When the prince saw him, he asked the princess, "Is
this your sire?"

And she replied, "Yes."

*And Scheherazade noticed that dawn was approaching
and stopped telling her story. When the next night arrived,*

*however, she received the king's permission to continue
her tale and said,*

All at once, the prince sprang to his feet, seized his
sword, and shouted at the king with such a terrible cry
that the king became utterly confused. Indeed, the prince
would have attacked the king with his sword, but the
king realized that the young man was more stalwart than
he was, so he sheathed his scimitar and dropped his arms
until the prince came up to him. Then the king said,
"Young man, are you a human or a jinnee?"

"If I did not respect your right as my host and cherish
your daughter's honor," said the prince, "I'd seal your
fate right here and now! How dare you associate me with
devils, me, a prince of the royal Chosroës, who, if they
wished to take your kingdom, could make you tremble,
and you'd feel as if an earthquake had hit you and
consumed your realm!"

Now, when the king heard his words, he was overcome
with fear and awe, and he replied, "If you are indeed the
son of kings, as you claim, how come you've entered my
palace without my permission and besmirched my honor
by making your way to my daughter and pretending that
I've given her to you as your wife? I'll have you know
that I've slain kings and sons of kings who sought her
hand in marriage! Even now, who could save you from
my might and majesty if I were to order my slaves and
servants to put you to the vilest of deaths? Who could
save you from my power?"

When the prince heard the king's speech, he answered,
"Truly, I'm surprised by you and your lack of sense! Tell
me, do you think you could possibly find a husband for
your daughter more handsome than I am? Have you ever
encountered a man with a stouter heart or one better
suited for a sultan or more glorious in rank than I?"

"Nay, by Allah!" responded the king. "Still, you should
have acted according to the custom of kings and asked
me whether you could be her husband before witnesses
so that I might have wed her to you in a public ceremony. Yet, even now, if I were to marry her to you in
private, you've dishonored me in front of her."

"All this is true," the prince said, "but if you summon
your slaves and soldiers, and they slay me, as you claim

they can, you would but only make known your own disgrace, and the people wouldn't know whether to believe you or me. Therefore, it seems to me that you'd do well to listen to my advice."

"And what is that?" asked the king.

"I propose," the prince declared, "that either you meet me in personal combat, and whoever slays the other shall have complete claim to the kingdom; or else leave me alone this night, and when dawn arrives, call out your cavalry, infantrymen, and servants against me. But first tell me how many there are."

"There are forty thousand in the cavalry," said the king, "and just as many in my infantry."

"When day breaks," the prince said, "you can set them against me and say to them: 'This man is a suitor for my daughter's hand, and he may only have her if he fights you all alone and wins, for he claims that he can defeat you and put you to rout.' After you say this, let me fight them, and if they slay me, your secret and honor will be protected forever. If I overcome them, then a king could have no better son-in-law."

And Scheherazade noticed that dawn was approaching and stopped telling her story. When the next night arrived, however, she received the king's permission to continue her tale and said,

After hearing this proposal, the king agreed to it. Despite the fact that he was awed by the prince's bravery, the king was certain that he would perish in the fray, and therefore he would not have to fear being dishonored. So he called the eunuch and ordered him to go to his vizier right away and tell him to assemble the whole army and prepare for battle. The eunuch carried the king's order to the minister, who immediately summoned the captains of the army and lords of the realm and commanded them to prepare for battle. The king himself sat for a long while conversing with the young prince and was pleased by his wise talk, good sense, and fine breeding. When it was daybreak, the king returned to his throne, commanded his merry men to mount, and ordered them to saddle one of the best of the royal steeds with handsome trappings and to bring it to the prince.

But the young man said, "Your majesty, I won't mount a horse until I review your troops."

"As you wish," replied the king. Then the two went to the parade ground, where the troops were assembled, and the prince looked them over and noted their great number. At this point, the king declared to them, "Listen, all you men! This young man has come to ask for my daughter's hand in marriage. Quite truthfully, I've never met a finer lad, nor anyone with a stouter heart or a stronger arm, for he claims that he can overcome you single-handedly and put you to rout. Indeed, he's declared that even if you were a hundred thousand, he would prevail. Now, when he charges at you, I want you to greet him with your sharp pikes and sabers and show him that he's taken on much more than he can handle." Turning now to the prince, the king said, "Get on with it, my son. It's time to do your duty!"

"Your majesty," the prince replied, "you're not being fair with me. Am I to go against your men on foot while they are mounted?"

The king responded, "I asked you to mount before. Well then, choose any of my horses you like."

"None of your horses pleases me," the prince stated. "I'll only ride the horse that I came on."

"Well, where's your horse?" the king asked.

"On top of the palace," said the prince.

"In what part of my palace?"

"On the roof."

Now when the king heard these words, he cried, "Stop this nonsense! This is the first sign you've given that you're mad. How can the horse be on the roof? But we'll see at once if you're telling the truth." Then he turned to one of his chief officers and said, "Go to my palace and bring me whatever you find on the roof."

All the people gathered at the assembly were astounded by the prince's words, and they began murmuring, "How can a horse come down the steps from the roof? We've never heard of a thing like this before!" In the meantime the king's messenger returned to the palace, climbed the stairs to the roof, and found the horse standing there. Never had it looked more handsome, but when the officer drew near and examined it, he saw that it was made of ebony and ivory. Now this man was accompanied by other officers, who began laughing when they saw that the horse was wooden. "Was this the horse that the young man meant? He must be mad. Well, we'll soon see, no matter what."

And Scheherazade noticed that dawn was approaching and stopped telling her story. When the next night arrived, however, she received the king's permission to continue her tale and said,

Then they lifted the horse and carried it to the king. Once they set it down before him, all his lords flocked around it to marvel at its beauty and the rich saddle and bridle. The king, too, admired it and was astounded by it. Then he asked the prince, "Young man, is this your horse?"

"Yes," he responded, "this is my horse, and you'll soon see how wonderful it is."

"Then take it and mount it," commanded the king.

"I won't mount it until your troops withdraw a bit," he replied.

So the king ordered them to retreat a good bow's shot from the horse, and the prince cried out, "Now watch, my king, for I'm about to mount my horse and charge your army and scatter them left and right!" Then the prince mounted while the troops arranged themselves in rows before him, and one soldier said to another, "When he comes between the rows, we'll greet him with the points of our pikes and sabers."

"By Allah," said another, "this is unfortunate. I find it difficult to slay such a handsome youth."

And a third continued, "You'll have to work hard to get the better of him, for I'm sure he's not doing this without knowing his own strength and potential."

Meanwhile after the prince got settled in his saddle, he pushed the button to take off, and all the people strained their eyes to see what he would do. Just then the horse began to heave and rock and sway and make the strangest movements that a steed ever made. Soon its belly was filled with air, and it took off with its rider soaring high into the sky. When the king saw this, he cried out to his men, "Woe to you! Catch him, catch him before he escapes!"

But his viziers and viceroys yelled back, "Oh king, can a man overtake a flying bird? This man is surely some mighty magician or jinnee, and may Allah save you from him!"

After watching the prince's feat, the king returned to the palace, where he went straight to his daughter and told her what had happened on the parade ground. He found her very much distressed because of the prince's departure, and all at once she fell violently sick and took to bed. Now, when her father saw her in such a miserable state, he embraced her, kissed her on her forehead, and said, "My daughter, praise the Almighty Allah and thank Him for delivering us from this cunning enchanter, this villain, this thief, who thought only of seducing you!" And he repeated to her the story of the prince and how he had disappeared in the sky, and he cursed him, not knowing how dearly his daughter loved him. But she paid no attention to his words and kept on weeping and saying to herself, "By Allah, I'll neither eat nor drink until Allah reunites me with him!"

Consequently, her father became greatly concerned about her condition, and no matter how he tried to soothe her, her longing for the prince only increased.

And Scheherazade noticed that dawn was approaching and stopped telling her story. When the next night arrived, however, she received the king's permission to continue her tale and said,

Now when Prince Kamar al-Akmar had risen high in the sky, he turned his horse's head toward his native land, and all he could do was to think about the beauty of the lovely princess. Since he had asked some of the king's people what the name of the city was, he knew that the city was called Sana'a and kept its location in mind. Meanwhile, he journeyed as fast as he could to the capital of his own country, and after circling the city, he landed on the roof of his father's palace, where he left his horse. Then he descended into the palace, and upon seeing that the threshold was strewn with ashes, he thought that one of his family had died. As was his custom, he entered the large salon and found his father, mother, and sisters clad in black mourning garments, and all of them were haggard and had pale faces. When his father caught sight of him and was sure that it was his son, he uttered a great cry and fell down in a fit. After a while he came to himself and embraced the prince with great joy. Then they all began to ask him what had happened to him, and he told them everything from first to last.

"Praise be Allah for bringing you home safe and sound," the king said, and he ordered his servants to prepare a great festival while the good news spread throughout the city. Drums and cymbals proclaimed the event. The mourning clothes were discarded. The streets and markets were decorated. The people vied with one another as to who should be the first to make the king even more jubilant than he was. In the meantime the king announced a general amnesty and ordered all the prisoners to be released. Moreover, he had banquets prepared for the people of the city, and for seven days and seven nights everyone ate and drank all he wanted, while the king rode around on horseback with his son so that the people could see the prince and rejoice.

After a while, the prince asked his father, "What's happened to the man who made the ebony horse?"

And the king replied, "I rue the very day that I set eyes on him! He was the cause of your separation from us, my son, and he has been in jail ever since your disappearance." However, now the king ordered the sage to be released from prison, and after sending for him, he presented him with clothes befitting his dignity and treated him generously and kindly, but he would not allow him to wed his daughter. Consequently, the sage became furious and regretted that he had given the king the horse, especially since he knew that the prince had learned the secret of the steed and how to control its movements. Despite the fact that the prince had managed to operate the horse, his father said to him, "You'd do well not to go near the horse from here on, for you don't know all that it can do, and you may make a mistake if you mount it again."

Now the prince had told his father about his adventure with the king of Sana'a and his daughter, and his father remarked that if the king had intended to kill him, he would have done so, but his hour had not yet arrived. In the meantime, the celebrations had come to an end, and the king and his son returned to the palace, where they sat down to eat, drink, and make merry. While they were sitting there, one of the king's beauitful slave girls, who was skilled in playing the lute, began to sweep her fingers across the strings and sing a song about the separation of lovers. When the prince heard these verses, the sparks of longing flamed up in his heart, and he yearned for the daughter of the king of Sana'a. So he rose right away, and after eluding his father's sight, he went up to the roof of the palace, where he mounted the horse and pushed the takeoff button, and the horse soared toward the upper regions of the sky. Some time later his father wondered where he was, and after climbing to the roof of the palace, he saw his son high in the firmament and was greatly troubled and regretted that he had not taken the horse and hidden it. Then he said to himself, "By Allah, if my son returns to me, I'll destroy the horse so that he'll be forced to stay on the ground, where he belongs, and I won't have to worry about him anymore." And he began to weep and moan.

And Scheherazade noticed that dawn was approaching and stopped telling her story. When the next night arrived, however, she received the king's permission to continue her tale and said,

While the king was weeping, his son kept flying through the sky until he came to the city of Sana'a and landed on the roof as he had done before. Then he crept downstairs quietly and, finding the eunuch asleep as usual, he raised the curtain and entered the alcove of the princess's chamber. To be on the safe side, he stopped to listen and heard her shedding tears and reciting some verses, while her women slept soundly all around her. Soon, however, some of them woke up because of her weeping and said, "Mistress, why are you mourning for someone who doesn't mourn you?"

"You fools!" she replied, "Do you think he's the kind who forgets or who can be forgotten?" And she began to weep and wail again until sleep overcame her.

Upon hearing and seeing all this, the prince's heart melted. So he entered her chamber and saw that she was

lying asleep without a cover and touched her hand, causing her to open her eyes and look at him.

"Why all this crying and mourning?" he asked.

And when she realized that it was he, she threw herself
upon him, gave him a kiss, and said, "Because of you
and because we were separated."

"My lady," he stated, "I, too, have been desolate
because of our separation!"

"Then why did you leave me?" she asked. "If you had
stayed away any longer, I would have died!"

"But think about my predicament with your father and
how he treated me," he answered. "If it had not been for
you, love of my life, I would have certainly slain him, but
because I love you, I'll love him for your sake."

"But you still shouldn't have left me," she said. "Did
you really believe that I could continue having a sweet
life after meeting you?"

"Let us forget what's happened. That's all past," he
declared. "Now I'm hungry and thirsty."

So she ordered her maidens to bring in something to
eat and drink, and they began eating, drinking, and conversing until the night was almost over. When day broke,
he rose to say goodbye to her before the eunuch would
awake. But Shams al-Nahar asked him, "Where are you
going?"

"To my father's house," he responded, "and I give you
my word that I'll come to you once a week."

However, she wept and said, "I beg you, by Allah the
Almighty, take me with you. I'll go wherever you go.
Don't make me suffer the bitter separation again."

"Will you really go with me?" he asked.

"Yes."

"Then," said he, "let's rise and depart."

So she got up right away, went to a chest, and adorned
herself in her richest and dearest trinkets and jewels.
Then, without telling her maidens where she was going,
she left the chamber with the prince, who took her up to
the roof of the palace. After he mounted the ebony
horse, he lifted her up behind him and tied her to him
with some strong rope. When everything was set, he
pushed the takeoff button, and the horse rose high in the
air. When her slave girls saw this, they shrieked aloud
and ran and told her father and mother, who rushed to

the rooftop only to see the magic horse fly away with the prince and princess. In his anguish, the king cried out, "Prince, I beg of you, by Allah, have mercy on us, and don't take away our daughter!"

The prince did not reply, but he thought to himself that the lady might regret being separated from her mother and father, and he asked her, "Oh beauty of the age, do you want me to take you back to your mother and father?"

"By Allah, my lord," she said, "my only wish is to be with you. I am so consumed by my love for you that I don't mind being separated from my mother and father."

Upon hearing these words, the prince rejoiced and made the horse fly carefully and gently so as not to disquiet her. Indeed, they kept flying until they caught sight of a green meadow with a spring of running water. Here they landed and ate and drank. Then they remounted and flew until they were in sight of his father's capital. The prince was filled with joy at seeing the city and thought that he would show to his beloved his father's dominions so that she would see that they were greater than those of her sire. So they landed in one of his father's gardens outside the city, and he carried her into a summerhouse with a dome. He left the ebony horse at the door and told the damsel to keep watch over it while he was away. "Sit here," he said, "until my messenger comes to you. I'm going to my father to ask him to prepare lodgings for you, and then I'll show you the royal estate."

She was delighted when she heard these words and said, "As you wish."

And Scheherazade noticed that dawn was approaching and stopped telling her story. When the next night arrived, however, she received the king's permission to continue her tale and said,

The prince's words indicated to her that he wanted to prepare everything for her so she could enter the city with due honor and respect according to her rank. So she was quite pleased. In the meantime, the prince went to the palace of his father, who rejoiced at his return. Then the prince said to him, "I've brought the king's daughter with me, the lovely damsel I told you about the other day. I've left her outside the city in the summer garden, and I'd like you to prepare a royal procession for her and go out to meet her in majestic array with all your troops and guards."

"I'm more than happy to do this," replied the king, and he immediately gave orders to have the town decorated. Then he went and mounted his horse and rode out in all splendor and majesty leading a host of high officers and servants followed by a band with drums, kettledrums, fifes, trumpets, and all kinds of instruments. In the meantime, the prince went to his treasury and took out jewelry, rich apparel, and whatever else kings generally keep in a safe place, and he set up a splendid display of his wealth. Moreover, he ordered the servants to prepare a litter with a canopy of green, yellow, and red brocade, and he ordered Indian, Greek, and Abyssinian slave girls to sit inside. Then he left the litter and went to the pavilion where he had set the princess down. Yet, neither she nor the horse was there. When he saw this, he slapped his face, tore his garments, and began wandering around the garden as if he had lost his mind. Eventually, however, he came to his senses and asked himself, "How could she have discovered the secret of the horse? I didn't tell her anything. Maybe the Persian sage who made the horse happened to come upon her and flew off with her in revenge for the way my father treated him." Then he sought out the guards of the garden and asked them if they had seen anyone enter the grounds. "Tell me the truth and the whole truth, or I'll have your heads cut off right away!"

"No one has entered," they said, "except for the Persian sage, who came to gather some herbs for healing."

So the prince was sure that it was indeed the sage who had flown off with the maiden.

And Scheherazade noticed that dawn was approaching and stopped telling her story. When the next night arrived, however, she received the king's permission to continue her tale and said,

Confused and bewildered, the prince was ashamed when the king and his entourage arrived. Turning to his sire, he told him what had happened and said, "Take the troops and march back to the city with them. As for me, I'll never return until I've cleared up this affair."

When the king heard this he was distressed and wept. "My son," he said, "calm yourself. Try to get over your sorrow and come home with us. I can arrange a wedding with some other king's daughter."

But the prince paid no attention to his words, and after bidding his father farewell, he set out on a journey, while the king returned to the city, and their joy was changed into sadness.

Now, it was due to destiny that, after the prince had left the princess in the garden house and gone to his father's palace, the Persian entered the garden to gather some special herbs. But when he smelled the sweet aroma of musk and other perfumes that emanated from the princess and impregnated the whole place, he followed his nose until he came to the pavilion, where he saw the horse that he had made with his own hands. His heart was filled with joy, for he had bemoaned its loss a great deal since giving it away. So he went up to it, and after examining every part, he found it in perfectly good shape. Just as he was about to mount it and ride away, he said to himself, "Perhaps I should look at what the prince has brought here with the horse before I ride away." So he entered the pavilion, and when he saw the princess sitting there as though she were the sun shining serenely in the sky, he knew at first glance that she was some highborn lady and was certain that the prince had left her in the pavilion while he had gone to the city to prepare a splendid state procession for her. So he went up to her and kissed the ground before her. Startled, she looked at him and was taken aback by his atrocious appearance and manners.

"Who are you?" she asked.

"My lady," he answered, "I am a messenger sent by the prince who has asked me to bring you to another garden nearer the city, because the queen cannot walk this far and does not want to be robbed of the pleasure of welcoming you."

"Where's the prince?"

"He's in the city with his father," said the Persian, "and he will soon come to meet you in great state."

"Tell me, slave," said the princess, "couldn't he have found someone more handsome than you to bring this message to me?"

The sage laughed loudly when he heard this and replied, "To tell the truth, he doesn't even have a mameluke in his service uglier than I am. But don't let my ugly looks deceive you, my lady. He has benefited greatly from my services. Indeed, he chose me as his messenger to you because he is so jealously in love with you, and my loathsome and ugly looks don't threaten him. Otherwise, he has an enormous number of handsome mamelukes, Negro slaves, pages, eunuchs, and attendants."

When the princess heard this, it made sense, and she believed what the sage had told her. So she got up right away.

And Scheherazade noticed that dawn was approaching and stopped telling her story. When the next night arrived, however, she received the king's permission to continue her tale and said,

As the sage took her hand to help her, she asked, "What have you brought me to ride on?"

"My lady," he said, "you can ride the horse you came on."

"I can't ride it by myself," she said.

Her reply caused him to smile, for he now knew that he was in complete control of her. So he said, "I'll ride with you myself." So he mounted and then lifted her behind him and bound her to him as firmly as he could manage. Of course, she did not know what he was going to do with her. Then he pushed the takeoff button so that the belly of the horse became full of air, and it swayed back and forth like a wave of the sea. Soon the horse rose and soared into the sky until it was out of sight of the city. Now when Shams al-Nahar saw this, she asked him, "Hold on, you! What's going on? I thought the prince sent you to me!"

"May Allah damn the prince!" answered the Persian. "He is a mean miserly knave!"

"Woe to you!" she cried out. "How dare you disobey my lord's orders?"

"He's no lord of mine!" replied the sage. "Do you know who I am?"

"The only thing I know about you is what you've told me."

"What I told you was untrue," said the Persian. "It was a trick, for I've lamented the loss of this horse a long time. It was I who constructed it and learned how to master it. And now that I've regained control and have control over you as well, I'll scorch the prince's heart just as he's ravaged mine! I'll never let him have the horse again. Never! So don't fret and don't weep, for I can be of more use to you than he was. I'm just as generous as I am wealthy, and my servants and slaves will obey you as their mistress. I'll adorn you in the finest raiment and your every wish will be fulfilled."

When the princess heard this, she slapped her face and cried out, "I might as well die! Not only have I lost my mother and father, but I've lost my beloved as well!"

And she wept bitter tears over what had happened to her, while the sage kept the horse flying through the air until he came to the land of the Greeks and landed in a verdant meadow with streams and trees. Now this meadow was located near a city which was ruled by a powerful king, and it so happened that he had gone out hunting that day. As he passed by the meadow, he saw the Persian standing there with the damsel and the horse by his side. Before the Persian was aware of what was happening, the king's slaves seized him and took him, the lady, and the horse to their master. Since the sage's atrocious looks were such a striking contrast to the beauty of the girl, he asked, "My lady, what is your relationship to this old man?"

The Persian tried to intervene with a quick reply: "My lord, she's my wife and the daughter of my father's brother."

But the lady was quick to reveal his lie: "By Allah, I don't know this man, and he's certainly not my husband! No, he's a wicked magician who's abducted me by force and fraud."

On hearing these words, the king ordered his servants to give the Persian a beating, and they thrashed him until he was almost dead. Then the king commanded them to carry him to the city and throw him into jail. On the other hand, he kept the damsel with him and put her in his seraglio, while the horse was stored in his treasury, even though he did not know its secret and how valuable it was.

In the meantime, Prince Kamar al-Akmar journeyed from city to city and country to country asking the people he encountered whether they had seen the princess and the magic horse. Of course, everyone was amazed by his talk and thought he was somewhat touched in the head. Though he continued doing this for a long time, he did not obtain any news of her. At last he came to her native city of Sana'a, but nobody had any idea where she was, and her father was still mourning her loss. Therefore, he turned back and headed for the land of the Greeks and continued to make inquiries along the way.

And Scheherazade noticed that dawn was approaching and stopped telling her story. When the next night arrived, however, she received the king's permission to continue her tale and said,

As chance would have it, the prince stopped at a particular khan and saw a group of merchants sitting and talking. So he sat down near them and heard one of them say, "My friends, let me tell you about this marvelous thing that I recently witnessed."

"What was it?" they asked.

"I was visiting a district in the nearby city, and I heard the people talking about an event that had happened not too long ago. It so happened that their king went out hunting one day with his courtiers, and they came to a meadow where they found an old man with a woman and a wooden horse made out of ebony. The man was atrocious, but the woman was amazingly beautiful, elegant, and graceful. As for the wooden horse, it was miraculous. No one had ever seen anything as perfectly made as this horse was."

"And what did the king do with them?" they asked.

"Well," said the merchant, "the king questioned the man, who claimed to be the woman's husband, but she denied this right away and declared that he was a sorcerer and a villain. So the king took her from him and had him beaten and thrown into jail. As for the ebony horse, I don't know what happened to it."

When the prince heard the merchant's story, he drew closer to him and began questioning the merchant discreetly and asked him about the names of the king and the city. Once the prince found out all he wanted to know, he spent the night full of joy. As soon as it was dawn, he set forth until he reached the city, but just as he was about to enter it, the gatekeepers stopped him and intended to bring him before the king so his majesty could question him about the craft he practiced and the reason why he had come to the city. Such was the custom of their ruler. However, it was suppertime when he entered the city, and it was impossible to see the king or to ask for instructions as to what to do with the stranger. So the guards took him to jail, thinking that it would be best if he spent the night there. But when the wardens saw how handsome and dignified he was, they could not find it in their hearts to imprison him. Instead, they made him sit with them outside the walls, and when their food was brought to them, they allowed him to share their meal. As soon as they had finished eating, they turned to the prince and said, "What country do you come from?"

"I come from Persia," he answered, "the land of the Chosroës."

When they heard this, they laughed, and one of them said, "Oh Chosroan, I've heard men tell stories and have checked to see how much truth there was in them, but never have I seen or heard a bigger liar than the Chosroan who's in our jail right now."

"And never have I seen a face and figure as hideous as his," said another guard.

"What has he been lying about?" asked the prince.

"He claims that he's a sage!" one of the guards said. "The king found him one day when he was out hunting. The old man had a beautiful woman and a remarkable ebony horse with him. As for the damsel, she is with the king, who's fallen in love with her and wants to marry her. But she's mad, and if the old man were really so wise, he could heal her, but he can't, and the king has been doing his utmost to discover a cure for her disease. He's spent an enormous amount of money this past year for physicians and astrologers on her account, but nobody has found a way to cure her. As for the horse, it's in the royal treasury, and the ugly man is with us in prison. Every night, as soon as it gets dark, he begins to weep and won't let us sleep."

And Scheherazade noticed that dawn was approaching and stopped telling her story. When the next night arrived, however, she received the king's permission to continue her tale and said,

After listening to what the guards had to say about the Persian prisoner, the prince thought of a way to free the princess. In the meantime, the guards became tired, and since they wanted to sleep, they took the prince inside the jail and locked the door. Once there, the prince overheard the wails and moans of the Persian sage, who said in his own language, "Alas! How I repent my sins, for I've sinned against myself and the king's son. I should never have abducted the damsel! I haven't gained a single thing from it. Truly, I should know by now not to reach for things that are above my station in life!"

Now when the prince heard this, he approached the Persian and said, "How long will this weeping and wailing last? Tell me, do you think that what's happened to you has never happened to anyone else?"

Since the Persian did not recognize the prince, he made friends with him and began to tell him all about his misfortunes. And as soon as morning arrived, the guards took the prince to their king and informed him that he had entered the city on the previous night at a time when an audience was impossible.

"Where do you come from?" the king asked the prince. "What is your name and trade, and why have you traveled here?"

"As to my name," the prince answered, "I'm called Harjah in Persian, and I come from Persia. As to my profession, I practice the art of medicine and heal the sick and those whom the jinn drive mad. In order to learn all there is to know, I travel from country to country and try to learn more by healing new patients."

Now, when the king heard this, he was extremely glad

and said, "Oh excellent sage, you've come just at the right time." Then he told him about the princess and added, "If you cure her and she recovers from her madness, you may have anything you want from me."

"May Allah give his blessings to the king," said the prince. "Describe to me all the symptoms of her insanity, and tell me how long it's been since she had this malady. You must also recount how you found her, the horse, and the sage."

So the king told him the whole story from first to last, and he added, "Right now, the sage is in jail."

"And what have you done with the horse?" asked the prince.

"I still have it," he said. "I've put it in my treasury."

Hearing this, the prince said to himself, "I'd better see the horse first and make sure that it's in good condition. If it is, all will be well, and all will end well. But if its motor has been destroyed, I must find some other way of rescuing my beloved." So he turned to the king and said, "I must see the horse in question, for I may need it to help the damsel recover from her madness."

"With all my heart," said the king, and he took him by the hand and led him to the place where the horse was being kept. The prince went around it, examining its condition, and found it in perfect condition. Therefore, he was full of joy and said to the king, "May Allah bless you! Now I would like to go and examine the damsel to see what her condition is like, for I hope to heal her through the means of this horse."

Then he ordered them to take good care of the horse, and the king led him to the princess's chamber. While the king remained outside, the prince went in and found her wringing her hands, writhing, beating herself against the ground, and tearing her garments to tatters. But there was really no madness of the jinn in her, and she did this only to keep people away from her. When the prince saw her acting like this, he said, "Nobody's going to harm you, my beauty," and he went on to soothe her and speak sweetly to her until he could whisper, "I'm Kamar al-Akmar," whereupon she uttered a loud cry and fainted out of joy. The king thought this was epilepsy brought on by her fear of him. Then the prince put his mouth to her

ear and said, "Oh Shams al-Nahar, be careful, for our
lives are at stake. Be patient and on your guard. We
must plan everything carefully to escape from this tyrannical king. My first move will be now to go out to him
and tell him that you are possessed by a jinnee and hence
your madness. Nevertheless, I'll tell him that I can heal
you and drive the evil spirit away, but he must untie your
bonds right away. Then, when he enters here, speak
nicely to him so that he'll think that I've cured you. Then
we'll be able to do whatever we want."

"Don't worry," she whispered, "I'll do just as you
say."

So the prince went out to the king in a joyful mood
and said, "Majesty, I've been fortunate to locate the root
of her disease, and I've also managed to cure her for you.
In fact, you may now go in to see her, but speak to her
gently and treat her kindly. Make sure you promise her
whatever she wants, and you will receive your just
rewards."

*And Scheherazade noticed that dawn was approaching
and stopped telling her story. When the next night arrived,
however, she received the king's permission to continue
her tale and said,*

So the king entered the chamber, and when she saw
him, she rose and kissed the ground before him. Then
she welcomed him by saying, "I'm grateful that you've
come to visit your servant today."

The king was ecstatic and ordered the waiting women
and eunuchs to attend her and take her to the Hammam
and get various rich garments ready for her. So they, too,
entered the chamber and saluted her, and she returned
their sālaams with the most polite language and pleasant
comportment. Thereupon they clad her in royal apparel,
and after putting a necklace of jewels around her neck,
they took her to the bath and attended to her every need
there. Then they brought her out, glistening like the
radiant moon itself, and when she came into the king's
presence, she saluted him and kissed the ground before
him, whereupon he rejoiced and said to the prince, "Doctor, all this is due to your great gifts. May Allah enable
us to profit even more from your healing spirit!"

"My king," the prince replied, "in order to complete the cure, it is necessary for you and your troops to return to the place where you found her, and you must bring the black wooden horse with her, for there is a devil in it, and unless I exorcise the satanic creature, he'll torment her at the beginning of every month."

"I'm only too happy to comply with your advice," said the king, "for you are the prince of all philosophers and the most learned of all who see the light of day."

Then the king ordered the ebony horse to be brought to the meadow and rode there with all his troops and the princess, nor did he have the slightest inkling about the prince's plans. Now, when they came to the appointed place, the prince, still dressed as a physician, ordered them to set the princess and the steed together and as far away from the king and his troops as possible. Once this was done, he turned to the king and said, "With your permission I'll now proceed to fumigate the enemy of mankind so that he'll never return to her again. After this I'll mount this wooden horse, which seems to be made of ebony, and set the damsel behind me. The horse will shake and sway back and will eventually head directly for you. At that point the affair will be at an end, and you'll be able to do with the damsel whatever you like."

When the king heard these words, he was ecstatic. So the prince left him and went to the horse. After mounting it and lifting the princess behind him, he tied her to him tightly, while the king and his troops observed. Then he pushed the takeoff button, and the horse sprang into the air and soared with them on high until they disappeared from sight. After this, the king stayed put for half the day expecting them to return, but they did not reappear. Eventually he gave up hope and regretted everything he had done and grieved over the loss of the damsel. Since there was nothing he could do, he went back to the city with his troops and sent for the Persian, who was in the prison, and said to him, "You traitor! You villain! Why did you hide the secret of the ebony horse from me? Now a swindler has come and stolen it from me along with your lady, whose ornaments are worth a mint, and I'll never see anything of them again!"

So the Persian related to the king everything that had happened to him in the past from the first to the last, and the king became so terribly furious that he almost died. He locked himself up in his palace for a while and kept mourning until his viziers came to him and comforted him. "Your majesty," they said, "truly, the man who took the damsel is an enchanter, and praise be to Allah, for He has rescued you from his sorcery!" And they did not stop talking to him in this way until he became reconciled to the fact that he had lost the princess forever.

In the meantime, the prince continued flying toward his father's capital in great joy until he landed on the terrace of the palace. After setting down the princess in safety, he went to his father and mother, saluted them, and told them that he had brought the princess back to the palace. Of course, they were extremely happy, and great banquets were prepared for the people of the city.

And Scheherazade noticed that dawn was approaching and stopped telling her tale. When the next night arrived, however, she received the king's permission to continue her tale and said,

The celebration of the prince's return lasted an entire month, and at the end of this time he married the princess, and they enjoyed each other with great delight on the wedding night. However, the king broke the ebony horse in pieces and destroyed the mechanism that enabled it to fly. Moreover, the prince wrote a letter to the princess's father telling him about everything that had happened to his daughter and informing him that she was now married to him and was safe and happy. This letter was sent by a messenger who carried valuable presents and rare articles for the king. When he arrived at the city of Sana'a and delivered the letter and presents, the king rejoiced and bestowed honors on the messenger. In addition, he sent rich gifts to his son-in-law via the same messenger, who returned to his master and reported everything that had happened, and the prince was glad. After this he wrote a letter every year to his father-in-law and sent him presents until, in the course of time, his own father, King Sabur, died, and he succeeded him to the throne. The new King Kamar al-Akmar was a just ruler, and he treated his lieges fairly and wisely so that his subjects became exceedingly loyal to him. Indeed, Kamar al-Akmar and his wife, Shams al-Nahar, led a life of joy and solace until they were finally visited by the Destroyer of delights and the Sunderer of societies.

No sooner had Scheherazade concluded her tale than she said, "And yet, oh king, this story is no more wondrous than the tale of Ali Baba and the Forty Thieves."

Ali Baba and the Forty Thieves

Once upon a time there were two brothers named Kasim and Ali Baba, who lived in a certain city of Persia. When their father died, they each received an equal share of his wealth and lost no time in spending and wasting it all. The elder brother, Kasim, however, married the daughter of a rich merchant, so that when his father-in-law passed away, he became the owner of a large shop that contained valuable merchandise and a storehouse of precious goods. Moreover, he inherited a great deal of gold buried in the ground. Thus, he became known throughout the town as a prosperous merchant.

Meanwhile, Ali Baba had married a poor and needy woman and lived with her in a dismal hovel. He eked out a scanty livelihood by gathering wood in a forest and selling it for fuel on his three asses in the bazaars around town.

Now, one day it so happened that Ali Baba had cut some dead branches and had placed the load on his donkeys when suddenly he perceived a cloud of dust high in the air and moving rapidly toward him from the right. When he took a closer look, he was able to distinguish a troop of horsemen, who would soon reach him, and this sight caused him great alarm, for he was afraid that they might be bandits who would slay him and drive off his donkeys. So he began to run, but since he could not possibly escape the forest in time to avoid them, he drove his donkeys into some nearby bushes and scampered up a huge tree, where he hid himself behind some leaves. Fortunately, he could observe everything beneath him without fear of being seen by the people below, and the first thing he noticed was an immense rock that towered above the tree. When the horsemen finally arrived, it was right in front of this rock that they dismounted, and he could see that they were all young and strong. Moreover, it was clear from their looks and demeanor that they were a group of robbers, about forty in all, who had just attacked a caravan and had carried off the spoils and booty to this place with the intention of hiding it safely in some cache.

Indeed, the saddlebags which the men took from their horses proved to be full of gold and silver, and the men slung their bags over their shoulders. Then the robber who appeared to be their captain led the way and pushed through thorns and thickets until he came to a certain spot, where he uttered, "Open, Sesame!"

All at once a wide doorway appeared in the face of the rock, allowing the robbers to enter, and then the portal shut by itself. Although they were now inside the cave, Ali Baba remained perched on the tree, for he knew that the robbers could come out of the cave at any moment and slay him if they caught him descending the tree. Nevertheless, after waiting for a long time, he became tired and decided to mount one of their horses, herd his donkeys together, and then head toward the town. Just as he reached his decision, the portal flew open and the chief emerged. Standing at the entrance, he counted his men as they came out, and finally he spoke the magic words "Shut, Sesame!" and the door closed by itself. After he inspected his men, they all slung their saddle-bags onto their horses and bridled them. As soon as they were ready, they rode off, and their chief led them in the direction that they had come from.

However, Ali Baba did not budge from the tree until they were clean out of sight, for he was afraid that one of them might return and spot him. When he finally descended, he thought to himself, "Why not try those magic words and see if the door will open and close at my bidding?" So he called aloud, "Open, Sesame!" And no sooner had he said those words than the portal flew open, and he entered a large, vaulted cavern through the portal about the size of a man, and hewn in stone. There was also light that came though air holes and bull's-eyes in the upper surface of the rock that formed the ceiling.

He had expected to find nothing but a dark and gloomy den and therefore was surprised to see the whole cave filled with bales of all kinds of material, heaped from floor to ceiling with camel loads of silks, brocades, embroidered cloths, and mounds of different-colored carpets. In addition, he came across countless gold and silver coins, some piled on the ground and others bound in leather bags and sacks. Upon seeing such an abundance of goods and money, Ali Baba concluded that the thieves must have been storing their loot in this place for many decades and not just the last few years.

Although the door to the cave had closed once he had entered, Ali Baba was not dismayed, because he remembered the magic words, which he used to open the door once again so he could carry out some of the spoils. He paid no attention to the precious materials but rather concentrated on gathering as many sacks of coins as he thought his donkeys could carry. Then he loaded them on the beasts and covered his plunder with sticks and branches so that nobody would detect the bags. Finally, he cried out, "Close, Sesame!" and immediately the door shut, for the spell had been so conceived that if anyone entered the cave, its portal shut automatically behind him, and if he wanted to leave the cave, the door would not open again unless he uttered the words, "Open, Sesame!"

Now that Ali Baba had loaded his asses, he drove them toward the town as fast as he could, and after reaching his home, he led them into the yard and shut the outer door. Then he took off the sticks and branches from the donkeys and carried the bags of gold to his wife, who immediately began feeling what was inside. When she realized that they were full of coins, however, she suspected that Ali Baba had robbed some people and began reproaching him for having done such an evil thing.

And Scheherazade noticed that dawn was approaching and stopped telling her story. When the next night arrived, however, she received the king's permission to continue her tale and said,

Upset by his wife's reaction, Ali Baba told her that he

had not robbed anyone, and that instead of berating him, she should rejoice with him at their good fortune. Thereupon, he told her about his adventure and began to pour heaps of gold on the floor right before her eyes so that she was dazzled by the sight and delighted by his account of the events in the forest. Then she stooped down and began counting coin after coin until Ali Baba said, "Silly woman, how long are you going to do that? Let me dig a hole to hide this treasure so that nobody will know about it."

"That's a good idea," she replied. "But I'd still like to weigh the coins and get an idea of their worth."

"As you please," he said, "but make sure you tell nobody about the money."

So off she went in haste to Kasim's home to borrow a scale to weigh the coins and determine their value. When she could not find Kasim, she said to his wife, "I'd appreciate it if you could lend me a scale for a while."

"Do you need the bigger or smaller scale?" her sister-in-law replied.

"Just the smaller one," she answered.

"Stay here a moment while I try to find what you need."

It was under this pretext that Kasim's wife went off and secretly smeared wax and tallow on the pan of the scale so that she could discover what Ali Baba's wife intended to weigh. By doing this she could be certain that whatever it was, some little piece of it would stick to the wax and fat. Once she knew that her curiosity would be satisfied, she gave the scale to Ali Baba's wife, who carried it home and began to weigh the gold. In the meantime, Ali Baba kept digging, and when the money was weighed, they stored it in the hole, which they carefully covered with dirt. Then the good wife took the scale back to her sister-in-law, not realizing that a coin had stuck to the pan of the scale. So when Kasim's wife saw the gold coin, she fumed with envy and wrath and said to herself, "Well now, they've borrowed my scale to weigh coins!" And she was quite puzzled as to how such a poor man as Ali Baba had obtained so many coins that he had to weigh them with a scale. This matter occupied her thoughts for a long time, and when her husband returned home in the evening, she said to him, "You may consider yourself a prosperous man, but your brother, Ali Baba, is much richer than you are. In fact, he's an emir in comparison to you. He's got such heaps of gold that he has to weigh his money with scales, while you must content yourself with counting your coins."

"How do you know this?" Kasim asked.

Then his wife told him all about the scale and how she had found a gold coin stuck to it. To prove her point she showed him the gold coin, which bore the mark and inscription of some ancient king. Consequently, Kasim became so envious and jealous that he could not sleep that night, and early the next morning he arose, went to Ali Baba's house, and said, "Brother, it would seem that you are a poor and needy man, but in truth, you have so much wealth that you're compelled to weigh your gold with scales."

"What are you saying?" responded Ali Baba. "I don't understand you. Make your point clear."

"Don't pretend to be ignorant, and don't think you can fool me!" Kasim cried out angrily and extended the palm of his hand, revealing the ancient coin. "You must have thousands of these coins if you needed my scale. My wife found this one stuck to a pan."

Then Ali Baba understood how both Kasim and his wife knew that he had a great many coins and he realized that it would be to no avail to deny it, since his denial would only cause ill will and mischief. Therefore, he told his brother all about the bandits and also about the treasure in the cave. After hearing the story, Kasim exclaimed, "I want you to tell me exactly where you found the money and also the magic words to open and shut the door. And I warn you, if you don't tell me the whole truth, I'll inform the chief of police, and you'll have to give up all your gold and spend the rest of your days in jail."

Under such threats, Ali Baba revealed the magic words and the location of the cave. As a result, Kasim, who had noted everything carefully, set out for the cave the very next day with ten donkeys that he had hired. He had no difficulty in finding the place, and when he came to the rock, he cried out in great joy, "Open, Sesame!" Then all at once, the portal yawned wide, and Kasim entered and saw the piles of jewels and treasures lying all around him. As soon as he was fully inside the cave, the door shut after him as it was accustomed to do. Meanwhile, Kasim walked about in ecstasy, marveling at the treasures, and when he finally became tired of gaping, he gathered together enough bags of coins for his mules to carry and placed them by the entrance ready to take outside and load on his beasts. But by the will of Allah Almighty, he had clean forgotten the cabalistic words and cried out, "Open, oh Barley!" However, the door refused to budge. Astonished and confused, Kasim began calling out all the names that had something to do with grain except sesame, which had slipped from his memory as though he had never heard the word. In his distress, he neglected the gold coins that lay in heaps at the entrance. Instead, he paced back and forth inside the cave worrying about his predicament. The great treasures that had once filled his heart with joy and gladness were now the cause of bitter grief and sadness.

And Scheherazade noticed that dawn was approaching and stopped telling her story. When the next night arrived, however, she received the king's permission to continue her tale and said,

Kasim abandoned all hope for his life and regretted that he had risked his life out of greed and envy. Indeed, it so happened that the robbers returned to the rock by noon and saw the mules standing beside the entrance from afar. Unfortunately, Kasim had failed to tether them, and they had strayed about the forest, browsing here and there. Nevertheless, the thieves paid scant attention to the strays, nor did they bother to catch them and tie them to stakes. They were only puzzled as to how they had managed to wander so far from the town. After the robbers dismounted, the chief went up to the door and repeated the magic words, causing the door to fly open at once.

Now, Kasim had heard within the cave the sound of the horses drawing nearer and nearer, and he fell down on the ground in a fit of fear, never doubting that it was the clatter of the bandits, who would certainly slaughter him. Nevertheless, he summoned his courage, and when the door flew open, he rushed out, hoping to make good his escape. But the unfortunate man ran smack into the chief, who stood in front of the band and knocked Kasim to the ground. Immediately thereafter, one of the robbers drew his sword and cut Kasim in two with one slash. Then the bandits rushed into the cave and carried the bags of coins back to the spot where they had been before. Fortunately, they did not miss the ones that Ali Baba had taken, so stunned and amazed were they to discover that a stranger had gained entry to the cave. They all knew that it was impossible for anyone to drop through the skylights, because they were as tall and steep as the rock's face, which was too slippery to climb. They also knew that it was impossible to enter by the portal unless one knew the magic words to open it. Nevertheless, they decided to quarter Kasim's dead body and hang two parts on the right and two parts on the left of the door so that the sight would be a warning of doom to all those who might dare to enter the cave. After they finished this task, they left the cave, closed the door to the treasure hoard, and rode off to do their usual work.

Now, when night fell, and Kasim did not come home, his wife became uneasy. So she went to Ali Baba and said, "Your brother hasn't returned home. You know where he went, and I'm afraid that something terrible has happened to him."

Ali Baba also suspected that some accident had occurred to prevent his brother's return. Nonetheless, he tried to comfort his sister-in-law with words of cheer and said, "I'm sure that Kasim is just being cautious and has chosen a roundabout road to avoid the city. That's probably the reason why he's late. I'm sure he'll be here very soon."

After hearing these words, Kasim's wife felt comforted and went home, where she sat and awaited her husband's return. But when half the night had passed and he still had not come home, she was most distraught. She was afraid to cry aloud out of grief because the neighbors might hear her and come and learn the secret. So she wept in silence, scolded herself, and began thinking, "Why did I ever disclose the secret of the coins to him and make him jealous of Ali Baba? Now I've reaped nothing but disaster!" She spent the rest of the night in bitter tears, and early the next morning she rushed as fast as she could to Ali Baba and begged him to go and search for his brother. Again he comforted her and then set out right away with his asses for the forest. Once he reached the rock, he was startled to see fresh bloodstains, and since he could not find his brother or the ten donkeys, he was convinced something terrible had happened. So he went to the door and said, "Open, Sesame!" and when he entered, he saw Kasim's dead body, two parts hanging to the right, and the rest to the left of the entrance. To be sure, he was frightened beyond belief, but he wrapped the quarters in the two cloths and set them upon one of his asses, hiding them carefully with sticks and branches so that nobody could see them. Then he went in and took some more bags of gold, which he placed upon the other two animals, and covered them carefully as he had done before. When everything was ready, he closed the door to the cave with the magic words and set off for home with all due caution. Soon after his arrival, he told his wife to bury the bags of gold with utmost prudence, but he did not tell her about the condition in which he had found his brother. Then he took the other donkey with the corpse to the widow's house and knocked gently at the door.

Now, Kasim had a slave girl named Morgiana, who was extremely shrewd, and she quietly lifted the bolt and let Ali Baba and the ass into the courtyard. After he took the corpse from the beast's back, he said, "Quick, Morgiana, get everything ready to bury your lord. I'll return quickly to help you, but first I must go and tell the bad news to your mistress."

When Kasim's widow saw her brother-in-law, she exclaimed, "Oh, Ali Baba, what news do you have about my husband? Alas, I see grief written upon your face! Tell me quickly what's happened."

So he told her what had happened to her husband, how he had been slain by the robbers, and in what condition he had brought the dead body home.

"My lady," he said, "we cannot change what has happened, but we must keep this matter secret, for our lives depend upon it."

The widow wept bitter tears and then responded, "Fate dictated what was to become of my husband, and now for safety's sake, I give you my word that I won't reveal anything about this affair."

"There's nothing one can do when Allah decrees what is to happen," he stated. "Be patient until the days of your widowhood have expired. Then I'll take you as a wife, and you will live in comfort and happiness. And you don't have to worry that my first wife will be angry at you or jealous, for she is kind and tender."

"As you wish," she said.

While she continued weeping and mourning over her husband's death, Ali Baba said farewell and rejoined Morgiana. They discussed the best way to manage the burial of his brother, and he told her exactly what to do before he left the matter in her hands and went home. As soon as Ali Baba had departed, Morgiana went quickly to a druggist's shop, and in order to conceal the matter, she asked for a drug that was often administered to people with a dangerous distemper. The druggist gave it to her but said, "Who's become so ill at your house that he needs this medicine?"

"It's my master, Kasim, who's sick," she said. "He's not said a word or eaten anything for many days now, and we're afraid he may die."

The next day Morgiana went again and asked the druggist for more medicine given to the sick to help them rally when they may be on the brink of death. The man gave her the potion, and as she took it, she sighed loudly, wept a few tears, and said, "I fear that he may not even have the strength to drink this draught. I think it will be all over for him before I reach the house."

Early on the second day, Morgiana covered her face with a veil and went to a man named Baba Mustafa, an old tailor, who made shrouds and sewed cloths together, and as soon as she saw him open his shop, she gave him a gold coin and said, "I want you to let me bind a kerchief over your eyes and then to come along with me."

When Mustafa hesitated, she placed a second gold coin in his palm and pleaded with him to follow her. Since he was a greedy man, he finally agreed, and she tied a kerchief over his eyes and led him by the hand to the house in which the dead body of her master was lying. Then after taking off the kerchief in the darkened room, she told him to sew the quarters of the corpse, limb to limb, and after throwing a cloth over the body, she said, "Make haste and sew a shroud according to the size of this dead man, and I'll give you another ducat."

Baba Mustafa quickly made the cloth so that it fit the body, and Morgiana paid him the promised gold coin. Then she tied the kerchief around his eyes once more and led him back to his shop. After this she returned home as fast as she could, and with the help of Ali Baba, she washed the body in warm water and then covered the corpse with the shroud and placed it upon a clean place ready for burial. When all 'this was done, Morgiana went to the mosque and notified an imam, a leader of prayer, that a funeral was awaiting the mourners in a certain household, and she requested that he come and read the prayers for the dead. The imam consented and returned with her. Then four neighbors lifted the bier, carried it on their shoulders, and went forth with the imam and others, who customarily gave their assistance at such obsequies. After the funeral prayers had ended, four other men carried off the coffin, and Morgiana walked before it with a bare head, striking her breast and wailing loudly, while Ali Baba and the neighbors followed behind. Finally they entered the cemetery in this order, and buried him. Then, leaving him to Munkar and Nakir—the Questioners of the Dead—they all made their way to their homes.

According to the custom of the city, the women of the neighborhood soon gathered together in the house of mourning and sat with Kasim's widow, comforting her until she was somewhat resigned to her fate and felt better. Meanwhile, Ali Baba stayed forty days at home in ceremonial lamentation for the loss of his brother. So nobody in the town except himself, Kasim's widow, and Morgiana knew anything about the secret. When the forty days of mourning were over, Ali Baba moved all the property that had belonged to the deceased to his own house and publicly married the widow. Then he appointed his nephew, his brother's eldest son, to take charge of Kasim's shop and carry on the business, for he had lived with a wealthy merchant a long time and had learned all about matters concerned with trade, such as selling and buying.

And Scheherazade noticed that dawn was approaching and stopped telling her story. When the next night arrived, however, she received the king's permission to continue her tale and said,

*   *   *

Now, one day, the robbers happened to return to the cave and were extremely startled to find no sign or trace of Kasim's body, and they also noticed that much of the gold had been carried off.

"We must look into this matter right away," said the chief, "or else we'll suffer more losses, and our treasure that we and our forefathers have amassed over the course of many years will disappear."

All the robbers agreed, and they came to the conclusion that the man whom they had slain had known the magic words to open the door. Moreover, they believed that someone besides him had knowledge of the spell and had carried away the body and much of the gold as well. Therefore, they decided that they had to make discreet inquiries to find out who the man might be. To begin their search, they thought it best to choose one of the more cunning robbers among them to disguise himself in the dress of some merchant from a foreign country. He was to go into the city and move from quarter to quarter and from street to street to find out whether any townsman had recently died. If so, he was to learn where he lived, and with this clue they might be able to find the scoundrel they sought. When they had fully finished discussing their plans, one of the robbers said, "I'd like your permission to take on this task. I'll go into town and try to dig up all the information we need, and if I fail, you may take my life."

Thereupon, this bandit disguised himself as a foreigner and snuck into the city during the night. Early the next morning he went to the market square and saw that the only shop open was that of Baba Mustafa, the tailor, who sat upon his working stool with thread and needle in hand. The thief wished him a good morning and asked, "How can you see what you're sewing? It's still dark."

"Well, I can see that you're a stranger and don't know my reputation!" said the tailor. "Despite my years, my eyesight is so keen that only yesterday I sewed together a dead body while sitting in a very dark room."

The bandit immediately realized that he had stumbled onto something important, and in order to obtain some further clues, he said, "I think you're just joking with me. How could you possibly stitch a cerecloth for a corpse or sew shrouds?"

"I don't care whether you believe me," said the tailor. "And don't ask me any more questions."

Thereupon, the robber put a gold coin in his hand and continued, "I'm not interested in discovering what you're hiding. However, you can rest assured that my breast, like every honest man's, is the grave of secrets. The only thing I want to learn from you is the house in which you did your work. Can you direct me to it or lead me there?"

The tailor took the gold greedily and replied, "A certain slave girl led me to a place which I know quite well, and there she put a kerchief around my eyes and guided me to some tenement. After that she led me to a dark room where the dead body lay dismembered. Then she untied the kerchief and told me first to sew the corpse together and afterward the shroud. When I finished my job, she blindfolded me again and led me back to the place where she had brought me and left me there. So you see, I can't tell you the location of the house."

"Even though you don't know the dwelling," the robber said, "you can still take me to the place where you were blindfolded. Then I'll put a kerchief over your eyes and lead you. Perhaps in this way you may hit upon the house. And if you do this favor for me, I'll reward you with another gold ducat."

The bandit slipped another coin into the tailor's palm, and Baba Mustafa put it into his pocket. Then he left his shop and walked with the robber to the place where Morgiana had tied the kerchief around his eyes. Here he told the robber to blindfold him and to lead him by the hand. Since Baba Mustafa was exceedingly clever, he was soon able to find the street where he had walked before, and after counting step by step, he suddenly came to a halt and said, "This is as far as I came with her."

And the two of them stopped in front of Kasim's house, which had now become the dwelling of his brother, Ali Baba.

Quickly the robber made some marks with white chalk upon the door so that he could easily locate it again. Then he removed the kerchief from the tailor's eyes and said, "Baba Mustafa, I want to thank you for this favor, and may Almighty Allah reward you for your favor. Please tell me now who lives in that house over there."

"Quite honestly," he responded, "I don't know, for I'm not very familiar with this part of the city."

Since the robber realized that he would not be able to obtain any more valuable information from the tailor, he dismissed him and sent him back to his shop. In the meantime, the bandit went back to the meeting place in the forest where his comrades were waiting for him.

Not long after his departure, it so happened that Morgiana was struck by the white chalk marks on the door when she went out on some errand. She stood there awhile deep in thought and soon suspected that some enemy had made the signs so that he would be able to recognize the house and do some harm against her master. Therefore, she chalked the doors of all her neighbors in the same way and kept the matter secret, never revealing it either to her master or mistress. Meanwhile, the robber told his comrades about his adventure in the city and how he had found the clue. So the captain and the rest of the bandits went to the city and entered it one by one in different ways. The robber who had marked Ali Baba's door accompanied the chief to point out the place, and when they reached the house, he exclaimed, "This is the place where our culprit lives!"

But when the captain looked around him, he saw that all the dwellings were marked by chalk in the same fashion, and he replied in a baffled manner, "How do you know that this is the right house when all the houses here have similar chalk marks?"

The robber was completely confounded and could not reply. Then he swore an oath and said, "I assure you that I marked one of the doors, but I don't know where all the other marks have come from. And now, I can't really tell you which is the right one."

Thereupon the captain returned to the marketplace and told his men, "All our work was in vain, because we can't find the right house. Let's return to our meeting place in the forest, and I'll join you there."

The thieves marched off in different directions and gathered together again inside the cave. When they were all assembled, the captain decided to punish the robber who had led them astray by locking him up. Then he said, "I'll give a special reward to whoever goes to town and brings me information that will allow us to capture the man who's plundered our property."

So another one of the robbers came forward and said, "I will, and you can count on me to fulfill your wish this time."

After giving this robber presents and promises, the captain sent him on his way. As destiny would have it, this second robber went straight to the house of Baba Mustafa, just like the first one, and he, too, persuaded the greedy tailor with gold coins to let him lead him blindfolded in a certain quarter of the city. Once again, this thief was led to Ali Baba's door, which he marked with red chalk to distinguish it from the others, which were still marked with white. Then he stole back to the group of thieves in the forest. However, Morgiana also spotted the red signs on the entrance of the house, and with great foresight she marked all the other doors in the same way and did not tell a soul about what she had done. Meanwhile the bandit could not help boasting, "Captain, I've found the house, and I put a sign on it that will clearly distinguish it from all the others in the neighborhood."

And Scheherazade noticed that dawn was approaching and stopped telling her story. When the next night arrived, however, she received the king's permission to continue her tale and said,

Once again the captain and his men went into city, but this time they found all the houses marked with red chalk. So they returned disappointed to the cave, and the chief was extremely irritated and locked his spy in jail with the other robber. Then he said to himself, "Two men have failed to find the house and have been duly punished for leading us astray. Probably nobody else in my band will dare now to follow up their work. So I believe it's up to me to go and find the culprit's house." Therefore, he went back into the city, and with the help of the tailor Baba Mustafa, who had accumulated a good deal of gold coins by now, he hit upon the house of Ali Baba, but he did not mark it with a sign. Instead he memorized where it was and stamped it on the tablet of his heart. Soon afterward he returned to the forest and said to his men, "I know exactly where it is and have memorized the place. So now we won't have any trouble in finding it. Therefore, I want you to go right away and purchase nineteen mules, one large leather jar of mustard oil, and thirty-seven vessels of the same kind, but they must be empty. Without me and our two comrades locked up in our jail, you number thirty-seven, and I intend to hide you with your weapons in the jars. Then I'll load two of you on each mule. On the nineteenth mule there will be a man in one of the jars and oil in the other. I'll disguise myself as an oil merchant and drive the mules into the town. Since it will be nighttime, I'll ask the master of that house if I can stay there until morning. After this we'll look for an opportunity in the darkness to attack and slay him. When he's dead, we'll recover the gold treasure that he robbed from us and bring it back on the mules."

This plan pleased the robbers, who went off and purchased the mules and huge leather jars and did everything the captain had instructed them to do. After waiting three days, they arose shortly before dawn and hid themselves in the jars. The chief then disguised himself in some merchant's garments and loaded the jars onto the nineteen mules. When all this was done, he drove the beasts before him and reached Ali Baba's place by nightfall.

It so happened that the master of the house was strolling back and forth in front of his home after having enjoyed his supper. When the captain saw Ali Baba, he saluted him with the salaam and said, "I've come from a distant village with some oil, and unfortunately I've arrived too late and don't have lodgings for the night. Please have pity on me, my lord, and allow me to stay in your courtyard. I need to give my mules some rest from carrying the jars and to feed them."

To be sure, Ali Baba had heard the captain's voice when perched upon the tree, and he had seen him enter the cave. However, because of the disguise, he was not able to recognize the thief. So he gave him a hearty welcome and granted him permission to spend the night in his courtyard. He then led him to an empty shed where the mules could be tethered and ordered one of his slave boys to fetch grain and water. He also informed Morgiana that a guest had come to spend the night and said, "Make a supper for him as soon as possible and get the guest bed ready."

After the captain had unloaded all the jars and had fed and watered his mules, Ali Baba received him with courtesy and kindness. Summoning Morgiana, he said in her presence, "See to it that our stranger has everything he desires. Tomorrow morning I want to go to the Hammam and bathe. So give my slave boy Abdullah a suit of clean white clothes that I'll wear after my bath. Moreover, I want you to prepare a broth tonight that I'll be able to drink after I return home in the morning."

"I'll get everything ready for you as you wish," she replied.

So Ali Baba retired for the night, and the captain finished his supper, went to the shed, and made sure that all the mules had food and drink for the night. Then he whispered to his men who were hiding in the jars, "When you hear my voice at midnight, open the jars quickly with your knives and come out right away."

When he returned to the house, Morgiana led the chief through the kitchen to the guest room, where she had prepared a bed for him.

"If you need anything else, my lord," she said, "just call me, and I'll be at your service."

"There's nothing else I need," he answered, and after putting out the light, he lay down on the bed to relax and sleep until the time came to rouse his men and finish their work. Meanwhile, Morgiana did as her master had ordered her. First she took out a suit of clean white clothes and gave it to Abdullah, who had not gone to sleep yet. Then she placed the pipkin on the hearth to boil the broth and fanned the fire until it burned briskly. After a short wait she had to see if the broth was boiling, but by that time all the lamps had gone out, and she found that there was no more oil left and could not get a light, no matter where she looked. Abdullah noticed that she was irritated and said to her, "Why are you making such a fuss? There are many jars of oil in the courtyard shed. Why don't you just go and take as much as you need?"

Morgiana thanked him for his clever suggestion, and Abdullah, who was relaxing in the hall, went off to sleep so that he might awake on time and help Ali Baba with his bath. Meanwhile, Morgiana took an oil can and walked to the shed, where the jars were arranged in rows. As she approached one of the vessels, the thief, who was hiding inside it, heard the footsteps and thought that it was his captain, whose command he was awaiting. So he whispered, "Is it time now for us to come out?"

Morgiana was startled and frightened by the voice, but since she was bold and alert, she replied in a disguised voice, "It's not time yet." Then she said to herself, "Something strange is going on here. These jars aren't filled with oil. I think the merchant is plotting something treacherous against my lord. May Allah the Compassionate protect us from his snare!" Once again she made her voice sound like the captain's and said to the robber in the jar, "Be patient. It's not time."

Then she went to the next jar and gave the same reply to the robber inside and so on until she had spoken to all the robbers in the vessels. "My God!" she said to herself. "My master extended his hospitality to this man because he thought he was an oil merchant, but he's actually taken in a band of robbers, who only await the signal to attack and kill him and plunder the place!" When she finally came to the last jar, she found it brimming with oil. So she filled her can, returned to the kitchen, trimmed the lamp, and lit the wicks. Next, she took out a large caldron and set it over the fire. After filling it with oil from the jar, she heaped wood on the hearth and fanned it to a fierce flame to make sure that it would boil its contents. When this was done, she bailed it out in potfuls and carried the boiling liquid into the courtyard, where she poured the seething-hot contents into the leathern jars one by one. Since the thieves were unable to escape, they were scalded to death, and every jar contained a corpse. Thus the clever Morgiana used her keen wit to make a clean end of everything without anyone in the house knowing what had happened.

Now, when she was certain that each and every man had been slain, she went back to the kitchen, shut the door, and continued brewing Ali Baba's broth. No more than an hour passed before the captain woke from his sleep, and after he opened his window, he saw that everything was dark and silent. So he clapped his hands as a signal for his men to come out of the jars, but not a sound was heard in return. After a while he clapped again and called out loud, but got no answer. And when he cried out a third time without a reply, he was perplexed and went out to the shed, where the jars were standing. He thought to himself that they might have all fallen asleep. But since the time for action was at hand, he felt he had to wake them without delay. So he approached the nearest jar and was startled by the smell of oil and seething flesh. Upon touching the outside of the vessel, he felt it reeking hot. Then he went to the others one by one and found them all in the same condition. It did not take him long to figure out what had happened to the members of his band, and fearing for his own safety, he climbed over the wall into a nearby garden and made his escape in high gear and with great disappointment.

Morgiana waited awhile for the captain to return from the shed, but he did not appear. Therefore, she realized that he had probably scaled the wall and had taken flight because the street door was double-locked. Since she knew the thieves could not cause any more trouble that night, Morgiana lay down to sleep in perfect contentment and with an easy mind.

Two hours before dawn, Ali Baba awoke and went to the Hammam, knowing nothing about the nocturnal adventure, for the gallant slave girl had not aroused him, nor had she deemed such action expedient. Indeed, if she had sought an opportunity to tell him about her plan, she most likely would have lost her chance, and the entire project would have been spoiled.

The sun was high above the horizon when Ali Baba walked back from the baths, and he was astounded to see the jars still standing under the shed. So he asked Morgiana, "How is it that my guest hasn't taken his jars of oil to the market?"

And Scheherazade noticed that dawn was approaching and stopped telling her story. When the next night arrived, however, she received the king's permission to continue her tale and said,

When Morgiana heard Ali Baba's question about his guest, she replied, "May Allah Almighty grant you three-score years and ten of safety! I'd like to have a private talk with you about this merchant."

So Ali Baba went off to the side with his slave girl,
who took him into the courtyard and locked the door
behind her. After showing him a jar, she said, "Please
look inside, and tell me whether there's oil or something
else."

After Ali Baba peered inside, he perceived a man, but
the sight of the corpse scared him so much that he almost
fled in fright.

"There's no need to fear this man," Morgiana said.
"He's no longer capable of harming you. He's stone
dead."

Upon hearing these comforting words, Ali Baba asked,
"Morgiana, what evil things was he planning, and how
did this wretch come to suffer this fate?"

"Praise be to Allah," she responded. "I'll tell you the
whole story, but you must keep quiet and not speak so
loud, or else the neighbors will learn about our secret.
First, take a look into all the jars, one by one."

So Ali Baba examined them and found that they each
contained a man, armed to the teeth, but scalded to
death. To say the least, he was so amazed that he became
speechless and could only stare at the jars. Soon, however, he recovered his composure and asked, "Where is
the oil merchant?"

"That villain was not a trader," Morgiana replied, "but
a lying crook whose sugar-coated words were intended to
lead you into a trap. But before I tell you what he was
and what has happened, you should drink some of this
broth for your health and to sooth your stomach, since
you've come fresh from the Hammam."

So Ali Baba went inside his house, and Morgiana
served him the broth, whereupon he said, "I'd like to
hear this wondrous story now. Please tell it to me, and
set my heart at ease."

So the slave girl began by saying, "Master, when you
told me to boil the broth and then retired for the evening, I obediently took out a suit of clean white clothes
and gave it to Abdullah. After that I kindled the fire and
set the broth on it. As soon as it was ready, I needed to
light a lamp so that I could see to skim it, but all the oil
was gone. When Abdullah heard me complaining, he
advised me to take some of the oil from the jars that
stood under the shed. Therefore, I took a can and went

to the first vessel, when I suddenly heard a voice whisper cautiously, 'Is it time for us to come out?' I was amazed by this and suspected that the so-called merchant was plotting to kill you. So I replied, 'It's not time yet.' Then I went to the second jar and heard another voice, and I gave him the same answer. And so it went with the rest. I was now certain that these men were only waiting for some signal from their chief, who was the guest you had received into you house. Moreover, I was sure that he had brought these men to murder you and plunder your goods. But I gave him no opportunity to fulfill his wish. After taking some oil from the last jar, I lit the lamp and put a large caldron on the fire. Next I filled it up with oil which I brought from the jar and made a blazing fire underneath. When the contents were seething hot, I took out various cans, filled them with the liquid, and went to pour the boiling liquid on them one by one. After scalding them all to death, I returned to the kitchen, put out all the lamps, and watched how the traitorous merchant would act next. Not long after I had taken my place by the kitchen window, the robber captain awoke and signaled to his men. Since they did not reply, he went downstairs and into the courtyard. Finding that all his men were slain in the jars, he fled over the garden wall, and I don't know where he's gone. After I was sure that he had disappeared, I double-locked the door, and with my heart at rest, I slept."

After telling this story to her master, Morgiana added, "I've told you the complete truth, but I must say that I've had an inkling for some days that there was mischief in the air. However, I didn't say anything to you because I didn't want the neighbors to know anything. Now I must tell you why I was so concerned. One day, as I came to the house door, I spotted a white chalk mark on it, and the next day there was a red sign beside it. Although I didn't know how the marks had been made, I put others on the entrances of various neighbors' doors, for I felt that some enemy was plotting something evil against my master. And these other marks were just like the one on your door. I'm convinced that these thieves were the ones who marked our house so that they'd be able to recognize it again. Of the forty thieves there are two remaining, and I don't know where they are. So you had better beware of them, and of course, you'd best beware of their captain, who's the most dangerous of the lot. If you should fall into his hands, he'll definitely murder you. Of course, I'll do all I can within my powers to save you from harm and your property from damage. Indeed, you may depend on me to serve you as best I can."

Upon hearing these words, Ali Baba rejoiced and said to her, "I am most pleased by the way you acted. But now you must tell me what I can do in your behalf, for I'll never forget the brave deeds you've done for me as long as I live."

"Before we talk about this," Morgiana said, "we'd better bury these bodies in the ground so that we can keep everything secret."

Heeding her advice, Ali Baba took his slave boy Abdullah into the garden, and there they dug a deep pit for the corpses of the thieves, and after taking away their weapons, they dragged the bodies to the grave and threw them into it. Then they covered the remains of the thirty-seven robbers with dirt, and they made the ground appear just as level and clean as it used to be. They also hid the leather jars, the gear, and the weapons, and thereafter, Ali Baba sent the mules by ones and twos to the bazaar and sold them all with the capable aid of his slave boy Abdullah. Thus, the matter was hushed up and never reached the ears of any of his neighbors. However, Ali Baba remained ill at ease because he thought the captain or the two surviving robbers would seek revenge. He took pains to keep everything private and made sure that nobody learned anything of what had happened and how he had managed to obtain his wealth from the bandits' cave.

Meanwhile the captain of the thieves was living in the forest full of rage and extremely upset. He had great trouble controlling his feelings, and after thinking about the matter over and over again, he finally decided that he had to take Ali Baba's life, otherwise he would lose the entire treasure, because Ali Baba knew the magic words and could return and take anything he wanted. Furthermore, the captain was resolved to undertake this task alone, and once he had gotten rid of Ali Baba, he would assemble a new band of thieves and would pursue his career of brigandage as indeed his forebears had done for many generations. So he lay down to rest that night, and after rising early in the morning, he donned some garments of suitable appearance. When he arrived at the city, he stopped at a khan, thinking to himself, "I'm sure that the murder of so many men has reached the wali's ears and that Ali Baba has been imprisoned and brought to justice. His house must be leveled by now and his goods confiscated. The townsfolk must surely have heard all about this." So, without hesitating, he asked the keeper of the khan, "What strange things have been happening in the city during the last few days?"

And the other man told him all that he had seen and heard, but the captain did not learn a thing about what concerned him most. Thus, he realized that Ali Baba was very shrewd and wise, and that he had not only carried away a good deal of the treasure and destroyed many lives, but done all this without being scathed. Furthermore, the captain realized that he himself had better keep on his toes so as not to fall into the hands of his foe and perish.

With all this in mind, he rented a shop in the bazaar, to which he brought whole bales of the finest material and expensive merchandise from the cave in the forest. Soon he took his seat inside the store and began doing business as a merchant. By chance, his place was directly across from the booth of the deceased Kasim, where his son, Ali Baba's nephew, now conducted his business. The captain, who now called himself Khwajah Hasan, soon formed an acquaintance and friendship with the shopkeepers around him and treated everyone with profuse politeness, but he was especially gracious and cordial to the son of Kasim, a well-dressed, handsome youth. Sometimes he would sit and chat with him for hours.

A few days after the robber captain had set up his business, Ali Baba chanced to come by and visit his nephew, whom he found sitting in his shop. The captain recognized him right away, and one morning he asked the young man, "Please, tell me, who is that man who comes to visit you every now and then at your shop?"

"He's my uncle," responded the young man.

From then on the captain showed him even greater favor and affection in order to make use of him when the time came. Indeed, he gave the young man presents and had him dine with him and fed him with the most delicious dishes. Soon, Ali Baba's nephew thought it was only right and proper that he should invite the merchant to have supper with him. However, his own house was small, and since he could not make a show of splendor, as had Khwajah Hasan, he asked his uncle for some advice.

And Scheherazade noticed that dawn was approaching and stopped telling her tale. When the next night arrived, however, she received the king's permission to continue her tale and said,

So Ali Baba told his nephew, "It's best to treat your friend in the same splendid way that he's treated you. So, since tomorrow is Friday, shut your shop as all the distinguished merchants do. Then, after the early meal, take Khwajah for a stroll, and as you are walking, lead him to my house. Meanwhile, I'll tell Morgiana to get a meal ready for his arrival with the best of viands and everything else necessary for a feast. Don't worry about a thing. Just leave the matter in my hands."

Accordingly, on the next day, Ali Baba's nephew took Khwajah for a walk in the large park. And as they were returning, he led him to the street where his uncle lived. When they came to the house, the youth stopped at the door, and after knocking, said, "My lord, this is my second home, and since my uncle has heard me speak a great deal about you and the kindness you have shown me, he would like to meet you. Therefore, I'd appreciate it if you would agree to visit him with me."

To be sure, the robber captain rejoiced in his heart that he had now found a way to gain access to his enemy's house and carry out his treacherous plot. But he hesitated at that moment and tried to find some excuse to walk away. However, when the door was opened by the porter, Ali Baba's nephew took his companion's hand, and after a great deal of persuasion, he led him inside. So the robber chief acted as though he were very pleased and honored when the master of the house received him with respect and said, "My lord, I am grateful to you for showing favor to the son of my brother, and I can see that you regard him with even more affection that I myself do."

Khwajah Hasan replied with pleasant words, "Your nephew has caught my fancy, and I am very pleased with him. Although he is young, Allah Almighty has endowed him with a great deal of wisdom."

Thus the two had a friendly conversation, until the guest rose to depart and said, "My lord, I must bid you farewell right now. But on some future occasion, I hope to see you again."

However, Ali Baba would not let him leave and asked, "Where are you going, my friend? I'd like to invite you to enjoy a meal with us. Afterward you can go home in peace. Perhaps my dishes will not be as delicious as those which you are accustomed to eating, but I beg you to grant my request and have dinner with me."

"My lord," replied Khwajah Hasan, "I am obliged for your gracious invitation, and I'd like to accept your offer with pleasure. However, there is a special reason why I must refuse at this time. Therefore, please allow me to depart."

To this the host responded, "Please tell me, my lord, what is it that's so urgent and important that you can't dine with me."

And Khwajah Hasan answered, "The reason is this: my physician cured me of some malady and ordered me not to eat meat prepared with salt."

"If this is all it is," said Ali Baba, "do not deprive me of the pleasure and honor of your company. If the meat has not been cooked yet, I'll tell the cook not to use any salt. Just wait here a moment, and I'll return right away."

So Ali Baba went into the kitchen and told Morgiana not to put any salt in the dishes she was preparing. Puzzled by her master's instructions, she asked him, "Who is this person that doesn't eat meat with salt?"

"What does it matter to you who it is?" Ali Baba responded. "Just do as I say."

"As you wish," she said, but she still wondered who it was that had made such a strange request and wanted very much to get a look at him. Therefore, when all the meat was ready to be served, she helped the slave boy Abdullah to spread the table and set the meat on it. No sooner had she seen Khwajah Hasan than she knew who he was even though he had disguised himself in the dress of a foreign merchant. Furthermore, when she looked more closely at him, she noticed a dagger hidden under his robe. "So, that's it!" she said to herself. "This is the reason why the villain doesn't want to eat salt. He's looking for an opportunity to slay my master! Well, I'll beat him to the punch and take care of him before he has a chance to harm my master."

Now, Morgiana went back to the kitchen and began thinking of a way to get rid of the robber captain. Meanwhile, Ali Baba and Khwajah Hasan had eaten their fill of the meat, and Abdullah brought word to Morgiana to serve the dessert. Therefore, she cleared the table and set down fresh and dried fruit in trays. Then she placed a small tripod for three cups with a flagon of wine next to Ali Baba, and lastly, she went off with Abdullah into another room as though she wanted to eat her supper there. At this point, the robber captain thought the coast was clear and felt extremely good. "The time has come for me to take full vengeance," he said to himself. "With one thrust of the dagger I'll kill this wretch, and then I can make my escape through the garden. If his nephew tries to stop me, I'll stab him and settle his accounts on earth. However, I must still wait awhile until the slave boy and cook have eaten and gone to rest in the kitchen."

Unknown to him, Morgiana watched him carefully, and since she read his intentions, she said to herself, "I must not allow this villain to take advantage of my lord. There must be some way I can stop him and put an end to his life." Accordingly, the trusty slave girl quickly changed her dress and put on some clothes that dancers generally wear. She veiled her face with a costly kerchief, bound her head with a fine turban, and tied a sash embroidered with gold and silver around her waist, in which she stuck a dagger with a jeweled hilt. After disguising herself like this, she said to Abdullah, "Take your tambourine, and let us sing and dance in honor of our master's guest."

So he did as she requested, and the two of them went into the room, the young boy playing the tambourine followed by Morgiana. Making a low bow, they asked permission to perform, and Ali Baba granted it and said, "Do your best and dance so that our guest will enjoy himself."

"My lord," said Khwajah Hasan, "you are truly entertaining me in a most pleasant way."

Then Abdullah began to strike the tambourine, while Morgiana performed with graceful steps and moves. Suddenly, she drew the dagger from her sash and paced from side to side, and this spectacle pleased them most of all. At times she stood before them, clapping the sharp-edged dagger under her armpit and then setting it against her breast. Finally, she took the tambourine from Abdullah, and while still holding the poniard in her right hand, she went around for gifts of money, as was the custom among entertainers. First she stood before Ali Baba, who threw a gold coin into the tambourine, and his nephew did likewise. As she approached Khwajah Hasan, he began to pull out his purse, and taking courage, she plunged the dagger into his heart quick as lightning, and the scoundrel fell back stone dead.

Ali Baba was dismayed and cried out angrily, "What have you done? This will be the ruin of me!"

But she replied, "No, my lord, I have slain this man to prevent him from harming you. Undo his garments and see what you will find there."

So Ali Baba searched the dead man's clothes and found a dagger concealed there. Then Morgiana said, "This wretch was your mortal enemy. Look at him carefully, for he is none other than the oil merchant and captain of the robbers. He came here to take your life, and when he would not eat your salt and you told me about this, I suspected something was wrong. After I got a look at him I was certain that he was the robber captain and that he had come to kill you. Praise be to Allah, for it was exactly as I thought it was."

Then Ali Baba lavished thanks upon her and said, "You have saved me from his hand two times, and now I grant you your freedom. And as a further reward for your fidelity, I am going to wed you to my nephew." Then, turning to the youth, he said, "Do as I bid you, and you will prosper. I want you to marry Morgiana, who is a model of duty and loyalty. You see now how this man only sought your friendship so that he could take my life, but this maiden, with her good sense and wisdom, has slain him and saved us."

Ali Baba's nephew consented to marry Morgiana on the spot. After reaching this agreement, the three of them lifted the dead body and carried it carefully into the garden, where they buried it as quickly as possible. For many years thereafter, nobody knew a thing about this.

In due time, Ali Baba married Morgiana to his nephew in great pomp and held a sumptuous wedding feast for his friends and neighbors. It was a joyful event with singing, dancing, and other entertainment. Thereafter, Ali Baba prospered in everything he undertook, and time smiled upon him as new sources of wealth were opened to him. For fear of the thieves, he did not return to the cave for a long time after his brother's death.

But one day, after some years had passed, he mounted his horse and journeyed there with care and caution. Since he did not find any signs of man or beast, he ventured to draw near the door. Then he got off his horse, tied it to a tree, and went to the entrance, where he pronounced the words, which he had not forgotten: "Open, Sesame!" As usual, the door flew open, and after entering, Ali Baba saw the goods and hoard of gold and silver untouched and lying exactly as he had left them. So he was convinced that none of the thieves remained alive, and with the exception of himself, there was not a soul who knew the secret of the place. Therefore, he carried a load of coins outside, put them in his saddlebags, and took the gold home with him. In the years that followed he showed the hoard to his sons and grandsons and taught them how the door could be opened and shut. Thus, Ali Baba and his family lived all their lives in wealth and joy in that city where he had once been a pauper. Thanks to the blessed secret treasure, he rose to a respectable position and became a dignified man.

No sooner had Scheherazade concluded her tale than she said, "And yet, oh king, this tale is no more wondrous than the remarkable story of 'Aladdin and the Magic Lamp.'"

Aladdin and the Magic Lamp

A long time ago in a city of China there lived a poor tailor with his only son, Aladdin. Now this boy had been obstinate and lazy ever since the day he was born, and when he became ten, his father wanted him to learn a proper trade, but since he lacked the money to pay for his son's apprenticeship in another craft, he had to take the boy into his own shop and teach him how to use a needle. However, since Aladdin was so stubborn and idle and preferred to play with the scamps in the neighborhood, he did not spend a single day in the shop. Instead, he would wait for his father to leave the shop for some reason or other, like paying a debt, and then he would run off at once to the gardens to be with some other little scoundrels. Such was his situation, and neither punishment nor good advice would help. He would not obey his parents or learn a trade. As a result his father became so sick due to his son's vicious personality and indolence that he died.

Despite his father's death, Aladdin continued to carry on as badly as he had done in the past, and when his mother saw that her son would not change, she sold the shop with all its contents and began spinning yarn to make a living. This work enabled her to feed herself and Aladdin, who became increasingly more lazy and wayward, especially when he no longer had to fear his father's stern reproaches. Indeed, the only time he came home was for his meals. Otherwise, his poor mother continued to toil for the both of them, while he persisted in his idle ways until he turned fifteen.

One day, while Aladdin was playing in the neighbor-

hood with some of the other vagabonds, a dervish from
Maghrib, the Land of the Setting Sun, came by and
began gazing at the boys. However, he did not appear to
notice anyone except Aladdin and kept staring at him.
Now, this dervish, a Moor from the interior of Morocco,
was a sorcerer whose magic powers were so powerful that
he could turn mountains upside down. Moreover, he was
adept in astrology, and after looking at Aladdin very
closely, he said to himself, "This is the boy I've been
searching for ever since I left my native land." So he
took one of Aladdin's friends aside and began asking
questions about him, such as who his father was. And he
tried to learn all he could about Aladdin and the circumstances of his life. Once he was satisfied, the magician
walked up to Aladdin, drew him aside, and asked, "My
son, aren't you the son of the tailor Mustafa?"

"Yes, my lord," the boy answered, "but he died a long
time ago."

Upon hearing these words, the Moor threw his arms
around Aladdin, embraced him, and begin kissing him,
while tears trickled down his cheeks. Of course, the boy
was surprised by the magician's behavior, and he asked,
"Why are you weeping, my lord? Did you know my
father?"

"How can you ask me a question like that, my son?"
replied the Moor. "Don't you realize how sad it makes
me to learn that your father, who was my brother, is now
dead? I was living in exile for many years and looked
forward with joy to seeing him again and talking about
the past, but now you've told me that he's passed away.
But blood is thicker than water, and I had a feeling that
you were my brother's son. I recognized you at once
among all the boys. Of course, when I left the country
your father had yet to marry. Unfortunately I've lost the
joyous opportunity of seeing my brother again and have
also missed the funeral services. But this was all due to
the fact that I was far away and that Almighty Allah had
decreed that this was the way it was to be—and there is
no tinkering with fate. Now, my son, you are my only joy
and comfort, and you are his replacement. As the saying
goes, 'He who leaves an heir does not die.' "

After the Moor had spoken these words, he stuck his
hand into his purse, pulled out ten gold pieces, and gave

them to Aladdin. "My son, take this money and give it to your mother with greetings from me. Let her know that your uncle has returned from exile and that, God willing, I'll visit her tomorrow to see the house where my brother lived and also to have a look at his burial site."

Thereupon Aladdin kissed the Moor's hand, and after running at full speed and with great joy to his mother's house, he entered and surprised her, for he never came home except at mealtimes. "Mother!" he exclaimed in his delight. "I've come to bring you good news about my uncle, who's returned from his exile and has sent me to greet you."

"My son," she replied, "you're mocking me. Who is this uncle of yours? And since when have you ever had a living uncle?"

"How can you say that I don't have living uncles or relatives when this man is my father's brother?" Aladdin cried. "Indeed, he embraced and kissed me. And when he heard about my father's death, he wept bitter tears, and then he told me to inform you about his arrival."

"My son," she responded. "I know very well that you had an uncle once. But he's dead, and I was not aware that you had another."

The next morning the magician went looking for Aladdin, for his heart could not bear to be separated from him. As he wandered about the city, he finally encountered him, playing in the streets with other scamps and vagabonds, as he usually did. When the Moor approached him, he took Aladdin's hand, embraced him, and kissed him. Then he pulled two dinars from his pocket and said, "Go to your mother and give her these ducats. Tell her that your uncle intends to eat with you this evening and that she should prepare a delicious supper for us. But before you do this, show me the way to your house once more."

"Just follow me, uncle," said Aladdin, and he ran ahead, pointing out the street leading to the house.

Then the Moor left him and went his way, while Aladdin ran home and gave the ducats and the news to his mother. So she arose right away and went to the market, where she bought all that she needed. After returning to her dwelling, she borrowed pans and platters from her neighbors, and when the meal was cooked and suppertime came, she said to Aladdin, "My child, the meat is ready, but perhaps your uncle does not know the way to our dwelling. So go out and meet him on the road."

"As you wish," he replied, but before the two could finish their conversation, they heard a knock at the door, and when Aladdin opened it, the Moor stood there attended by a eunuch, who was carrying wine and fruit. So the boy let them in, and the slave went about his business. After entering, the Moor greeted his sister-in-law with a salaam, began to shed tears, and said, "Show me the place where my brother used to sit."

She pointed to the place, and the Moor went to it, prostrated himself in prayer, and kissed the floor. "How meager is my satisfaction!" he cried out. "How unfortunate I am, for I've lost you, brother, light of my eyes!"

And he continued weeping and wailing like this until he fainted. Consequently, Aladdin's mother was convinced that he was sincere and that he really was her husband's brother. She went over to him, and after lifting him up from the floor, she said, "Please stop, or else you'll kill yourself."

And Scheherazade noticed that dawn was approaching and stopped telling her story. When the next night arrived, however, she received the king's permission to continue her tale and said,

Aladdin's mother began consoling the Moor and led him to the couch. As soon as he was seated at his ease and was waiting for the food to be served, he began talking to her and said, "You must be wondering, my good sister-in-law, why you never saw me or knew anything about me while my late brother was alive. The reason for this is that I left this city forty years ago and wandered all over the lands of India, Sind, and Arabia and finally settled down in the magnificent city of Cairo in Egypt, which is one of the wonders of the world. Thereafter I traveled to the interior of Morocco, where I lived for thirty years. Then, one day, as I was sitting alone at home, I began thinking about my native land and my late brother, and my yearning to see him became so strong that I bemoaned my exile and the distance between my brother and myself. Finally, I decided to

return to my birthplace and to see my brother once
more, saying to myself, 'Oh you unhappy man, how long
will you wander like a nomad from your birthplace and
native land? You only have one brother and no more.
So, rise and return to him before you die. Who knows
what might happen to you and what changes might happen in the course of time? It would be most sad if you
died without ever seeing your brother again. Allah has
blessed you with ample wealth, and your brother might
not be as fortunate as you are, whereby you might be
able to help him in his distress.' So, I arose at once,
prepared myself for the journey, and recited the Fatihah.
After the Friday prayers ended, I mounted my steed and
traveled to this city, suffering many hardships and en-
countering all sorts of dangers along the way, but I patiently endured them and was blessed by the Lord's
protection, until I reached my goal. After I entered the
city, I wandered about, and the day before yesterday I
saw Aladdin playing with some boys on the street. By
God, the moment I saw him, my heart went out to him,
and I felt deep down that he was my nephew, for we are
of the same blood. In fact, as soon as I spotted him, I
forgot my trials and tribulations and became ecstatic.
However, when he told me about his father's death, I
fainted out of disappointment. Perhaps he has told you
how sorrowful I was and how I reacted. Nevertheless,
I'm somewhat consoled by the sight of Aladdin, my brother's son, for whoever leaves an heir does not die."

After hearing these words, Aladdin's mother began to
weep, and the Moor now sought a way to complete his
deception. So, while he comforted her, he turned to
Aladdin and asked, "My son, what craft have you learned?
What work do you do to support yourself and your
mother?"

The boy was abashed and put to shame. He hung his
head and lowered his eyes, but his mother spoke out,
"What work? Indeed, he's never learned a thing. I've
never seen such an ungrateful child as this one! Never!
He wastes the entire day with the other scamps and
vagabonds of the neighborhood like himself. He drove
his father to his grave, and he'll do the same with me,
too. I spin cotton and toil at the spinning wheel day and
night so that I can earn a couple of scones of bread that

we eat together. By the life of me, the only time I see my
son is at mealtimes and none other. Indeed, I've been
thinking about locking the house door and never opening
it to him again. Then he'll have to go and seek a livelihood and earn a living. After all, I've gotten on in years
and no longer have the strength to work the way I do. By
Allah, I'm forced to provide him with his daily bread
when I'm the one who should be provided for!"

Upon hearing this, the Moor turned to Aladdin and
said, "Why are you doing this, nephew? Why are you so
ungrateful? Your behavior is disgraceful and unworthy.
You're a sensible young man, and the child of honest
folk. Indeed, you should be ashamed that your mother at
her age should have to struggle to support you. Now that
you've reached manhood, it is incumbent upon you to
learn some trade and to support yourself. Praise be to
Allah, there are numerous craftsmen in this city, and
there are many different trades. So choose something
you would like to learn, and I'll help you get established.
Later, when you're grown up, you'll be able to support
yourself in your own business. Perhaps you didn't like
your father's profession, and if that's the case, then
choose some other craft that may suit you better. Then
let me know, and I'll help you as best I can."

However, Aladdin kept silent, and the Moor realized
that Aladdin preferred to continue living the life of a
freeloader and vagabond. So he said to the boy, "I did
not mean to be so harsh and severe, nephew. If you
really don't want to learn a craft, despite all that I've
said, I'll open a merchant's shop for you and furnish it
with expensive stuffs. Then you can deal and trade with
other merchants and become well known in the city."

Now, when Aladdin heard his uncle's words and his
plan of making him a merchant and gentleman, he rejoiced, for he was quite aware of the fact that these
people dressed in fine garments and had sumptuous meals.
So he looked at the Moor, smiled, and nodded his head
to show that he was content.

"Well now," said the Moor, "since you're willing to let
me open a shop for you and make a gentleman out of
you, then I'll take you to the bazaar first thing tomorrow
morning, God willing, and I'll have a fine suit of clothes

cut out for you like the one merchants wear. After that I'll look for a store for you, as I've promised."

Up to this point, Aladdin's mother still had some doubts as to whether the Moor was her brother-in-law, but when she heard his promise of opening up a merchant's shop for her son and providing him with stuffs and capital, she cast them to the wind and decided that the Moor was in truth her husband's brother, for a stranger would never do as much as he was doing for Aladdin. So she advised her son to mend his ways, get rid of his foolish ideas, and prove himself a man. Moreover, she told him to obey his excellent uncle as though he were the Moor's son and to make up for all the time he had wasted with his vagabond friends. After this she rose, set the table, and served the supper, whereupon they all sat down and began eating and drinking. During the meal, the Moor conversed with Aladdin about business matters and other similar topics so that later that night, after the Moor had departed and promised to return early the next morning, Aladdin could barely sleep for joy.

Indeed, as soon as dawn arrived, the Moor knocked at the door, and Aladdin's mother opened to let him in. However, the Moor would not enter. Instead, he asked permission to take the boy to the market, and Aladdin went straight to him, wished him good morning, and kissed his hand. Then the Moor took him to a clothier's shop at the bazaar and asked to look at expensive suits that were finely tailored and ready to wear. The merchant brought him what he desired, and the Moor said to the boy, "Choose whatever you like."

Aladdin was extremely happy about his uncle's generosity, and he picked out the suit that pleased him most, whereupon the Moor paid the merchant for the garments, and they left. Soon the Moor led the boy to the Hammam baths, and after they bathed, they drank sherbets together. Then Aladdin arose, put on his new garments with great joy, and went to his uncle, kissed his hand, and thanked him for all his favors.

When they left the Hammam, the Moor took Aladdin to the bazaar again and showed him how people traded at the market, buying and selling, and he said, "My son, it's important for you to become familiar with the people here, especially the merchants, so that you can learn their business, now that you are one of them." Then he showed Aladdin the city with its mosques and other interesting sights. Finally, they entered a cookery, where dinner was served to them on silver platters. After eating and drinking their fill, they continued on their walk, and the Moor took Aladdin to the parks, the magnificent buildings, and the sultan's palace, where they visited the grand and elegant apartments. Finally, they went to the khan of foreign merchants, where the Moor had taken his lodgings, and he invited various traders to have supper with them and told them that Aladdin was his nephew. By the time they had finished their meal, it was dark, and the Moor rose up and took the boy back to his mother, who mistook her son for a merchant but was extremely delighted when she recognized him. Immediately, she began expressing her gratitude toward her false brother-in-law for his kindness and said, "I can never thank you enough for your generosity. You're most kind."

"Please don't consider this mere kindness," said the Moor. "The boy is my own son, and it is incumbent on me to assume the role of my brother, his sire. So I hope you will be satisfied."

"May Allah bless you and grant you long life for my sake so that you may keep this orphan under your wing. And I hope that he will be obedient and do whatever you ask him to do."

"Aladdin has now become a man of good sense," the Moor replied. "I pray to Allah that he will follow in his father's footsteps and be a comfort to you in your old age. But I regret that tomorrow being Friday, I shall not be able to open his shop, since it is the day when all the merchants go to the parks and gardens after congregational prayer. On Saturday, however, we shall start his business, Allah willing. Meanwhile, tomorrow I'll come and take Aladdin for a pleasant stroll to see the parks and gardens outside the city that he has perhaps never seen before. He'll also be able to see the merchants and notables who go there and make their acquaintance."

After saying this, the Moor went away and spent the night at the khan.

* * *

And Scheherazade noticed that dawn was approaching and stopped telling her story. When the next night arrived, however, she received the king's permission to continue her tale and said,

Early the next morning the Moor arrived at Aladdin's house and knocked at the door. Now, after all the delights that the boy had experienced the day before, he had not been able to sleep a wink all night and could hardly wait until daybreak. So as soon as he heard the knock, he rushed to the door, opened it, and saw his uncle, the magician, who embraced and kissed him. Then, as they began walking, the Moor said to him, "Nephew, today I'm going to show you a sight that you've never seen before in your life." And he began to make the boy laugh and cheer him up with his pleasant talk.

Once they left the city gate, the Moor took him through the gardens and pointed out the fine buildings and marvelous pavilions. Whenever they stopped and stared at a mansion or palace, the Moor would ask Aladdin whether he liked it. Indeed, the boy was ecstatic and in seventh heaven because of the sights he had never seen in his entire life. Thus, they continued to stroll about and enjoy themselves until they became tired. Then they entered a huge wonderful garden that was nearby, a place that delighted their hearts and eyes, for it had a fountain that spouted water from the jaws of a golden lion, and the water flowed swiftly among an abundance of flowers. They found a nice place to sit down in the garden near a pond and rested a little while. Soon Aladdin began to jest with the magician and to have fun with him as though the Moor were really his father's brother. Then the Moor stood up, loosened his belt, and pulled out a bag full of dried fruits and other good things to eat.

"Perhaps you're hungry, nephew," he said. "Take whatever you'd like to eat."

Aladdin responded by sticking his hand into the bag, and the Moor ate with him. After they were refreshed and rested, the magician said, "Get up, nephew. If you're no longer tired, let's stroll onward and finish our walk."

Thereupon Aladdin arose, and the Moor accompanied him from garden to garden until they had left them all behind and reached the base of a huge and barren hill.

Since the boy had never gone beyond the city gates and had never taken such an extensive walk as this, he asked the Moor, "Where are we going, uncle? We've left the gardens behind us, and there's nothing but open country from here on. I'm tired and can't go on. So if there are no more gardens after this, let's return to the city."

"No, my son," said the magician. "This is the right way. You see, there are more gardens after this, and we're going to look at one that is more splendid than any royal garden in the world and beyond comparison with those you have just seen. So, pluck up your courage. You're a man now. Praise be to Allah!"

The Moor began to cajole the boy and to tell him wondrous tales, true stories as well as lies, until they reached the spot the magician had come all the way from Morocco to China to see. Upon arriving at their destination, the Moor said to Aladdin, "Nephew, sit down and take a rest, for this is the spot we've been looking for. If Allah is merciful, I'll soon be able to show you marvelous things that nobody in the whole world has ever seen before. Indeed, no one has ever had the pleasure of viewing that which you are about to see."

After they had relaxed awhile, the Moor spoke again. "Once you have rested, my son, I want you to get up and look for some wood chips and dry sticks so that we can start a fire. Then I'll show you things beyond your imagination."

Now, when Aladdin heard these words, he longed to see what his uncle intended to do, and forgetting how tired he was, he arose right away and began gathering small wood chips and dry sticks until the Moor cried to him, "Enough, nephew! Enough!"

Soon the magician took out a small box from his breast pocket, and after opening it, he took some incense, set fire to the wood, and sprinkled the incense on the fire. Then he conjured and uttered some strange words, and the sky darkened. Suddenly there was a burst of thunder, and the ground split open. Aladdin was so startled and frightened that he wanted to flee, but the Moor saw this and grew extremely angry, for without the boy his work would come to nothing. It was only with Aladdin's help that he would be able to obtain and open the hidden treasure. So he got up and gave the boy such a hard smack on the back of his head that his back teeth were almost knocked out, and Aladdin fell to the ground in a swoon. After a while the Moor revived him with some magic, and Aladdin wept and asked, "Uncle, what have I done to deserve such a beating?"

In response, the Moor began to comfort him and said, "My boy, it is my intention to make a man out of you. Therefore, don't contradict me, for I'm your uncle, and you are like a son to me. Obey everything that I tell you to do, and soon you'll forget all your hardships and become absorbed by all the marvels I'm about to show you."

Then the Moor looked down into the crack in the ground and showed Aladdin a marble slab that had a copper ring attached to it. After striking a geomantic table, he turned to Aladdin and said, "If you do everything I tell you, you'll become richer than all the kings of the world. That's why I struck you. There is a treasure down there in your name, and you were about to run away and abandon it. But now, pull yourself together."

And Scheherazade noticed that dawn was approaching and stopped telling her story. When the next night arrived, however, she received the king's permission to continue her tale and said,

"The treasure is under that marble slab," the Moor continued, "so place your hand on the ring and raise the slab. Nobody but yourself has the power to open it, and no mortal on this earth except yourself may set foot in this hidden place, for the treasure has been destined for you. But you must follow all my instructions carefully and remember every word I tell you. All this, my son, is for your own good. The treasure is of immense value, and it is worth more than any king on this earth has ever accumulated. Bear in mind that we shall share all this together."

So poor Aladdin forgot the slap on his head and his tears. Indeed, he was dumbfounded and overjoyed that he was fated to become richer than a sultan. Therefore, he cried out, "Uncle, tell me what to do, and I'll obey all your orders."

"Nephew," replied the magician, "you are like my

own child and even dearer to me because you are my brother's son. Since I have no other relatives, you will be my heir and successor." After saying this, he went over to Aladdin and kissed him. "Now you know why I have done all this work. It has been all for your sake, my son. You will become a rich and great man. So do exactly as I tell you, and go to the ring and lift it."

"But, uncle," Aladdin answered, "the ring is much too heavy for me. I can't lift it all by myself. You must come and help me, for you're stronger than I am."

"Nephew," the Moor replied, "if I help you, all our work will be in vain. You must place your hand on the ring and pull it, and the slab will rise right away. Remember, I told you that nobody can touch the ring but you. However, while you are raising it, you must pronounce your name and the names of your father and mother, and you'll see that you'll be able to lift the slab with ease."

Thereupon the boy mustered up his strength and set his mind to the task. He followed the Moor's instructions carefully, and before he knew it, he had lifted the slab and had cast it aside. Right below him was a stairway with twelve steps that led to a subterranean cave.

"Aladdin," the Moor said, "get a grip on yourself and do exactly what I tell you. I want you to descend the stairs to the vault as carefully as possible. Once you are at the bottom, you will find a space divided into four apartments, and in each one of these you will see four golden jars and other valuable articles made of gold and silver. Beware of all these things! Do not touch them or allow your garments to even brush the jars or the walls! Leave them where they are and continue walking forward until you reach the fourth apartment. If you don't do what I say, you'll be turned into a black stone. Now, when you reach the fourth apartment, you'll find a door, which you will open, and after pronouncing the words that you spoke over the slab, you're to enter and go through a garden adorned by fruit trees. The path that you're to take is about fifty yards long, and it leads to a terrace that has a ladder with some thirty rungs. And you will also see a lamp hanging from the ceiling of the terrace. You're to climb the ladder and take the lamp. After pouring out the contents, place it in your breast pocket. You don't have to worry about damaging your clothes, since the contents are not made of common oil. On your return, you may pluck whatever you want from the trees, for they are yours as long as the lamp is in your hands."

Now, when the Moor finished giving his instructions to Aladdin, he drew a ring from his finger, placed it on one of Aladdin's, and said, "My son, this ring will protect you from all harm and threat, but only on the condition that you bear in mind all that I've told you. So it's up to you now. Go to it, and be brave and determined. You're a man now and no longer a child. And very soon, you'll be the richest man in the world."

Eagerly, Aladdin descended into the cave, where he found the four apartments, each containing four jars of gold. He walked by them with utmost care and caution, just as the Moor had told him to do. From there, he entered the garden and walked down the path until he came upon the terrace, where he mounted the ladder and took the lamp, which he extinguished by pouring out the oil. After placing the lamp in his breast pocket, he descended the ladder and returned to the garden, where he began gazing at the trees and noticed that the birds were singing songs in praise of the Great Creator. Now, he had not realized upon entering that all the trees were covered with costly gems as their fruit, Moreover, each one had a different kind of jewel with various colors of green, white, yellow, and red. They all glistened, and their radiance made the rays of the sun in its midday brightness appear pale in comparison. Indeed, the size of each stone was beyond description, and it was evident that there was not a king in the world who owned a single gem equal to the larger sort or who could boast of even one that was half the size of a smaller kind.

Aladdin began walking among the trees and was surprised and bewildered by what he saw. In place of common fruit, there were all sorts of fine jewels and precious stones such as emeralds, diamonds, rubies, spinels, balasses, pearls, and other gems that were dazzling to the eyes. And since the boy had never seen anything like this in all his livelong days, and since he had no idea of the worth of such valuables (he being still but a boy), he thought that all these jewels were made of glass or crystal. So he gathered them and began filling his pockets, checking to see whether they were fruit such as grapes or figs. However, he found that they were all made of some glassy substance and said to himself, "They'll make wonderful playthings when I get home." He continued plucking numerous gems and crammed them in his pockets until they were stuffed full. After that he picked others and placed them in his belt and the folds of his garments. Then he hurried back along the path for fear that his uncle might become angry with him. As he went through the four apartments and passed by the four jars of gold, he did not touch them, even though he would have been allowed to take some of the contents on his way back. Finally, when he came to the stairs of the cave, he began climbing until he reached the last step. However, finding that this one was higher than all the others, he needed help to mount it. So he said to the Moor, "Oh uncle, lend me a hand so I can climb out."

But the magician answered, "First give me the lamp and lighten your load. It's probably weighing you down."

"It's not the lamp that's weighing me down," Aladdin responded. "Just lend me a hand, and as soon as I reach the ground, I'll give it to you."

Since the Moor's only goal was to obtain the lamp and none other, he began to insist that Aladdin give it to him at once. But the boy had placed it at the bottom of his breast pocket and his other pockets were bulging with gems. Therefore, he could not reach it with his fingers to hand it over, causing the magician to explode with rage. Indeed, the Moor persisted in demanding the lamp, while poor Aladdin could not get at it. Thinking that the boy wanted to keep the lamp for himself, the magician was now convinced that he would not be able to obtain it. In his fury he ran over to the fire, threw more incense on it, and uttered some magic words. Within seconds the power of the magic caused the marble slab to slide over the entrance to the cave, preventing Aladdin's escape.

Now, as I mentioned before, the sorcerer was really a stranger and was not related to Aladdin in any way. He had lied to the boy and had used him only so that he could obtain the treasure that had been intended for Aladdin. This Moor was an African, born in the interior of Morocco, and from his childhood on, he had been addicted to witchcraft and had studied and practiced ev-

ery kind of occult science. Indeed, the city of Tunis itself
is notorious for this unholy lore, and he continued to
read and hear lectures there until he became a master in
all kinds of sorcery and spells that he had acquired after
forty years of study. Then one day he discovered through
a satanic inspiration that there was a treasure hidden in
one of the remote cities of China named Al-Kal'áas, a
treasure that no king on earth could ever match. The
most marvelous thing in this enchanted treasure was a
wonderful lamp, and whoever possessed this magic lamp
would become the richest man on earth and mightier
than any king of the universe. However, the magician
discovered that this treasure could only be opened by a
poor boy named Aladdin, who lived in that Chinese city,
and after he ascertained how easy it would be to obtain
the lamp through the boy, he traveled to China and did
what he did with Aladdin, thinking that he would become lord of the lamp. But when his attempt and hopes
were thwarted and all his work went to waste, he decided
to let the boy die there and heaped the soil on top of the
entrance while saying to himself, "I have not touched a
hand to him, and hence there is no murder." Once he
was sure that it would be impossible for the boy to escape
with the lamp, he made his way back to Africa, sad and
dejected.

So much for the magician.

As for Aladdin, he began shouting to the Moor when
he heard the earth being heaped on top of the marble
slab, for he still believed that the magician was his uncle.
He begged him to lend a hand so that he might get out of
the cave, but no matter how loudly he yelled, there was
no reply. Soon it became apparent to him that the Moor
had deceived him, and that the man was no uncle but a
liar and a wizard. Consequently, poor Aladdin became
desperate, for he was certain there was no escape. After
weeping awhile about his misfortune, he stood up and
descended the stairs to see if Allah Almighty had somehow provided him with a way of escape. He turned to the
right and to the left but saw nothing but darkness and
four walls, for the sorcerer had locked all the doors
through magic and had even cut him off from the garden
to make sure that the boy would die. Then Aladdin's
weeping became greater, and his wailing louder when he

found all the doors shut tight, especially since he had hoped to find some solace in the garden. So there was nothing to do but to return and sit upon the stairs that led to the entrance of the cave.

And Scheherazade noticed that dawn was approaching and stopped telling her story. When the next night arrived, however, she received the king's permission to continue her tale and said,

As Aladdin sat on the stairs in utter misery and wept about his predicament, he began rubbing his hands together, as people who are in trouble generally do, and he raised them in prayer to Allah and begged for mercy. While he was thus imploring the Lord and chafing his hands, his fingers chanced to rub the ring that the sorcerer had given to him for his protection. All at once, there was some smoke and an enormous jinnee appeared before him and said, "I'm at your service, master! Your slave has come. Ask whatever you want, for I am the thrall of whoever wears my lord and master's ring."

Aladdin trembled at the sight of this ifrit, for he was as huge and terrifying as one of Solomon's jinn. However, when he recalled that the ifrit was to obey him because he was wearing the ring, he recovered his spirits. In fact, he was overjoyed and cried out boldly, "Slave of the ring, I want you to carry me to the face of the earth."

No sooner had he spoken than the ground split open, and he found himself outside at the entrance to the treasure in full view of the world. Since he had been sitting in the darkness of the cave for three whole days, the bright light of the sun hurt his eyes, and he was unable to keep them open. So he had to accustom himself to the light gradually to regain his vision. Astounded to be above earth once more, he thought at first that he was at some other place than the entrance to the cave. But then he saw the spot where they had lit the fire of wood chips and dried sticks and where the magician had uttered the magic spells over the incense. Then he turned right and left and caught sight of the gardens from afar, and his eyes recognized the road that they had taken. So he thanked Allah Almighty, who had brought him back to the face of the earth and had freed him from death after he had given up all hope of living. Soon he arose and walked toward the city until he reached the streets and made his way home. When he went into his apartment and saw his mother, he was so overcome by joy and so relieved to be at home again that he fainted right in front of her.

Now his mother had been very sad since he had left her and had rejoiced when he entered the apartment. However, when he sank to the ground in a swoon before her eyes, she was extremely upset and rushed to sprinkle some water on his face. Then she obtained some scents from the neighbors that she had him sniff. When he came around a little, he asked her to bring him some food and told her, "It's been three days since I've had anything to eat."

Thereupon she fetched him what she had on hand, set it before him, and said, "Come, my son, eat and refresh yourself. After you've rested, you can tell me what happened to you. At this point, I won't ask you any questions, for you seem quite exhausted to me."

After Aladdin had finished eating and drinking and had recovered his spirits, he began scolding his mother for leaving him in the hands of the magician. "I want you to know, Mother," he said, "that he intended to take my life. That man, who you said was my uncle, was a scoundrel, and if Almighty Allah had not rescued me from him, I would have been destroyed. Mother, the man was a sorcerer, liar, and hypocrite. I don't think there's a devil under the earth worse than he is. His only wish was to use me so he could obtain what he wanted, and then he planned to do away with me. His fondness for me was all show, and he wasn't interested in my welfare at all. Listen to what he did."

Then Aladdin told her about everything that had happened and wept as he related his adventures to her. At one point during his story he took out the lamp from his breast pocket to show it to her along with the gems and jewels he had brought from the garden, still unaware of their great value. When he finally concluded his story, he heaped abuse on the magician with a burning heart and in great anger.

"Truly," his mother said, "that man is a dangerous criminal and hypocrite who murders people with his magic.

Praise be to Allah, who saved you from the magician's treachery. I honestly thought he was your uncle."

Then, since the boy had not slept a wink for three days and found himself nodding, he went to sleep, and his mother did likewise. Indeed, he did not awake until about noon on the second day, and as soon as he shook off his slumber, he asked his mother for some food. However, she replied, "My son, I have nothing in the house, since you ate everything there was the day before. Be patient and wait until I finish spinning some yarn. Then I'll carry it to the market and buy some food for you with the money I earn from selling it."

"Mother," said he, "keep your yarn. Don't sell it. Just fetch me the lamp I brought with me. I'll go and sell it and buy some food with the money I earn. I'm sure that it will bring in more money than what you can get for your yarn."

So Aladdin's mother arose and fetched the lamp for her son. But while she was doing it, she saw that it was exceedingly dirty and said, "My son, here's the lamp, but it is filthy. I think that it will sell for more if we wash and polish it."

Then, taking a handful of sand, she began to rub the lamp with it. However, all of a sudden, a gigantic jinnee appeared, and he was just as horrifying as he was huge.

"Tell me what you want, mistress," the jinnee cried. "I am your slave and beholden to anyone who holds the lamp. Not only am I your slave, but so are all the other slaves of the lamp."

Aladdin's mother was so overcome with fright that she became tongue-tied and could not respond. Never in her life had she seen such an awesome figure, and she fell to the ground in a swoon. Now, Aladdin was standing at some distance, and he had already seen the jinnee of the ring that he had accidentally rubbed while he had been in the cave. Therefore, when he heard the slave talking to his mother, he rushed over and snatched the lamp from her hand.

"Oh, slave of the lamp," he said, "I am hungry, and I want you to fetch me something to eat. And let it be something delicious and sumptuous."

The jinnee disappeared for a split second and then returned with a vast silver tray loaded with twelve golden platters of different kinds of meat, delicious dainties, and bread whiter than snow. Moreover, there were two silver cups and many flasks of clear wine of the very best vintage. After setting all these things before Aladdin, he vanished from sight. Then Aladdin went and sprinkled rose water on his mother's face and revived her with some pure and pungent perfumes.

"Get up, Mother," he said, "and let us eat this food that Allah Almighty has provided for us."

But when she saw the vast silver tray, she was astounded and asked, "Who is this generous benefactor that has decided to help against our hunger and poverty? We are truly obliged to him. I think it may even be the sultan, who most likely heard about our dire need and misery and sent us this tray of food."

"Mother," Aladdin said, "this is no time for asking questions. Arise, and let us eat, for we are both famished."

Accordingly, they sat down to the tray and began eating, and Aladdin's mother tasted meat that she had never had the pleasure of tasting before. Indeed, they devoured the food in front of them with an appetite fit for kings. Neither one of them knew how valuable the tray was, for never in their born days had they seen the likes of it. As soon as they had finished the meal (leaving just enough for supper and the next day), they got up and washed their hands and chatted for a while. Then the mother turned to her son and said, "Tell me, Aladdin, now that we've eaten, what you did with the jinnee. You no longer have the excuse of saying, 'I'm hungry.'"

So Aladdin told her all that had taken place between him and the slave while she had been unconscious on the ground. His story caused her to be very surprised, and she said, "It's true that the jinnees do appear to humans, but I myself never saw one before this. He's probably the same one who rescued you while you were in the cave."

"It's not the same one, Mother," Aladdin replied. "The ifrit you saw is the slave of the lamp. The other was the slave of the ring and had a different shape."

When his mother heard these words, she cried, "You mean that accursed one who appeared before me and almost killed me is attached to the lamp?"

"Yes," he replied.

"Then, I beg you, my son," she said, "by the milk with

which I suckled you, throw away the lamp and the ring! They can only cause us a great deal of terror, and I couldn't bear to look at that jinnee a second time. Moreover, it is unlawful to have relations with them. Remember that the Prophet warned us against them, and may Allah bless and preserve him!"

"I shall take your concern to heart, Mother," Aladdin responded, "but it's impossible for me to part with the lamp or the ring. You yourself have seen how well the slave provided for us when we were famished. Moreover, that liar, the magician, sent me down into the cave not for the silver or the gold that filled the four apartments. Rather he wanted the lamp and nothing else, because he had learned about its priceless value. If he hadn't been sure about this, he would not have gone to so much trouble and suffered so much hardship, nor would he have traveled from his own country to ours in search of it. Indeed, he wouldn't have buried me in the cave after he had given up hope of obtaining the lamp from me. Therefore, we must keep this lamp and make certain not to disclose its secret powers to anyone. It is now the means of our livelihood and will make us rich. The same is true about the ring, which I shall never withdraw from my finger, since without it I would not be with you here today. Indeed, I would have died with the treasures in the cave. So how could you possibly ask me to remove it from my finger? And who knows what troubles and predicaments I may have in the future? I may need this ring to save my life again. However, since I know how you feel, I'll hide the lamp from your sight so that you'll never have to lay your eyes on it again."

When his mother heard his words and thought about them, she knew that he was right and said, "Do as you wish, my son. As far as I am concerned, I don't ever want anything to do with them, nor do I ever want to see that frightful sight again."

And Scheherazade noticed that dawn was approaching and stopped telling her story. When the next night arrived, however, she received the king's permission to continue her tale and said,

Aladdin and his mother continued eating the food that

the jinnee had brought them the next two days until it was all gone. Then Aladdin took one of the platters that the slave had brought upon the tray to the bazaar in order to sell it. He was still unaware that it was made of the finest gold imaginable, and he approached a Jew, who was shrewder than the devil himself to offer it for sale. When the Jew caught sight of it, he took the boy aside so that nobody might see him, and he examined the platter until he was certain that it was made of gold. However, since he did not know whether Aladdin realized its actual value or was naive, he asked him, "How much do you want for this platter?"

"You know what it's worth," replied the boy.

The Jew debated with himself as to how much he should offer, because Aladdin had given him a cunning reply. At first he thought of a small sum, but at the same time, he feared that the boy might be expecting a considerable amount. So he said to himself, "I had better make him a halfway decent offer even though he might be an ignoramus." So he pulled out a dinar from his pocket, and when Aladdin eyed the gold coin, he hastily took it from the Jew's palm and went his way. Thereupon the Jew realized that the boy had no idea of the platter's worth and regretted that he had not given him a copper carat instead of a gold dinar. In the meantime, Aladdin went straight to the baker's shop, where he bought bread and changed the ducat. Then he went to his mother and gave her the scones and the change from the ducat.

"Mother," he said, "take this money and buy whatever we need."

So she arose, walked to the bazaar, and brought back whatever they needed for the household. Afterward they had a fine meal and were refreshed. And whenever the food ran out, Aladdin would take another platter and carry it to the accursed Jew, who bought each and every one of them at the pitiful price of a dinar. He would even have tried to lower this price to next to nothing, but seeing how he had paid a dinar for the first platter, he feared to offer a lesser sum in case the boy might go to one of his rivals and he would lose his huge profits.

When all the golden platters had been sold, the silver tray was the only thing that remained. Because it was so large and heavy, Aladdin brought the Jew to his house and produced the article. When the buyer saw its size, he gave Aladdin ten dinars and went his way. Thereafter, the boy and his mother lived off this money for a while until it was fully spent. Consequently, Aladdin took out the lamp and rubbed it, and immediately the slave made his appearance once again.

"Ask, my lord, for whatever you want," the jinnee said. "I am your slave and the thrall of whoever possesses the lamp."

"Since I am famished, I want you to bring me a tray of food like the one you brought me before," the boy said.

In the wink of an eye the slave produced a similar tray carrying twelve platters of the most sumptuous food with pure white bread and various bottles of fine wine. Now, Aladdin's mother had gone out when she knew that he was about to rub the lamp so that she would not have to see the jinnee again. But after a while, when she returned and saw the tray covered with the gold platters and smelled the savory meat, she was astonished and pleased.

"Look, Mother!" cried Aladdin. "You wanted me to throw away the lamp, but look at its virtues."

"My son, may Allah reward the jinnee," she replied, "but I never want to see him again."

Then the boy sat down with his mother, and they ate and drank until they were satisfied. Then they put away the rest of the food for the next day. As soon as the food had been consumed again, Aladdin arose, hid a platter beneath his garments, and went off with the intention of selling it to the Jew. However, by chance, he passed the shop of an old jeweler, an honest and pious man who feared Allah. When the sheikh saw the boy, he asked him, "What are you doing here, my son? I've seen you pass by here many times. Moreover, I've seen you making deals with a Jewish man and exchanging various articles with him. It seems to me that you have something for sale and are looking for a buyer. But you probably don't know, my boy, that the Jews do not respect the laws of the Moslems and are always cheating them, especially this accursed Jew with whom you've been bartering. If you indeed have something to sell, you just have to show it to me. Never fear, by Allah, I'll pay you the true price."

Thereupon Aladdin took out the platter and gave it to the old goldsmith, who weighed it on his scales and asked the lad, "Did you sell something similar to this to the Jew?"

"Yes," Aladdin answered, "and others as well."

"What price did he pay you?"

"One dinar."

"What a thief that man is to rob Almighty Allah's servants in this way!" the goldsmith exclaimed. Then, looking at the boy, he remarked, "My son, that tricky Jew has cheated you! In truth, he's made a laughingstock out of you. This platter is pure gold, and it's worth seventy dinars. If you agree to this price, you may have the money."

Accordingly, the sheikh counted out seventy gold pieces, which Aladdin accepted and at the same time thanked him for exposing the Jew's treachery. And after this, whenever he needed to sell another platter, he would bring it to the goldsmith and so he and his mother were soon in better circumstances. Nevertheless, they did not stop living in their customary way as middle-class folk, for they did not squander or waste their money. Moreover, Aladdin had now changed his ways: he no longer associated with the scamps and vagabonds of the neighborhood, and he began to meet good honest men. He went to the market street every day, where he conversed with the merchants, both great and small, asking them about their trade and learning the price of investments and so forth. Likewise, he frequented the bazaars of the goldsmiths and jewelers, where he would sit and enjoy himself by examining their precious stones and noting how jewels were bought and sold. Soon he became aware that the fruit with which he had filled his pockets in the subterranean garden was neither glass nor crystal, but made up of rich and rare gems. Indeed, it dawned on him that he had acquired immense wealth that surpassed that of actual kings. This discovery became even more evident when he examined all the precious stones in the jewelers' quarter and found that their biggest gem could not even match his smallest.

Several years went by, and Aladdin kept frequenting the bazaars, where he became known and loved by most of the folk there. He bought and sold, traded the dear and the cheap, until one day, after rising at dawn and heading for the jewelers' bazaar as was his custom, he heard the town crier announcing something important in the streets: "By command of our magnificent master, the king of the time and the lord of the age and the tide, let all the people close their shops and stores and retire behind the doors of their houses. The Lady Badar al-Budur, the sultan's daughter, desires to visit the Hammam. Whoever does not respect this order will be punished by death and his blood will be upon his own head."

And Scheherazade noticed that dawn was approaching and stopped telling her story. When the next night arrived, however, she received the king's permission to continue her tale and said,

Since the Badar al-Budur's beauty and loveliness were the talk of the entire town, Aladdin began thinking of some way to catch a glimpse of the princess. At last, he decided that it would be best if he took a place behind the Hammam door, where he might see her face as she entered. With this plan in mind, he went straight to the baths before she was expected and stood behind the entrance, a place where none of the people happened to be looking. Now, when the sultan's daughter had made the rounds of the city and its main streets and had amused herself by sightseeing, she finally reached the Hammam, and upon entering, she raised her veil, and her face glittered like a bright sun or a pure white pearl.

After Aladdin saw how lovely she was, he muttered to himself, "Truly, she is a tribute to the Almighty Maker who has adorned her with such amazing beauty and loveliness." From the moment he saw her, he fell helplessly in love with her. His thoughts were distraught. His gaze was dazed. His entire heart was gripped by her. Later, when he returned home to his mother, he was in a state of ecstasy. His mother asked him why he was so delirious, but he would not respond. After she prepared the morning meal, he continued to act very strangely, and she asked again, "My son, what's happened to you? Tell me, is anything wrong? Let me know if something bad has happened to you, for it's not like you to remain silent when I speak to you."

Thereupon, Aladdin, who used to think that all women resembled his mother, and who did not know what "beauty" and "loveliness" meant, even though he had heard about the charms of the sultan's daughter, turned to his mother and shouted, "Let me be!"

However, she continued to plead with him at least to sit down and eat. So he did as she requested but hardly touched the food. After that he lay down on his bed and spent the night in deep thought until the next day. His condition remained the same that day, and his mother was distressed because she was not able to learn what was bothering her son. Since she thought he might be sick, she approached him and said, "My son, if you are feeling pain or something else, let me know so that I can go and fetch a doctor. In fact, the sultan summoned a doctor from the land of the Arabs, who has already arrived, and it is said that he is extremely skillful. If you want, I'll go and bring him to you."

"I'm feeling well, Mother," Aladdin replied. "I'm not in the least bit sick. The only thing is that until yesterday, I had always thought that all women resembled you. However, I've seen the Lady Badar al-Budur, the sultan's daughter, as she was going to the baths. And now I know differently." And he related to her everything that had happened to him and added, "You've probably heard the crier announce that no man was to open his shop or stand in the street so that the Lady Badar al-Budur could retire to the Hammam without anyone seeing her. But now you know that I have seen her as she is, for she raised her veil at the door. And when I caught sight of her and saw the noble work of the Creator, I became ecstatic and fell deeply in love with her. In fact, I'm now determined to win her hand, and I can't sleep a wink without trembling and thinking about her. Therefore, I intend to ask the sultan for permission to marry her in lawful wedlock."

When Aladdin's mother heard her son's words, she told him he was out of his mind and cried, "My child, may Allah protect you! It seems you've lost your head. You must try to regain your senses and stop acting like a madman."

"No, Mother," he responded, "I'm not out of my mind, nor am I a maniac. There is nothing that you have said or can say that will change how I feel and think. I can't rest until I've won the darling of my heart, the beautiful Lady Badar al-Budur. Believe me, I'm determined to seek her hand from her sire, the sultan."

"If you value my life," his mother replied, "don't talk this way! Somebody might hear you and declare you insane. Get rid of all these foolish ideas! Who would ever dare request such a thing from the king? Indeed, even if you persist, how would you go about making such a request? Who would represent you at the court?"

"Nobody else but you, Mother," Aladdin stated. "There's nobody fonder of me than you. And there's nobody whom I trust more than you. So my plan is that you will present my petition for me to the sultan."

"May Allah protect me and keep me from doing anything of the sort!" she exclaimed. "Do you think that I've lost my mind like you? Get that idea out of your head! Remember whose son you are, my child. You're the orphan boy of a tailor, the poorest of the tailors who toiled in this city. And I, your mother, also come from a poor family. How then can you dare to ask to marry the daughter of the sultan, who would never let his daughter marry anyone except a prince of the same rank and majesty? Even if a suitor were noble but a degree lower than his daughter, he would forbid a marriage!"

"Mother, everything you've told me is common knowledge," said Aladdin. "Moreover, I'm quite aware that I'm the child of poor parents. Despite all this, I'm not going to let myself be deterred. If you truly love me, I hope that you'll grant me this favor and present my petition. Otherwise, you'll destroy me. I shall die if I can't win the darling of my heart. Remember, Mother, I am your son."

Upon hearing these words, his mother wept and said, "Yes, indeed, I am your mother, and you are my only son. And my greatest desire is for you to marry. But even here, let us suppose that I would try to find a wife for you from a family that is our equal. Her parents would ask at once whether you have any property, merchandise, or trade to support their daughter. What can I reply then? I would be at a loss for words. And if I cannot possibly answer the poor like ourselves, how can I be so bold as to ask for the daughter of the sultan of China, who has no peer? Think about this. Who would ever dare ask the sultan to wed his daughter to the son of a tailor! If I ever did such a thing, our misfortunes would increase, and our lives would be in mortal danger from the sultan. It might even mean death for you and me. As far as I am concerned, how could I possibly gain access to the sultan? And even if I should succeed, what could I say when they ask me about your livelihood? The king would probably think that I'm a madwoman. And lastly, suppose that I obtain an audience with the sultan, what gift could I possibly bring to his majesty?"

And Scheherazade noticed that dawn was approaching and stopped telling her story. When the next night arrived, however, she received the king's permission to continue her tale and said,

After pausing a moment, Aladdin's mother continued trying to persuade her son to abandon his plan to marry the sultan's daughter, and she said, "It's true, my son, that the sultan is mild and merciful. He never rejects anyone who requests justice or protection from him, nor anyone who asks him for alms. He is most generous and kind and bestows favors on people near and far. But he grants favors only to those who deserve them, to men who have proved themselves in battle under his eyes or men who have rendered great service as civilians to his estate. But you haven't done anything! What deed have you performed before him or in public that merits his grace? Moreover, this favor that you intend to request from him cannot be granted to anyone of our rank. As I told you before, whoever goes to the sultan and asks for his daughter in marriage must offer him something that suits his exalted position."

"Mother, everything you've said thus far is true," Aladdin replied. "And it's a good thing that you've reminded me of all these things and made me think about them. However, my love for the Princess Badar al-Budur has inflamed my heart, and I can't rest unless I win her. When you brought up the subject of a gift, it was something I had not thought about, but it is this very thing that I can indeed offer the sultan. You see, Mother, I can offer the king something that no other monarch in the world has ever seen or possessed. If you remember, I brought back some glass and crystal from the cave that I thought was worth nothing. Well, it turns out that they are precious stones, and there is not a king in the world who can match even the smallest gem that I possess. Ever since I began associating with the jewelers, I've learned that they are priceless gems. So you don't have to worry whether we have an appropriate gift. There is a porcelain bowl in our house, and I'd like you to fetch it for me so that I may fill it with these jewels, which you will carry to the king as a gift. Then you will submit my petition to him, and I am sure that with such a gift as this, you will have no trouble. If you are unwilling to do this, Mother, I shall surely die. Just remember that this gift is one of the priceless gems, and in my many visits to the jewelers' bazaar, I observed the merchants selling jewels, whose beauty was not worth one quarter carat of what we possess. Therefore, I know for sure how priceless our gems are. Now, please bring me the bowl so that I can put some of them in there and arrange them in a splendid way."

So she stood up and fetched the bowl. As she was bringing it back to him, she said to herself, "I'll be able to know what to do after I see whether he was telling me the truth." Then she set the bowl before her son, who pulled some of the stones out of his pockets and put them into the bowl. He arranged all sorts of gems in the bowl until he had filled it, and his mother was astonished by the sight. Indeed, their radiance was so dazzling that she was bewildered. However, she was still not certain that they were indeed priceless, even though her son might have been telling the truth when he said that nothing like them could be found even among kings.

Then Aladdin turned to her and said, "You see how magnificent this present is for the sultan? I'm sure that it will enable you to be received with respect and honor by the king. Now you have no excuse. So, collect yourself and arise. Take this bowl, and bring it to the palace."

But his mother responded, "My son, it's true that the present is extremely valuable and precious, and that there is nothing like it in the world. But who can be so bold as to go and ask the sultan for his daughter? I can't imagine myself saying to him, 'I would like to request the hand of your daughter for my son.' I'd be tongue-tied in front of him. And even granting that Allah comes to my aid and gives me enough courage to say to him, 'I'd like to arrange a marriage between your daughter, the Lady Badar al-Budur, and my son, Aladdin,' they will surely think that I'm demented and cast me out in disgrace and disgust. Moreover, both you and I will be in danger of losing our lives from then on. Nevertheless, because I love you so much, I shall summon my courage and go to the court. Perhaps the king will receive me and honor me on account of the gift, but what shall I say when he asks me how much property you own and what you do for a living?"

"I don't think that the sultan will ask such questions when he gets a look at the jewels," Aladdin answered. "Don't worry yourself about things that may never happen. All you have to do is set this present of precious stones before him and ask his permission to wed me to his daughter. Don't make things difficult. Remember, I have the lamp that provides us with a stable income and whatever else I need. If indeed the sultan does ask you those questions, my hope is that the lamp will furnish me with the right answers."

Then Aladdin and his mother talked all night long about what she was to do, and when the next morning came, she arose and mustered up all her courage. Indeed, she felt somewhat better after Aladdin had explained to her how powerful the lamp was and that it could supply them with whatever they needed. However, now Aladdin was worried that his mother might tell people about the lamp and all its magical powers. So he said to her, "Mother, beware that you don't tell anyone about the powers of the lamp, since this is our most important possession. Be on your guard so that you don't tell anyone about it, no matter who it is. Otherwise, we shall probably lose it and lose the fortune and benefits that we expect from it."

"Have no fear," his mother said, and she arose and took the bowl full of jewels, which she wrapped up in a fine kerchief, and went straight to the divan before it became too crowded. When she entered the palace, she saw the viziers and various nobles go into the audience chamber, and after a short time, the divan was filled by the ministers, high officials, chieftains, and emirs. Finally, the sultan entered, and everyone bowed in respect. Then the king seated himself on the throne, and all who were present at the audience stood before him with crossed arms waiting for his command to sit down. When they received it, each man took his place according to his rank. Then the petitioners went before the sultan, and he judged each case according to its merits in his customary way until the divan came to an end. At this point the king arose and withdrew into the palace, and the people went their way.

And Scheherazade noticed that dawn was approaching and stopped telling her story. However, when the next night arrived, she received the king's permission to continue her tale and said,

Even though Aladdin's mother had been among the earliest to arrive at the sultan's court, she had not been able to find anyone to intercede for her before the king and was unfamiliar with the way the divan was held. Therefore, she was obliged to leave the palace and return home. As soon as Aladdin spotted her with the bowl in her hands, he thought that something unfortunate had happened, but he did not want to ask her until she came into the apartment and sat down. Thereupon, she told him what had occurred and said, "Praise be to Allah, my child, that I had enough courage to attend the audience today. And even though I was too scared to speak to the king today, I shall definitely do so tomorrow. There were many people like me today who could not get an audience with the sultan. Don't fret, my son, tomorrow I shall speak to him, and let come what may come."

When Aladdin heard his mother's words, he was relieved with joy, and although he had hoped the matter would be settled by then, he controlled himself with patience. They slept well that night, and early the next morning, Aladdin's mother went with the bowl to the king's court, which she found closed. So she asked the people what the matter was, and they told her that the sultan did not hold an audience every day but only three times a week. So she had to return home. After this, whenever the sultan held court, she appeared there and waited for someone to help her. However, nobody came to her assistance, and she continued to attend the audiences without success for one whole month.

Now, the king had noticed her presence at every audience, and on the last day of the month, when she took her usual place, her courage failed her, and she allowed the divan to come to a close without uttering a syllable. In the meantime, while the king was preparing himself to enter the harem accompanied by the grand vizier, he turned to him and said, "For the past few weeks I've noticed that old woman over there at every session, and she always seems to be carrying something under her mantilla. Do you know anything about her or what she wants?"

"My lord," the vizier responded, "women are very often petty-minded, and most likely this woman has come to make a complaint about her husband or one of her relatives and neighbors."

However, the sultan was not satisfied by this reply, and he told the vizier to bring the woman before him if she attended the next audience.

"As you command, your majesty," replied the vizier, placing his hand on his brow.

So the next time that Aladdin's mother attended the divan, the king caught sight of her and said to his grand vizier, "That's the woman we were talking about yesterday. Bring her to me so that I can find out what she wants and grant her request."

Accordingly, the minister brought her forward to be introduced to the sultan, and she kissed the ground before him in respect, wishing him glory, prosperity, and long life.

"Woman," said the king, "for some days now I've seen you at my audiences, and yet you've yet to say a word. So tell me now if there is a request that I may fulfill."

Aladdin's mother kissed the ground a second time, and, after blessing him, she said, "Truly, my lord, there is something I would like to request, but before I do this, I would like you to grant me immunity, because your highness may find my petition highly unusual."

Since the king wanted to know her request and was a man of exceptional mildness and clemency, he gave her his word that she would have immunity. Furthermore, he dismissed everyone at the court and allowed only his grand vizier to remain. Then he turned toward his petitioner and said, "Tell me your request, for you are under the protection of Allah Almighty."

"Your majesty, I also need your pardon," she said.

"May Allah pardon you as I myself do," he replied.

"Great king," she resumed, "I have a son named Aladdin, and one day some time ago, when he heard the town crier commanding all the people to close their shops and get off the streets because the Lady Badar al-Budur, the sultan's daughter, was going to the Hammam, he felt an uncontrollable urge to look at her and hid himself in a place behind the doors of the baths to catch sight of her. When she entered, he saw her, but it was too much for him. Ever since the time he looked at her, your majesty, he has not had a moment's peace. Moreover, he has demanded that I go and ask permission from your highness for him to wed your daughter. I tried to get him to drive this idea out of his head, but it was impossible. His love for your daughter has gripped him so deeply that he's told me he'll die if he cannot win your daughter for his bride. Therefore, I hope your highness will be merciful and mild and pardon my boldness and that of my son, and I beg you not to punish us."

After the sultan heard her tale, he regarded her with compassion, and laughing aloud, he asked her, "Tell me, what is that you've been carrying in your mantilla?"

Relieved that the sultan was laughing and was not angry at her, she immediately opened the mantilla and set the bowl of jewels before him. All at once, the audience hall was illuminated as though the chandeliers and torches had been lit. Indeed, the king was dazed and amazed by the radiance of the rare gems, and he marveled at their size, beauty, and quality.

"Never in my life have I seen anything as beautiful and superb as these jewels!" cried the king. "I don't think that I have a single one in my treasury like these." Then he turned to his minister and said, "What do you say? Have you ever seen such fine jewels as these before?"

"Never," replied the vizier. "I don't think you have anything in your treasury to match these."

"Indeed," resumed the king, "whoever makes a present like this to me deserves to become the bridegroom of my daughter. As far as I can see, nobody is more worthy than this man."

When the vizier heard the sultan's words, he was tongue-tied and highly distressed, for the sultan had promised to allow his son to marry the princess. So, after a while, he whispered, "Great king, your highness promised me that the Lady Badar al-Budur would wed my son. Therefore, I find it only just that your highness grant my son a delay of three months during which time he might find a gift more valuable than this."

Although the king knew that such a thing could not be done, not even by the vizier himself or any of his nobles, he granted him the desired delay out of kindness. Then he turned to Aladdin's mother and said, "Go to your son and tell him that I've pledged my word that my daughter shall marry him. First, however, he shall have to wait three months while I make the proper preparations for the wedding."

Aladdin's mother thanked the king and blessed him, and after leaving the palace, she rushed home in joy. When her son saw her enter the apartment with a smile on her face, he knew it was a sign of good news, especially since she had returned without the bowl.

"Allah willing, I hope you've brought me good news, Mother," he said. "Perhaps the jewels have done their job, and the king has received you with kindness and granted your request."

In response, she told him the whole story—how the sultan had treated her favorably and had marveled at the extraordinary size of the jewels and their superb quality, as had the vizier. Then she concluded by saying, "And he promised his daughter would be yours. However, I heard the vizier whisper something about a private contract made between him and the sultan. So the king granted him a delay of three months, and I am somewhat fearful that the vizier will not be kindly disposed toward you and will attempt to change the sultan's mind."

And Scheherazade noticed that dawn was approaching and stopped telling her story. When the next night arrived, however, she received the king's permission to continue her tale and said,

*　　*　　*

Despite the delay of three months, Aladdin was over-joyed by the news, and told his mother, "Inasmuch as the king has given his word, I am extremely pleased and want to thank you with all my heart. Before this, I felt as though I were dead, and now you've restored my life. Praise be to Allah, for there is no man on the face of this earth happier or more fortunate than I am!"

Aladdin showed great patience during the next two months and looked forward to the wedding. Then, one day toward sundown, his mother went to the bazaar to buy some oil, and she found all the shops shut and the whole city decorated. The people were hanging wax candles and flowers in their windows, and she saw soldiers and mounted troops in processions and carrying torches. Surprised by such a marvelous sight and glamorous scene, she went into a store that carried oil and that was still open, and as she was buying the supplies she needed, she asked why there was such a commotion.

"You must be a stranger in town," the shopkeeper replied.

"Not at all," she said.

"You're from this town, and you don't know that this is the wedding night of the sultan's daughter with the son of the grand vizier?" the shopkeeper asked. "How is that possible? Right now he's in the Hammam, and all these soldiers are standing guard and waiting for him to come out. Then they will escort him in the bridal procession to the palace, where the princess is expecting him."

When Aladdin's mother heard these words, she was extremely upset and also at a loss as to how to inform her son about this distressing news. She knew that the poor boy had been looking forward to his marriage with the princess, hour by hour, and could hardly wait until the three months would elapse. But she knew she had to tell him about this quickly, and when she returned home, she said, "My son, I must tell you some bad news that will cause you a great deal of suffering."

"Tell me right away," he said.

"The sultan has broken his promise to you," she said. "The grand vizier's son is to marry his daughter this very night. For some time I had suspected that the minister would change the king's mind, for I noticed how he whispered something to the sultan when your request was granted."

"And how did you learn that the vizier's son is to marry the princess tonight?" Aladdin asked.

Then she told him the whole story, how she had seen the closed shops, the decorations, the soldiers, and the processions, and Aladdin was overcome by grief and jealousy. However, after a short time, he remembered the lamp and recovered his spirits.

"Upon your life, Mother," he said resolutely, "I don't believe that the vizier's son will enjoy the princess tonight. But let's drop the subject. Please get up and serve me my supper. After that, I'm going to retire to my room. Don't worry, everything will turn out well."

After eating his meal, Aladdin locked himself in his room. Then he brought out the lamp and rubbed it. Immediately the jinnee appeared and said, "Ask whatever you want, for I am your slave and beholden to whoever holds the lamp, I and the other slaves of the lamp."

"Hear me!" Aladdin commanded. "I asked the sultan for his daughter's hand, and he gave his word that I could marry her after three months. But he has not kept his word and has given her to the vizier's son. Indeed, this very night the vizier's son is to enjoy her. Therefore, I order you, if you are indeed a trustworthy slave of the lamp, to carry the bride and bridegroom to this room tonight once they have gotten into bed. This is all I ask for the present."

Thereupon the slave disappeared, and Aladdin rejoined his mother to spend the rest of the evening with her. But at the hour when he knew that the slave would be coming, he arose and retired to his room. After a little while, the marid arrived and brought with him the newlyweds in their bridal bed. Aladdin rejoiced to see them and cried out to the slave, "Carry that scoundrel into the privy and put him to sleep!"

The jinnee did as he was commanded right away, but before leaving the vizier's son in the privy, he blew such a cold blast on him that the bridegroom shriveled and looked pitiful. Then the slave returned to Aladdin and said, "If you require anything else, just call me."

"Return to me in the morning," Aladdin said, "so that you can take them back to the palace."

"As you command," the jinnee said and vanished.

Soon Aladdin got up, hardly believing that the affair had been such a success, but when he looked at the Lady Badar al-Budur lying under his own roof, he knew everything had actually happened as he had planned it. However, he did not allow his burning desire to get the best of him and treated her with respect.

"Oh, most beautiful of princesses," he said, "don't think that I've brought you here to dishonor you. Heaven forbid! No, it was only to prevent the wrong man from enjoying you, for your sire, the sultan, promised you to me. Have no fear and rest in peace."

Now, when the Lady Badar al-Budur saw herself in that dark and dismal apartment and heard Aladdin's words, she began to tremble and was so petrified that she could not utter a reply. Soon the young man moved toward her, and after stripping off his outer dress, he placed a sword between them and lay down beside her. He did not come near the princess or do anything indecent, for all he wanted to do was to prevent the consummation of her nuptials with the vizier's son. On the other hand, the Lady Badar al-Budur spent a terrible night in bed and did not sleep a wink. The same was true of the vizier's son, who lay in the privy and did not dare to stir for fear that the jinnee might harm him.

As soon as it was morning, the slave appeared before Aladdin without the lamp being rubbed and said to him, "My lord, if you require anything, command me, and it will be done immediately."

"Go and return the bride and bridegroom to their apartment," said Aladdin.

So the slave carried out his order in the twinkle of an eye and carried the pair in their bed to the palace without their being able to see who was transporting them. Both were terribly frightened, and the marid had barely time to set them down again and disappear when the sultan came to visit and congratulate his daughter. Of course, as soon as the vizier's son heard the doors thrown open, he sprang quickly from the bed and got dressed, for he knew that it could only be the king who would enter at that hour. Nonetheless, it was extremely difficult for him to leave his bed, in which he would have preferred to warm himself after spending the night in the cold and damp privy.

And Scheherazade noticed that dawn was approaching and stopped telling her story. When the next night arrived, however, she received the king's permission to continue her tale and said,

After entering the apartment, the sultan kissed his daughter on her forehead, wished her good morning, and asked whether she was satisfied with the bridegroom. But her only reply was a scowl, which forced him to repeat his question a few times. However, she refused to answer. So the king left the room, and after going to the queen, he informed her of what had taken place between him and his daughter. Since the mother did not want her husband to stay mad at their daughter, she said, "This is just the way young married couples are nowadays, at least during the first few days of marriage. They're bashful and somewhat coy. So be patient and excuse her. After a while she'll become herself again and speak with people just as she did before. To be on the safe side, I'll go and see how she is."

So the queen arose and donned her dress. When she entered her daughter's room, she went over to her and gave her a kiss on her forehead. However, the princess did not respond, causing the queen to say to herself, "Something strange has definitely happened, otherwise she wouldn't be so troubled." Now she spoke directly to her daughter and said, "Tell me what's the matter. I've come to wish you a good morning, and all I get is silence for an answer."

Thereupon the Lady Badar al-Budur raised her head and said, "Pardon me, Mother, I've neglected my duty. I know I should have greeted you with respect, seeing that you have honored me by this visit. However, I want you to know the reason why I am in such a terrible mood, and how I have just experienced the most vile night of my life. You see, no sooner had we gotten into bed than some invisible creature came, lifted our bed, and transported it to some dark and dismal place." After that the princess related to her mother all that had happened that night: how the bridegroom had been taken away from her, how she had been left alone, and how another young man had come and lain down next to her after placing a sword between them. "In the morning," she resumed, "the creature who had carried us off came and returned us to the palace. But as soon as we arrived and he disappeared, my father entered, and I had neither the heart nor the tongue to speak to him, for I was still trying to get over my fright and terror. I'm sure that my poor behavior has made him angry. So I hope, Mother, that you will explain to him why I acted the way I did and that he will pardon me for not answering him the way I should have."

When the queen heard her daughter's story, she said to her, "My child, pull yourself together. If you tell this story, people will probably say that the sultan's daughter has lost her mind. And you've done the right thing by not recounting your adventure to your father. Beware, and again I say, beware of telling him anything about what happened last night."

"Mother," the princess replied, "I've told you the truth. I'm not crazy. This is what happened to me, and if you don't believe me, ask my husband."

"I want you to get up right away," the queen said, "and banish all such thoughts from your mind. Put on some clothes and go and watch the bridal festivities they've organized for you throughout the city. Listen to the drumming and the singing, and look at the decorations that were all created in your honor."

After saying this, the queen summoned the servants, who dressed and prepared the Lady Badar al-Budur. In the meantime she went to see the sultan and assured him that their daughter had suffered from some bad dreams and nightmares during the wedding night.

"Don't be severe with her for not answering you this morning," she said.

Thereafter she secretly sent for the vizier's son and asked him what had happened and whether what the Lady Badar al-Budur had said was true. However, since he feared losing his bride, he said, "My lady, I don't have the slightest clue about what you've just said."

The queen was now certain that her daughter had either hallucinated or was suffering from bad dreams.

The marriage festivities lasted the entire day, with professional dancers and singers performing to the accompaniment of all kinds of instruments with great mirth. Meanwhile the queen, the vizier, and the vizier's son did their very best to make sure that the princess would enjoy herself. That day they left nothing undone to increase her pleasure and make her forget everything that had been bothering her. Yet it was all in vain, for she watched the spectacles in silence. Indeed, for the most part she was downcast and brooded about everything that had happened to her during the past night. It is true that the vizier's son had suffered much more than she had, since he had spent the night in the privy. However, he had refused to tell the truth and repressed the incident for fear of losing his bride and the connection with the royal family that brought him so much honor. Moreover, everyone envied him because he had won such a lovely and beautiful young woman as the Lady Badar al-Budur.

In the meantime, Aladdin also went out that day to enjoy the festivities, which extended throughout the city as well as the palace. When he heard the people talk about the high honor that the vizier's son had gained and how he would prosper by becoming the son-in-law of the sultan, he began to laugh. And he said to himself, "Indeed, you poor wretches, you don't know what happened to him last night. Otherwise you wouldn't envy him the way you do."

When darkness fell and it was time for sleep, Aladdin arose in his room, rubbed the lamp, and the slave appeared in a flash. Once again Aladdin ordered him to bring the sultan's daughter, together with her bridegroom, just as he had done on the previous night, before the vizier's son could take her virginity. So the marid quickly vanished and at the appointed time returned with the Lady Badar al-Budur and the vizier's son in the bed. Once again he carried the bridegroom to the privy and left him there in fear and trembling. Meanwhile Aladdin arose and placed the sword between the princess and himself and lay down beside her. When day broke, the slave transported the pair back to the palace, leaving Aladdin filled with delight at the condition of the minister's son.

Now, when the sultan woke up in the morning, he decided to visit his daughter again and see if she would treat him as she had on the past day. So, shaking off his sleep, he jumped up, clothed himself, and went to the apartment of the princess. Upon hearing the knocking, the vizier's son jumped up and began donning his garments while his ribs were still freezing because the jinnee had just returned them to the palace. The sultan moved toward the wedding bed, raised the curtain, and wished his daughter good morning. Then he kissed her forehead and asked her how she felt. However, she looked sad and sullen, and instead of answering, she just scowled at him as though she were angry and suffering from a terrible plight. Thereupon the sultan became extremely angry at her for not replying, and he suspected that something bad had happened to her. So he drew his sword and cried out to her, "What's come over you? Either tell me what's happened, or I'll take your life this very moment! Is this the way to pay your respect to me, by not talking to me?"

When the Lady Badar al-Budur saw her father brandishing his sword at her and how furious he was, she felt somehow released from the past that was hanging over her and she managed to raise her head.

"Don't be angry with me, dear father," she cried out. "Please calm down, for I'm not responsible for the way I've been acting, as you will soon see. Please, if you listen to what happened to me during these past two nights, I'm sure you'll pardon me and have pity on me, for I'm still your loving child."

Then the princess told him all that had occurred during the past two nights and added, "If you don't believe me, ask my husband, and he'll tell your highness the whole story. I don't know what they did with him when they took him away from me or where they kept him."

When the sultan heard his daughter's words, he became sad, and his eyes brimmed with tears. Then he sheathed his sword and kissed her.

"My daughter," he said, "why didn't you tell me yesterday what had happened to you the night before? Then I could have protected you from the terror that you suffered this past night. But it doesn't matter now. Get up and forget about it all. Tonight I'll have guards posted around your room so that you'll never have to go through anything like this again."

Then the sultan returned to his palace and summoned the grand vizier right away. When he arrived, the king asked him, "How do you view this whole matter? I'm sure your son has told you what happened to him and my daughter."

The minister replied, "Great king, I haven't seen my son for two days."

Thereupon, the sultan told him what the princess had suffered and added, "I want you to find out what's happened to your son and all the facts pertaining to this case. Since my daughter has had such a great shock and appears to be terrified, she may not really know what happened to her, although I think she's told me the truth."

So the grand vizier arose, went out, and summoned his son. When the young man arrived, his father asked him whether the princess had been telling the truth.

"Father," he said, "heaven forbid that the Lady Badar al-Budur would ever lie. Indeed, she told the truth. These past two nights have been the most vile in my life when they should have been the most pleasurable. What happened to me was even worse than what happened to her, because I was not allowed the pleasure of sleeping in a bed. Instead, I was stuck in a frightful black hole that had a horrible smell and was truly damnable. Moreover, my ribs were frozen cold."

In short, the young man told his father the whole story and added, "I implore you, Father, speak to the sultan and ask him to release me from this marriage. I confess that it's a great honor for me to be the sultan's son-in-law, and I've fallen terribly in love with the princess. But I have no strength left to endure what I've suffered these past two nights."

When the vizier heard these words, he became exceedingly sad, for his most cherished wish had been to wed his son to the sultan's daughter and help him advance in life. He thought about the entire affair a long time and was in a quandary about what to do. Indeed, it upset him to break off the marriage and he was reluctant to do so, especially since it had brought him such rare fortune. Consequently, he said, "Be patient, my son, until we see what happens tonight when we'll assign guards to protect your room. Don't be so quick to abandon the great distinction and honor that only you have achieved."

Then the vizier returned to the sultan and informed him that everything that the Lady Badar al-Budur had said was true. As a result, the king said, "Well then, given the situation, I must act immediately," and he commanded that all the festivities be stopped, and he annulled the marriage.

The people were stunned by this news, especially when they saw the grand vizier and his son leave the palace with miserable and angry faces. "Why was the marriage broken off?" They began to ask. "What happened?" Of course, nobody knew the truth except Aladdin, who claimed the princess's hand and laughed in secret joy. But even after the marriage was dissolved, the sultan forgot the promise that he had made to Aladdin's mother. The same was true with the grand vizier. Neither one of these men had an inkling of why and how everything had happened and did not link the incidents with Aladdin.

Aladdin waited patiently for the three months to elapse, and as soon as the term had expired, he sent his mother to the sultan to remind him of his promise. So she went to the palace, and when the king appeared in the divan and saw the old woman standing before him, he remembered his promise with regard to the marriage, and he turned to the minister and said, "That old woman over there is the one who gave me the jewels, and I gave her my word that when three months had elapsed, I would wed my daughter to her son."

The minister went over to her and brought her before the king, whom she saluted and blessed. In turn, the sultan asked her if there was anything he could do for her, and she answered, "Great king, the three months that you commanded me to wait have elapsed, and it is time to wed my son, Aladdin, with your daughter, the Lady Badar al-Badur."

The sultan was distraught at this request, especially since he saw that the woman was one of the poorest of his subjects. Nevertheless, the present she had brought him was magnificent and priceless. So he turned to the grand vizier and whispered, "What advice do you have for me? In truth, I did give my word. But it seems to me that they are poor and from the lower classes."

The vizier, who was mad with envy and bitter about what had happened to his son, said to himself, "How can someone like this wed the king's daughter and my son lose this high honor?" Therefore, he whispered to the king, "My lord, it will be easy to put off a poor devil like her son. He's certainly not worthy enough for your daughter, especially when you haven't even seen what he looks like."

"But how am I to do this?" the sultan asked. "I can't put off the man when I gave him my word. As you know, the word of kings is their bond."

"My lord," the vizier replied, "my advice is that you place another demand on him and ask for forty platters of pure gold filled with gems like the ones that this woman already brought you with forty white slave girls and forty black eunuch slaves to carry the platters."

"By Allah," the king answered, "that is good advice. It will be impossible for him to carry off such a feat, and then I'll be freed of my promise."

Then he turned to Aladdin's mother and addressed her loudly. "I want you to go and tell your son that I am a man of my word, but he can have my daughter only on the condition that he pay the dowry for my daughter. The settlement amounts to forty platters of pure gold, all brimful with gems, like those you've already brought me, with as many slave girls and black eunuchs to carry them. If your son can provide this dowry, then I'll marry him to my daughter."

Aladdin's mother departed, and on her way home she wagged her head and said to herself, "Where can my poor son procure these platters and jewels? Even if he were to return to the underground cave and pluck them from the trees, which I think is impossible anyway, how will he obtain the forty girls and black slaves?" Nor did she stop murmuring to herself until she reached her apartment, where she found Aladdin awaiting her, and she lost no time in saying, "My son, didn't I tell you to forget about the Lady Badar al-Budur and that people like us can't aspire to marriages with people of her rank?"

"Tell me what happened," Aladdin responded.

"The sultan received me with all due honor," she said,

"and it· seems to me that his intentions toward us are noble. But your enemy is that accursed vizier, for after I addressed the king in your name as you requested, he turned to the minister, who spoke to him in a whisper. After that the sultan replied with a list of demands." Then she told her son the conditions for the marriage to take place and concluded by saying, "He expects you to give him a reply right away, but I suppose that we have no answer for him."

And Scheherazade noticed that dawn was approaching and stopped telling her story. When the next night arrived, however, she received the king's permission to continue her tale and said,

"Mother, calm down and collect yourself," Aladdin said. "Please bring me something to eat, and after we have dined, Allah willing, you'll see my reply. The sultan thinks, like you, that he has demanded such an extraordinary dowry that he can deter me from marrying his daughter. The fact is that he's demanded much less than I had expected. But do me a favor, and go out to purchase the food for dinner, and leave me alone to procure the reply."

So she went out to the bazaar to buy what was necessary for dinner while Aladdin retired to his room, where he took the lamp and rubbed it. Immediately the slave appeared to him and said, "Ask, my lord, whatever you want."

"I've asked permission from the sultan to marry his daughter," Aladdin said, "and he has demanded forty platters of purest gold each weighing ten pounds and all to be filled with gems that come from the garden in the underground cave. Furthermore, they are to be carried on the heads of forty white slave girls to be attended by forty black eunuchs. I want you to bring them to me at once."

"As you request, my lord," said the jinnee, who disappeared for an hour or so and then returned with the platters, jewels, slave girls, and eunuchs. After setting them down before Aladdin, he said, "Here is what you desired. If you would like anything else, just tell me."

"I don't need anything else right now," Aladdin replied, "but if I do, I'll summon you and let you know."

The slave now disappeared, and after a little while, Aladdin's mother returned home, and when she entered the apartment, she saw the slave girls and blacks and exclaimed with wonder, "All this has come from that marvelous lamp! May Allah preserve it for my boy!"

But before she could take off her mantilla, Aladdin said to her, "Mother, this is the time that the sultan usually goes to his seraglio palace. So take him what he's demanded at once so that he'll know that I'm prepared to provide him with all he wants and more. Also, he'll realize that the grand vizier has beguiled him, and that it is fruitless to try to deter me."

Then he arose right away and opened the door to the apartment so that the slave girls and eunuchs could depart. When the people of the neighborhood saw such a marvelous spectacle, they all stood to gaze at it, and they admired the slave girls, who were beautiful and lovely, for each one of them wore robes lined with gold and studded with jewels worth no less than a thousand dinars apiece. The people also stared at the platters, and although they were covered by brocades studded with gems, their glitter pierced the brocades, and their gleam surpassed the rays of the sun. As Aladdin's mother walked forward, the slave girls and the eunuchs followed her in a fine procession, and people from all quarters gathered to gaze at the beauty of the damsels, glorifying God Almighty, until the procession reached the palace and entered it. Now, when the high dignitaries, chamberlains, and commanders caught sight of Aladdin's mother and her company, they were all astonished, especially when they laid their eyes on the slave girls, for each and every one of them could ravish the reason of a monk. And although the chamberlains and officials were men from distinguished and wealthy families, the sons of grandees and emirs, they were dazzled by the costly dresses of the slave girls and the platters that they were carrying on their heads. In fact, they had to veil their eyes when they looked at the stunningly bright platters. Then the nabobs went in and reported to the king, who commanded them to enter his chamber right away, and Aladdin's mother went in with them. When they all stood before the sultan, they saluted him with every sign of respect and worship and prayed for his glory and prosperity. Then the slave girls removed the platters from their heads and placed them at his feet, and once they took off the brocade covers, they stood with their arms crossed behind them. The sultan was extremely astonished and captivated by the incomparable beauty and loveliness of the slave girls. Moreover, he was totally bedazzled by the golden platters filled with gems and so bewildered by this marvelous sight that he became dumbfounded and was unable to utter a syllable for quite some time. When he considered that all these treasures had been collected within an hour or so, he felt completely stupefied. Soon, however, he commanded the slave girls to carry the platters to his daughter's chamber. When they left his presence, Aladdin's mother stepped forward and said to the sultan, "My lord, this small token is the least we could do to honor the Lady Badar al-Budur. Actually, she really deserves much more than this."

Upon hearing this, the sultan turned to his minister and asked, "What do you say now? Isn't a man who can produce such great wealth in so short a time worthy of becoming the sultan's son-in-law?"

Although the minister was stunned by these riches, even more than the king, he was dying with envy and extremely frustrated because he saw that the king was satisfied with the dowry. Therefore, he replied with the intention of preventing the king from going through with the marriage, "It isn't worthy enough for her. Not even all the treasures of the universe could match your daughter's pinky. I believe that your highness is overestimating these things in comparison with your daughter."

When the king heard the vizier's words, he knew that they were prompted by great envy. So he turned to Aladdin's mother and said, "Go to your son and tell him that I've accepted his dowry and shall keep my word. My daughter shall be his bride, and he my son-in-law. Furthermore, tell him that I want him to appear before me at once so that I can become acquainted with him. He will be received with honor and consideration, and this night will be the beginning of the marriage festivities. Only he must come here without delay."

Aladdin's mother returned home faster than a cyclone

in order to congratulate her son, and she was in ecstasy at the thought that her boy was about to become the son-in-law of the sultan. After her departure from the palace, the king dismissed the divan and went to the princess's chamber, where he ordered the platters and slave girls brought before him so that he could inspect them with his daughter. When the Lady Badar al-Budur looked at the jewels, she was astonished and cried out, "I don't think that there are any jewels in the world that can compare to these!" Then she looked at the slave girls and admired their beauty and loveliness. Since she was aware that they had been sent to her by her new bridegroom, she was very pleased. To be sure, she had been distressed by what had happened to her former husband, the vizier's son, but now she was overjoyed when she gazed upon the damsels and their charms. Furthermore, her father was just as glad as she was and particularly happy when he saw that his daughter was no longer melancholy. Then he asked her, "Are you pleased with these things? Personally I think that your new bridegroom is more suitable for you than the vizier's son. And very soon, Allah willing, you'll find your happiness with him."

So much for the king.

In the meantime, as soon as Aladdin saw his mother enter the house with a great smile of joy on her face, he cried out, "May Allah be praised! All that I've ever desired has now been fulfilled!"

"You'll be glad once you hear my news," his mother said. "The sultan has accepted your offer, I mean, your dowry, and you are now engaged to the Lady Badar al-Budur. You are to be married to her this very night, my son. The king has given me his word and has proclaimed to the world that you will be his son-in-law. However, he also told me to send you to him right away so that he can become acquainted with you and receive you with honor and respect. So here I am, my son, my work is done. Let what may happen happen. The rest is up to you."

Aladdin arose and kissed his mother's hand and thanked her for her kind service. Then he left her, went into his room, took the lamp, and rubbed it. Immediately the jinnee appeared and cried out, "At your service, my lord. Ask whatever you want."

"I want you to take me to the finest Hammam in the world," Aladdin said. "Then fetch me the most expensive and regal garments that surpass anything ever worn by a king."

"As you command," the marid replied, and he carried Aladdin to baths that even the kings of the Chosroës had never seen. The building was made entirely of alabaster and carnelian, and it was lined with marvelous and captivating paintings. The great hall was studded with precious stones, and not a soul was there. But when Aladdin entered, a jinnee in human shape washed and bathed him as he wished. After Aladdin left the baths, he went into a large room, where he found a rich and princely suit. Then he was served with sherbets and coffee flavored with ambergris. Once he was done drinking, a group of black slaves approached him, sprayed him with perfume, and clothed him in the costliest of clothing.

As we know, Aladdin was the son of a poor tailor, but anyone who had seen him then would have said, "This young man is the greatest progeny of the kings. Praise be to Him who changes others and who does not change Himself!" Soon the jinnee arrived and transported him back to his home.

"My lord," the ifrit asked, "do you need me for anything else?"

"Yes," Aladdin replied. "I want you to bring me forty-eight mamelukes. Twenty-four are to precede me, and the other twenty-four are to follow me, and I want all of them equipped with the best suits of armor, weapons, and horses. Indeed, their outfits are to be the costliest in the world. Then fetch me a stallion fit for a king of the Chosroës, and let his trappings be studded with gold and the finest jewels. I also want forty-eight thousand dinars so that each white slave can carry a thousand gold pieces. Since I intend to visit the sultan right away, don't delay. Without all these men and equipment, it will be impossible to appear before him. Furthermore, I want you to produce a dozen slave girls, incomparably beautiful and magnificently dressed so that they can accompany my mother to the royal palace. Let each one of the slave girls be robed in raiment that would fit a queen."

"As you command," the jinnee replied, and after disappearing for a split second, he brought everything that he had been ordered to bring. In addition, he gave Aladdin a stallion unrivaled by the finest of Arabian steeds, and its saddle cloth was a splendid brocade lined with gold. Immediately, Aladdin sent for his mother and gave her the garments that she was to wear. In addition, he placed her in charge of the twelve slave girls, who formed her escort to the palace. Then he sent one of the mamelukes ahead to see if the sultan had left the seraglio or not. The white slave went and returned faster than lightning and reported, "My lord, the sultan is awaiting you!"

Thereupon, Aladdin arose and mounted his horse with his mamelukes riding behind and in front of him. They looked so splendid that all who saw them had to exclaim, "Praise the Lord who created them and endowed them with such magnificence and beauty!" And they scattered the gold coins among the crowds of people who came to watch them and their master, who surpassed not only his men but also the finest of princes in his splendor and glory. Praise be to the Bountiful Giver, the Lord Eternal! All this was due to the power of the magic lamp, which provided the person who possessed it with the fairest looks, enormous wealth, and great wisdom. The people appreciated Aladdin's generosity, and they were all captivated by his charm, elegance, comportment, and dignified manners. They praised the Creator for such a noble creation, and each and every person blessed Aladdin, for although they knew that he was the son of a poor tailor, nobody envied him, and they all felt that he deserved his good fortune.

And Scheherazade noticed that dawn was approaching and stopped telling her story. When the next night arrived, however, she received the king's permission to continue her tale and said,

Now the sultan had assembled the lords of the land and had informed them of the promise that he had made to Aladdin. Moreover, he ordered them to wait for Aladdin's approach and then to go forth, one and all, to meet and greet him. Therefore, the emirs, viziers, chamberlains, nabobs, and officers took their stations at the palace gate. Aladdin would have dismounted at the outer entrance, but one of the nobles, whom the king had assigned this duty, approached him and said, "My lord, your highness the sultan has commanded that you ride your steed up to the divan door, where you are to dismount."

Then they all accompanied him to the appointed place, where they helped him dismount. After this, all the emirs and nobles went ahead of him into the divan and led him up to the royal throne. Thereupon the sultan came down from his throne to prevent Aladdin from prostrating himself, and after embracing and kissing him, he seated him to his right. Aladdin did what was customary in greeting a king by blessing him and wishing him a long life and prosperity. Then he said, "My lord, thanks to your generosity, you have promised me the hand of your daughter the Lady Badar al-Budur, even though I do not deserve the greatness of such a gift, since I am but the humblest of your slaves. Indeed, I pray that Allah preserve you and keep you prosperous. In truth, great king, I do not have the words to thank you for the enormous favor that you have bestowed upon me. And I hope that you will grant me a plot of land where I can build a pavilion suitable for your daughter."

The sultan was struck with admiration when he saw Aladdin in his princely suit. He noted how handsome and attractive he looked and how remarkable the mamelukes were who served him. His astonishment grew even greater when Aladdin's mother approached him in a splendid and costly dress, clad as though she were a queen, and followed by twelve slave girls, who attended her with great respect and reverence. Finally, he was most impressed by Aladdin's eloquence and polite speech, and so was everyone else at this gathering. Of course, the grand vizier was so enraged with envy that he almost exploded, and he felt even worse when the sultan clasped Aladdin to his bosom and kissed him after listening to the youth's eloquent and respectful speech.

"Alas, my son," said the king, "that I have not had the pleasure of conversing with you until this day."

After making this remark, the sultan commanded the music to begin. Then he arose, and taking Aladdin by hand, he led him into the palace, where supper had been prepared, and the eunuchs at once laid the tables. Once the king had sat down and seated Aladdin on his right side, the viziers and other officials took their places, each according to his rank. Meanwhile, the bands played and a splendid marriage feast was displayed in the palace. The king started making friends with Aladdin and conversed with the youth, who answered the sultan politely and eloquently, as though he had been bred in the palaces of kings or had lived with them all his life. The more they conversed with each other, the more the sultan was delighted and pleased by his son-in-law's wit and elegance. After they had eaten and drunk and the trays were removed, the king summoned the kazis and witnesses, who wrote out the marriage contract between Aladdin and the Lady Badar al-Badur. Then the bridegroom arose and would have gone away if his father-in-law had not prevented him and asked, "Where are you going, my son? The wedding festivities have just begun. The marriage is made. The knot is tied. The contract written."

"My lord," Aladdin responded, "it is my desire to build a pavilion for the Lady Badar al-Budur suitable for her status and high rank. Until I do this, I cannot visit her. But, Allah willing, the building will be finished within the shortest amount of time, for your slave will do his utmost in regard for your highness. Although I long very much to be with the princess and to enjoy her company, it is incumbent upon me first to show my respect for her and to complete this task."

"Look around you, my son," replied the sultan, "and choose whatever ground you deem suitable for your plans. I'll leave it up to you. But I think the best place would be to build your pavilion on that broad ground over there facing my palace."

"I could wish for nothing better than to be near to your highness," said Aladdin.

After saying this, Aladdin bade farewell to the king, mounted his horse, and rode from the palace with his mamelukes following him. Along the way, crowds of people shouted their blessings until he reached his home. Once there, he entered his room, took the lamp, and rubbed it. Immediately the slave appeared and said, "Ask whatever you want, my lord."

"I have an important and urgent task for you," Aladdin replied. "I want you to build me a pavilion in front of the sultan's palace right away. It must be marvelous and furnished royally with every possible comfort."

"As you command," said the jinnee and vanished.

Before daybreak, the jinnee returned to Aladdin and said, "My lord, the pavilion is finished as you desired. If you would like to inspect it, please get up and come with me."

So Aladdin arose, and the slave carried him in a split second to the pavilion, which impressed him a great deal. The building was made out of jasper, alabaster, marble, and mosaics. The treasury was full of gold, silver, and costly gems, worth more than can be imagined. From there, the jinnee led him to another place where Aladdin saw tables, plates, dishes, spoons, ladles, basins, covers, cups, and saucers, all made out of precious metal. Next they went to the kitchen, where they found the cooks provided with all the utensils they needed, made out of gold and silver. After that they visited a warehouse filled with chests packed with royal garments, incredibly beautiful stuffs such as gold-lined brocades from India and China and velvet and silk materials. Then the jinnee led Aladdin on a tour of the numerous apartments, which contained marvelous things beyond description. When they went outside to the stables, Aladdin saw that they contained magnificent steeds that could not be found anywhere on the earth, even in the stables of kings, and even the harness rooms were hung with costly trappings, saddles, and bridles studded with pearls and precious stones. And all of this was the work of one night.

Aladdin was wonder-struck and astounded by the magnificent display of wealth, which not even the wealthiest monarch on earth could produce. He was even more astonished to see his pavilion fully provided with eunuchs and slave girls whose beauty could seduce a saint. Yet, the major attraction of the pavilion was the upper dome of twenty-four windows all made of emeralds, rubies, and other gems. And one window remained unfinished, at Aladdin's request, so that he could prevail upon the sultan to complete it.

After Aladdin had inspected the entire edifice, he was exceedingly happy and pleased. Then turning to the slave, he said, "I still need one thing more, which I forgot to ask."

"Ask whatever you want, my lord," the jinnee said.

"I want a carpet made of the finest brocade and woven with gold," he said. "When it is unrolled, I want it to extend to the sultan's palace so that the Lady Badar al-Budur can walk upon it without treading on common ground."

The slave departed momentarily, and upon his return, he said, "My lord, I've brought you what you wanted."

Then the jinnee took him and showed him a carpet which completely overwhelmed him by its splendor and extended from the pavilion to the palace. After this, the jinnee lifted Aladdin and transported him back to his home.

As the sun began to shine, the sultan rose from his sleep and went to his window, from which he saw a new grandiose pavilion opposite his palace. At first he could not believe his eyes and rubbed them to make sure that he was not dreaming. However, soon he was certain that the building was real, and he was amazed by its grandeur and by the carpet that was spread between his palace and the pavilion. The royal doorkeepers and all the members of his household were also astonished by the spectacle. Meanwhile, the vizier entered the palace, and when he caught sight of the newly built pavilion and the carpet, he was stupefied as well. He and the king began talking about this marvelous sight, and they finally agreed that no king in the universe could ever build such a pavilion. Addressing the minister, the sultan asked, "Do you agree now that Aladdin is worthy enough to be the husband of my daughter? You realize, of course, that no ordinary man could have built such an opulent and magnificent pavilion as this."

However, the vizier was still envious and replied, "Great king, I don't care how rich or adroit he may be. He must have used magic to build such a splendid pavilion in one night."

"I'm surprised to see that you continue to have a bad opinion of Aladdin," said the sultan. "I attribute it to your envy and jealousy. You were present when I gave him the ground to build a pavilion for my daughter. However that may be, I ask you, why would it be impossible for the man who gave me such remarkable gems for my daughter's dowry to build such an edifice as this?"

When the vizier heard the sultan speaking about Aladdin that way, he knew that his lord loved Aladdin a great deal, and thus his envy increased. It was only due to the fact that he could do nothing against the young man that he refrained from saying anything.

In the meantime it was broad daylight and the appointed time had arrived for Aladdin's return to the palace, where his wedding was being celebrated, and the emirs, viziers, and grandees had assembled to be present at the ceremony. So Aladdin arose and rubbed the lamp. Immediately the jinnee appeared and said, "Ask whatever you want, my lord. I am at your service."

"I want to go to the palace right away," Aladdin said. "Today is my wedding, and I want you to bring me ten thousand dinars."

The slave vanished, and in the twinkle of an eye he returned with the money. After Aladdin mounted with his mamelukes behind and in front of him, he headed for the palace, scattering gold pieces along the way, and the people praised him and held him in high esteem. When he drew near the palace, the emirs, officials, and officers, who were waiting for him, noticed his approach, and they hastened right away to inform the king. Thereupon the sultan rose and met his son-in-law. After embracing and kissing him, he led him into his own apartment, where he sat down and seated Aladdin on his right. The city was all decorated, and music rang throughout the palace. The singers sang, until the king commanded that the noon meal be served. Then the eunuchs and mamelukes spread the tables and trays fit for kings, and the sultan and Aladdin were joined by the lords of the realm, who took their seats and ate and drank until they were satisfied.

The wedding festivities in the palace and the city were glorious, and both nobles and commoners rejoiced and were glad, while the governors of the provinces and the nabobs of various districts flocked from far away to witness Aladdin's marriage with all its processions and festivities. Moreover, when the sultan looked at Aladdin's mother, he was astounded by the change that had come over her, for he recalled how she used to visit him as a poor woman even though Aladdin had such immense wealth.

When the spectators, who crowded the royal palace to

enjoy the wedding festivities, gazed upon Aladdin's pavilion and saw how beautiful it was, they were tremendously surprised that such a vast edifice as that could have been built in a single night. Therefore, they blessed Aladdin and cried out, "May Allah reward him and bless him with prosperity and long life!"

When dinner was over, Aladdin rose and said farewell to the sultan. He mounted his horse and rode with his mamelukes to his pavilion so that he could make the preparations to receive his bride there. And as he passed, the people shouted their good wishes and blessings, and immense crowds conducted him to his new home while he showered gold on them along the way. When he reached his pavilion, he dismounted, entered, and sat down on the divan, while his mamelukes stood before him with arms folded. After a short while they brought him sherbets, and when he had drunk them, he ordered his slave girls, eunuchs, and mamelukes to get everything ready for the Lady Badar al-Budur.

As soon as noon arrived and the great heat of the sun had abated, the sultan ordered his officers, emirs, and viziers to go down to the parade ground, where he joined them on horse. And Aladdin also assembled his mamelukes and mounted a stallion who surpassed all the steeds of Arabia to ride to the parade ground. There he displayed what an expert horseman he was by excelling in the various games that were played. Badar al-Badur watched him from her balcony and was so impressed by his good looks and equestrian skills that she fell head over heels in love with him and was ecstatic with joy. After the games were finished, the sultan and his nobles returned to the palace, and Aladdin went back to his pavilion with his mamelukes.

Toward evening the viziers and nobles took the bridegroom and escorted him to the royal Hammam, where he was bathed and sprayed with perfume. As soon as he came out, he donned a suit more magnificent than his previous one and rode with the emirs and officers in a grand cortege surrounded by the viziers with their swords drawn. All the people and troops marched before him in a throng carrying wax candles and kettledrums, pipes, and other musical instruments, and they led him to his pavilion. Here he dismounted, and after entering, he sat down and offered seats to the viziers and emirs who had escorted him. Meanwhile the mamelukes brought sherbets that they also passed around to the people who had followed in the procession. There was a huge crowd outside, impossible to count, and Aladdin ordered his mamelukes to go out and shower them with gold coins.

In the meantime, when the sultan returned from the parade ground, he ordered his household to form a cavalcade for his daughter according to ceremony and to take the Lady Badar al-Budur to her bridegroom's pavilion. So the nobles and officers, who had followed and escorted the bridegroom, now mounted at once, and the slave girls and eunuchs went out with wax candles and made a splendid procession for the Lady Badar al-Budur. They marched in front of her, and Aladdin's mother was by her side, until they entered the pavilion. There were also the wives of the viziers, emirs, grandees, and nobles in front of the princess, and she was also attended by the forty-eight slave girls whom Aladdin had given to her as a present. Each one of them held a huge torch of camphor and amber set in a gold candlestick studded with gems. Upon reaching Aladdin's pavilion, they led the princess to her chamber on the upper floor, changed her robes, and displayed her. Then they accompanied her to Aladdin's apartment, and soon he paid her his first visit.

Now his mother was with the bride, and when Aladdin came up to the princess and took off her veil, the old woman was greatly taken by Badar al-Budur's beauty and loveliness. Moreover, she looked around the pavilion entirely illuminated by gold and gems with a gold chandelier studded with precious gems like emeralds and jacinths. Awed by what she saw, she said to herself, "Once upon a time I thought the sultan's palace was splendid, but this pavilion surpasses everything. I don't think a single king of the Chosroës ever accomplished anything like this. I'm even positive that nobody in the world could build something like it."

Then the tables were spread, and they all ate, drank, and enjoyed themselves. At the end of the meal, forty damsels came before them, each holding a musical instrument in her hand, and they deftly moved their fingers, touched the strings, and broke into song. Their tunes were very melodic and also melancholy and captivated all the listeners. The princess was particularly enchanted by the music and said to herself, "Never in my life have I heard such songs as these." Indeed, she was so enraptured that she refrained from eating in order to pay closer attention to the music. At last, Aladdin poured out wine for her and gave it to her with his own hand. In sum, it was a magnificent night, and not even Alexander the Great had ever enjoyed a feast like this one. When they had finished eating and drinking, and the tables were removed, Aladdin stood up and took his bride to his apartment, where he enjoyed her.

The next morning, Aladdin arose, and his servant brought him sumptuous garments and helped him get dressed. After drinking coffee flavored with amber, he ordered the horses to be saddled. Then he mounted with his mamelukes behind and in front of him and rode to his father-in-law's palace. When the sultan's eunuchs saw him approaching, they went in and reported his coming to their lord.

And Scheherazade noticed that dawn was approaching and stopped telling her story. When the next night arrived, however, she received the king's permission to continue her tale and said,

Informed that Aladdin was approaching, the sultan got up to receive him, and he embraced and kissed him as though he were his own son. After seating him on his right side, he blessed him and prayed for him, as did the viziers, emirs, and grandees of the realm. Soon the king commanded the attendants to serve the morning meal, and all the nobles at the court broke their fast together. After they had eaten and drunk to their satisfaction and the tables were removed, Aladdin turned to the sultan and said, "My lord, would your highness deign to honor me at dinner in the house of Lady Badar al-Budur, your beloved daughter, and bring with him all the ministers and grandees of the realm?"

The king was delighted by the invitation and replied, "You are most generous, my son!"

Then the sultan gave orders to his nobles, and, with Aladdin at his side, they all rode over to the pavilion. As the king entered it and gazed at its construction, architecture, and masonry, all jasper and carnelian, he was bedazzled by the grandeur and opulence. Turning to his grand vizier, he asked, "What do you say now? Have you ever seen anything in your entire life, even among the mightiest of the earth's monarchs, that can compare to such wealth of gold and jewels?"

"As I told your majesty before," the vizier said, "this feat could not have been accomplished by mortals, whether they be kings or commoners. No builders in the universe could have constructed a pavilion like this. All this could only have been produced by sorcery!"

"That's enough," replied the sultan. "Don't say another word. I know exactly what's prompted you to say what you've said."

Aladdin preceded the sultan and conducted him to the upper dome, where he saw its skylights, windows, and lattices, which were made of emeralds, rubies, and other gems. Once more, the sultan was stunned and astonished by all that his eyes encountered. He strolled around the dome and enjoyed himself by looking at the various sights until he came to the window that Aladdin had purposely left undone. When the sultan noticed that it was not finished, he cried out, "It's a shame, poor window, that you've been left unfinished!" Then, turning to his minister, he asked, "Why do you think that this window was left incomplete?"

"I imagine," said the vizier, "that Aladdin felt rushed by you and was in such a hurry to get married that he was unable to finish it."

Meanwhile, Aladdin had gone to his bride and informed the princess of her father's presence. When he returned to the dome, the king asked him, "My son, why was this window here left unfinished?"

"Great king," responded Aladdin, "the wedding was so sudden that I failed to find the artists who could finish it on time."

"I have a mind to complete it myself," said the sultan.

"May Allah grant your majesty perpetual glory!" exclaimed Aladdin. "This way your memory will endure forever in your daughter's pavilion."

At once the sultan ordered that jewelers and goldsmiths be summoned, and he commanded that they should be provided with everything they might need, such as gold and gems from his treasury. When the craftsmen were all assembled, he told them how he wanted the work to be completed in the dome window. Meanwhile the princess came forth to meet her father, who noticed her smiling face as she approached. So he embraced and kissed her, and then led her down into the pavilion.

By this time it was noon, and one table had been spread for the sultan, his daughter, and Aladdin, and a second one for the viziers, lords, chief officers, chamberlains, and nabobs. The king took his seat between the princess and her husband, and when he reached out his hand and tasted the food, he was struck with surprise by the savory flavor of the dishes and the sumptuous cooking. Moreover, there were eighty damsels who stood before him, and they were all so beautiful and radiant that each and every one of them could have said to the moon, "Move on so that I may take your place!" They all held musical instruments, which they played with great expertise, and they sang melodic songs that touched the heart of everyone who listened. The sultan had a wonderful time, and at one point he exclaimed, "Truly, all this is beyond the compass of either king or emperor!"

Everyone partook in the delicious meal, and the wine flowed until they had drunk enough. Then the sweetmeats and other desserts were served in another room, and they all moved there and enjoyed their fill. Soon the sultan arose so that he could inspect the work of his jewelers and goldsmiths. However, he noted a great difference, for his men were incapable of making anything like the windows in Aladdin's pavilion. They informed him how all the gems stored in his minor treasury had been brought to them, and they had used them to the best of their ability. However, since they were insufficient, the sultan now ordered that the gems from his major treasury be delivered to them, but they only sufficed to finish half the window. Therefore, the king ordered that all the precious stones owned by the viziers and grandees of the realm be brought to them. Yet, even here, they fell far short of the supply the craftsmen needed.

The next morning Aladdin arose to look at their work and noticed that they had not finished even a half of what they needed to do to complete the window. As a result, he ordered them to undo all they had done and restore the jewels to their owners. Accordingly, they pulled out the precious stones and sent those that belonged to the sultan back to him and the others to the viziers and grandees. Then the craftsmen went to the sultan and told him what Aladdin had ordered them to do. So he asked them, "What did he say to you? Why wasn't he content with your work? And why did he make you undo everything?"

"We have no idea, your majesty," they replied. "He just made us to take everything apart."

At once the sultan called for his horse, and after mounting it, he rode over toward the pavilion.

In the meantime, after Aladdin had dismissed the workers, he retired to his room and rubbed the lamp. Immediately the jinnee appeared and said, "Ask what you want. Your slave is at your service."

"I want you to finish the window that was left unfinished," said Aladdin.

"As you command," said the marid and vanished. Within seconds he returned and said, "My lord, I have carried out your command."

When Aladdin went upstairs to the dome, he found that the entire window had been finished. While he was still inspecting it, one of his eunuchs came to him and said, "My lord, the sultan has come to visit you and is at the pavilion gate."

So Aladdin went at once to greet his father-in-law, who, upon seeing him approach, cried out, "Why didn't you allow the craftsmen complete their work?"

"Great king," Aladdin replied, "I had purposely left this window unfinished. Indeed, I was perfectly capable of completing it. Certainly I did not intend to invite your majesty to a pavilion that was still deficient. And since I want to show you that I capable of making everything perfect, I would like you to accompany me upstairs to inspect the window."

So the sultan went up with him, and after entering the dome, he looked all over but saw nothing missing in the windows. Indeed, they were all perfect. Astounded by the sight, he embraced Aladdin and said, "My son, how did you accomplish this? How is it that you can finish something in a single night that my workers need months to finish? By Allah, there's no one in the world who can rival you!"

"May Allah grant you long life and prosperity!" Aladdin replied. "Your slave does not deserve such a compliment."

"My son," the sultan asserted, "you deserve all the praise in the world for a feat that no craftsman could ever accomplish."

Then the sultan went downstairs with him to the apartment of his daughter, where he relaxed for some time with her. He was pleased to see how much she enjoyed the glory and grandeur of the pavilion, and after reposing awhile, he returned to his palace.

Now, Aladdin was accustomed to ride through the city street every day with his mamelukes in front and behind him, and he would scatter gold among the people. There was not a person, native or foreigner, who did not love him for his generosity and kindness. Moreover, he increased the payments to help the poor and needy, and he himself helped distribute alms to them. Because of his good deeds, he won high renown throughout the realm, and most of the lords and emirs of the realm ate at his table. Everyone wished him well.

Aside from helping those in need, Aladdin continued enjoying such pastimes as riding and hunting. He would often go to the parade ground in the presence of the sultan and display his equestrian skills. And whenever the Lady Badar al-Budur watched him riding his magnificent steeds, her love for him grew, and she thought to herself that Allah had been most beneficent to her by causing what happened to the vizier's son and preserving her virginity for her true bridegroom.

Day by day Aladdin's fame grew, and his reputation became so great that everyone loved and admired him. Moreover, it so happened at that time that certain enemies of the sultan began to wage war against him. Therefore, the sultan equipped an army and made Aladdin the commander in chief. Before long he marched out with his men until he drew near the hostile forces, which were vast. When the action began, he bared his sword and charged at the enemy. The battle was violent, but at last Aladdin broke through the enemy's lines and put the foe to flight. His troops destroyed a good part of their army, and plundered their cattle, property, and possessions.

Moreover, Aladdin confiscated countless goods. Then he returned victorious to the capital, which had been decorated in his honor. The sultan went forth to meet him and embraced him in joy. Following this, there were great festivities held throughout the kingdom, and the king and his son-in-law retired to the pavilion, where they were met by the Princess Badar al-Budur, who rejoiced when she saw her husband again. After kissing him on his forehead, she led him to her apartment. After a while the sultan joined them, and they sat down while the slave girls brought them sherbets and desserts, which they drank and ate. Then the sultan commanded that the whole kingdom be decorated to celebrate the victory of his son-in-law over the invader.

By this time, all the soldiers and people of the kingdom looked only to Allah in heaven and Aladdin on earth. They loved him more than ever because of his generosity and kindness, his noble horsemanship and his success in defeating the foes of their country. Such then was the great fortune of Aladdin.

Now let us return to the magician, that Moor, who had traveled back to his own country after he failed to obtain the lamp. Once he was there, he spent his days bemoaning all the hardships that he had suffered in his attempt to win the lamp. It had been most frustrating for him to lose the lamp just when he was about to taste victory. Whenever he thought about it, he became enraged, and at times he would exclaim, "My only satisfaction is that the little bastard has perished in the cave, and I can only hope that someday I may still obtain the lamp, since it is still safe underground."

One day, he cast a geomantic table of sand and noted their figures so that he could transfer them to paper. After this, he studied them carefully, because he wanted to make sure of Aladdin's death and determine the exact position of the lamp beneath the ground. Soon he established the sequence of the figures, their origins and destinations, but he could not see the lamp. The result made him furious, and he made another try with the sand to ascertain Aladdin's death, but he did not see him in the enchanted cave. Now he almost exploded with anger when he realized that the boy had escaped from the underground and was somewhere on the face of the earth, alive and well. Moreover, it became clear to him that Aladdin must be the possessor of the lamp for which he himself had endured more hardship than any other man could possibly have endured for such a great object. "I have suffered more pain than any other mortal could bear because of that lamp, and that miserable creature did not have to do a thing for it to fall into his hands. If he has learned the virtues of the lamp, he must be the richest man in the world. All the more reason why I must destroy him!"

Then the Moor struck another geomantic table and examined the figures, which revealed to him that Aladdin had become immensely rich and had married the sultan's daughter. Therefore, his envy was fired with the flame of wrath, and without delay, he arose and equipped himself for a journey to distant China, where he arrived in due time.

Now, when he reached the king's capital, he took lodgings at one of the khans. After he had rested from his long and exhausting journey, he donned his suit and wandered about the streets. Wherever he went, he continually heard people praising the pavilion and its grandeur and vaunting the handsome features of Aladdin, his kindness, generosity, fine manners, and good morals. Soon he entered a tavern where men were drinking a warm beverage, and after approaching one man who was lauding Aladdin, he said to him, "Young man, who is this man you've been praising?"

"Apparently, you're a stranger," the man said, "and you've come from far away. But even if this is true, how is it that you've never heard of the Emir Aladdin, whose renown, I would imagine, has spread all over the universe and whose pavilion is known to people far and wide as one of the wonders of the world? How come you've never heard of the name of Aladdin and his fame, may Allah increase his glory?"

"It would be my greatest wish to see his pavilion," the Moor said. "In fact, I would be very much obliged if you could show it to me, since I am a foreigner."

"As you wish," the man said, and after bringing him to the pavilion, he departed.

When the Moor saw it, he realized at once that it was the work of the lamp. So he cried, "Ah! Ah! I'm going to dig the grave of this son of a tailor, who was such a rotten egg that he couldn't even earn his own living! If the fates are with me, I'll destroy his life and send his mother back to her spinning wheel." After exclaiming this, he returned to the khan in a downcast and furious mood. Once he was alone in his room, he took out his astrological equipment and geomantic table to discover where the lamp was being kept, and he learned that it was in the pavilion and that Aladdin was not carrying it with him. This disclosure made him feel happy, and he exclaimed, "Now it will be an easy task to take the life of this miserable wretch and obtain the lamp."

Then he went to a coppersmith and said to him, "Make me a set of lamps, and if you do a fast job, I'll pay you more than they're worth."

"Your wish is my command," said the coppersmith, and he began work on the lamps immediately. When they were finished, the Moor gave him what he demanded. Then he took them to the khan and put them in a basket. Soon thereafter he began wandering through the streets and markets of the city crying aloud, "Ho! Who will exchange old lamps for new lamps!"

When the people heard him cry out like this, they derided him and said, "He's surely mad! Who would offer new lamps for old ones?" Many people began following him, and little scamps ran after him and laughed at him from place to place. But he did not mind their treatment and derision. He kept walking about the streets until he came to Aladdin's pavilion, where he shouted with his loudest voice, and the boys screamed at him, "Madman! Madman!"

Now, as destiny would have it, the Lady Badar al-Budur was sitting near a window of the dome, and she heard the cries of the Moor and the children bawling at him. Since she did not understand what was going on, she gave orders to one of her slave girls to find out who was crying and why. The girl went outside and came upon a man crying, "Ho! Who will exchange old lamps for new lamps?" And there were boys chasing after him and laughing at him. When she returned and told the princess what was going on, Lady Badar al-Budur laughed loudly. Now Aladdin had carelessly left the lamp in his apartment without hiding it and locking it up in his strongbox, and one of the slave girls, who had seen it, said, "I think I noticed an old lamp in the apartment of my lord Aladdin. So why don't we take it down to the old man and see if he is telling the truth and will exchange with us?"

"Bring me the old lamp which you've seen in my lord's apartment," the princess said.

Lady Badar al-Budur knew nothing about the lamp and its secret powers that had enabled Aladdin to marry her and achieve such grandeur. She was merely bemused by the old man in the street and wanted to find out whether he would really exchange a new lamp for an old one. So when the slave girl returned from Aladdin's apartment with the lamp, she ordered a chief eunuch to go down and exchange the old lamp for a new one, not suspecting how cunning the Moor really was. The eunuch did as he was commanded, and after taking a new lamp from the Moor, he returned and placed it before his lady, who broke into laughter about the demented state of the man when she saw that the lamp was brand-new.

However, as soon as the Moor held the lamp in his hands, he knew it was the magic one from the enchanted cave, and he immediately stuck it into his breast pocket, leaving all the other lamps to the crowd of people that had gathered around him. Then he ran through the streets until he was clear of the city and could slow down. Once he reached the open plains, he felt more relaxed and waited for nightfall. There in the desert he took out the lamp and rubbed it. Immediately the jinnee appeared and said, "I am at your service. Ask whatever you want."

"I want you to lift up Aladdin's pavilion from its present place with all the people and contents in it, and then transport it along with me to my own country in Africa," said the Moor. "You know my home city, and I want the building placed in the gardens that are right near it."

"As you command," the marid replied. "Close your eyes and open your eyes, and you will find yourself together with the pavilion in your own country."

The Moor did this, and in the twinkle of an eye, the magician and the pavilion with everything in it were transported to Africa. Such, then, was the work of the Moor. But now let us return to the sultan and his son-in-law.

* * *

And Scheherazade noticed that dawn was approaching and stopped telling her story. When the next night arrived, however, she received the king's permission to continue her tale and said,

Because of the affection that the king had for his daughter, it was his custom to look out his window every morning after he got out of bed and to gaze at her abode. So, that day, he arose and did what he usually did. But when the king drew near his window this time and looked out at Aladdin's pavilion, he saw nothing. In fact, the site was as smooth as a well-paved street and just as it had been before. There was no edifice, nothing. He was so astonished and bewildered that he rubbed his eyes to make sure his vision was not impaired, but he was finally certain that there was no trace or sign of the pavilion. Nor did he have the slightest idea about why and where it had gone. His astonishment quickly turned to grief, and he wrung his hands while tears trickled down his cheeks and over his beard, for he was worried about his daughter. Then he sent out officials right away and summoned the grand vizier, who came to him at once. When he saw the sultan in such a miserable state, he said, "Pardon, your majesty, may Allah keep you from evil. Why are you so downcast?"

"Don't you know why?" asked the sultan

"Not at all," said the minister. "By Allah, I don't know anything."

"Then it's quite clear that you haven't looked at Aladdin's pavilion today."

"True, my lord, it must still be shut."

"Since you have no inkling of what has happened," said the king, "I want you to go over to the window and look over at Aladdin's pavilion and tell me whether it is still shut."

The vizier did what the sultan commanded, but he could not see anything. There was no pavilion nor anything else. Completely baffled, he returned to his lord, who remarked, "Now you know why I'm so distressed."

"Great king," the vizier said, "I told you before that the pavilion and all those other feats were brought about through magic."

On hearing this, the sultan fumed with rage and cried out, "Where is Aladdin?"

"He's gone hunting," answered the vizier.

Immediately the king ordered some of his chief eunuchs and officers to find Aladdin and bring him back in chains and manacles. So they went in search of him, and when they found him, they said, "My lord, excuse us and don't be angry with us. The king has commanded that we take you to him in chains and manacles. Those were his royal orders, and we must obey them."

Aladdin was greatly surprised by their words and baffled by the king's orders. At first he did not know what to say, but once he recovered from the shock, he said to the officers, "Do you know why the king is doing this? I know that I'm innocent and that I've never sinned against the king or his kingdom."

"My lord," they answered, "we have no idea whatsoever why the king has issued his orders."

So Aladdin dismounted from his horse and said to them, "Do whatever the king ordered you to do, for you are obliged to carry out his commands."

After the officers had bound Aladdin with chains and manacled him, they brought him back to the city. But when the people saw him in bonds, they realized that the king intended to cut off his head, and since they loved and admired him so much, they took out their weapons, swarmed out of their houses, and followed the soldiers to see what they could do. When the troops arrived with Aladdin at the palace, they entered and informed the sultan that they had found Aladdin. Thereupon the king ordered the executioner right away to cut off his son-in-law's head.

Now, as soon as the crowds of people were aware of this order, they barricaded the gates, closed the doors of the palace, and sent a message announcing to the king that they would level his palace and everyone in it if Aladdin was harmed in the slightest way.

So the vizier went to the sultan and reported, "Great king, your order is also our death warrant. I think that it would be a better idea if you pardoned your son-in-law, or else we shall have to pay the price. Your subjects love him far more than they love us."

The executioner had already spread the carpet of blood

and had compelled Aladdin to take his place on it. After tying a blindfold around his eyes, he walked around him three times awaiting the king's final orders. However, the king looked out the window and saw that his subjects had already begun storming the palace and were climbing over the walls. So he immediately ordered the executioner to stay his hand and commanded the herald to go out to the crowds and announce that he had pardoned Aladdin. But when his son-in-law found himself free and saw the sultan seated on his throne, he went up to him and said, "My lord, until recently you had treated me with extreme favor. Therefore, I beg you, be gracious enough to tell me how and why I have sinned against you."

"Traitor!" cried the king. "Do you pretend not to know your own sin?" And turning to his vizier, he said, "Take him to the window and make him look out. After that, let him tell us where his pavilion is."

After Aladdin saw that the pavilion had disappeared and the site was as level as a paved road, he was astonished and bewildered, since he did not know what had happened. When he returned to the king, his father-in-law asked, "Where is your pavilion and where is my daughter, the darling of my heart, my only child?"

"Your majesty," Aladdin answered, "I don't know anything about it, nor do I know what's happened."

"Then you must find out," answered the king. "I have pardoned you only so that you can look into this affair and find out what has happened to my daughter. Do not ever show your face here again unless you bring her back with you, and if you don't bring her back, I swear that I'll cut off your head!"

"As you command," Aladdin replied. "My only request is that you grant me forty days to do this. If I don't produce her within forty days, you can cut off my head and do with me whatever you wish."

"I shall grant you a delay of forty days," said the king, "but don't think you can ever escape me. No matter where you go on this earth, and even if you hide in the clouds, I'll find you and bring you back."

"Your highness, I've given you my word," said Aladdin. "If I don't bring her back within forty days, I'll return, and you can cut off my head."

Now, when the people saw that Aladdin was free, they were overcome with joy. But the way he had been put to shame before his friends and the exultation of his envious foes made him hang his head. So he went into the city alone and wandered about, perplexed by what had happened. He lingered in the capital for two days in the most sorrowful state, not knowing what to do. Indeed, he did not have the slightest idea of how to find his wife and his pavilion, and during this time various friends brought him something to eat and drink. After the two days had passed, he left the city and drifted aimlessly about the fields and open plains. As he walked, he came upon a path that led him to a river, where, because of the stress and sorrow, he abandoned himself to despair and thought about throwing himself into the water. However, being a good Moslem, who believed in the unity of the Godhead, he feared Allah in his soul, and standing upon the river bank, he prepared himself to perform the Wuzu ablution. But just as he was scooping up the water in his right hand and rubbing his fingers, he also chanced to rub the ring. All at once its jinnee appeared and said to him, "At your service. Your thrall has come. Ask me whatever you want."

Upon seeing the marid, Aladdin rejoiced and cried out, "Slave, I want you to bring back my wife and pavilion and everything that was inside it."

"My lord," replied the jinnee, "you're demanding a service of me that is impossible for me to perform. Only the slave of the lamp can do this. I can't and won't even dare to attempt it."

"Well, since the matter is beyond your power," Aladdin responded, "I won't demand this of you, but at least transport me to my pavilion, wherever it may be."

"As you command, my lord," said the jinnee, and after lifting him high in the air, in a split second he set Aladdin down beside his pavilion in Africa on a spot facing his wife's apartment.

Despite the fact that it was nighttime, he took one look and recognized that it was his home. Now all his cares and worries disappeared, and he regained trust in Allah after abandoning all hope of ever finding his wife again. Then he began to ponder the secret and mysterious ways of the Lord (all glory to His omnipotence) and how Allah had deigned to bless him and how the ring had come to his rescue just as he had thought he had been overcome by despair. Happy and relieved, Aladdin was also exhausted, for he had spent four days without sleep because of the stress he had been under. So when he approached the pavilion, he found a spot beneath a tree and slept near the building that had been set down among the gardens outside the city.

Although his head was full of worries, he managed to sleep soundly until morning, when he was wakened by the warbling of small birds. So he arose and went down to the bank of the river that flowed into the city and washed his hands and face. After he had finished his Wuzu ablution, he said the dawn prayer and then returned to sit beneath the window of his wife's apartment.

Now, the Lady Badar al-Budur had become extremely sad at being separated from her husband and father, and she suffered greatly from the misfortune that she had experienced at the hands of the accursed Moor. Since she could not eat or drink and found it difficult to sleep, she had become accustomed to rising with the dawn and sitting in tears by her window. Her favorite slave girl would enter her chamber at the hour of morning prayer in order to dress her, and this time, as destiny would have it, when she threw open the window to let her lady comfort herself by looking at the trees and hills, she caught sight of her master sitting below and quickly informed the princess.

"My lady! My lady!" she cried out. "My lord Aladdin is sitting at the foot of the wall."

So the princess arose hurriedly and went to the window, where she saw Aladdin, who caught sight of her just as he was raising his head. Immediately they greeted each other, and their hearts soared with joy.

"Come up to me through the secret door," she called out to him. "The accursed magician is not here now."

And she gave orders to the slave girl, who went downstairs and opened the door for him. Once Aladdin entered, he was met by his wife, and they embraced and kept kissing each other with delight until they wept for joy. After this, they sat down, and Aladdin said, "My lady, before anything else, I must ask you a question. I used to keep an old copper lamp in my apartment. Could you tell me what happened to it?"

When the princess heard these words, she sighed and cried, "Oh my darling, it was that very lamp which caused this catastrophe."

"How did it happen?" Aladdin asked.

And she answered by recounting everything that had occurred from first to last, especially how they had exchanged the old lamp for a new one. Then she added, "The next day at dawn we suddenly found ourselves in this land, and the man who deceived us and took the lamp informed me that he had accomplished everything through the magic lamp. He is a Moor from Africa, and we are now in his native country."

"What does this wretched criminal intend to do with you?" asked Aladdin. "What has he said to you? What does he want from you?"

"Every day he comes to visit me, just once," she said. "He has been wooing me and wants me to forget you. In fact, he insists on replacing you and wants me to marry him. He told me that my father had cut off your head, and that it was he who made you so rich, for at one time you were just the son of poor parents. Most of the times he has tried to use sweet talk with me, but he's only received tears and moans in reply. Not one kind word has passed through my lips."

"Tell me if you know where he keeps the lamp," Aladdin asked.

"He always keeps it on him," she answered. "It never leaves him. Once, when he was talking to me about it, he took it from his breast pocket and showed it to me."

When Aladdin heard these words, he was very pleased and said, "My lady, listen to me now. I intend to leave you right away, but I'll return after I change my clothes. So don't be alarmed when you see me in different garments. I want you to order one of your slave girls to stand by the secret door, and when she catches sight of me, she's to open it at once. Now I'm off to devise a plan to slay this damned madman."

Upon saying this, he arose and went through the secret door. Then he walked for a while until he met a peasant, to whom he said, "Friend, I would like to exchange clothes with you."

But the peasant refused, and Aladdin had to use force to strip him of his clothes, but he left the man with his own rich garments to wear. Then he followed the highway leading to the nearby city, and after entering it, he went to a bazaar where incense and drugs were sold. There he bought a rare and potent drug called bhang, and he returned by the same road in disguise until he reached the pavilion. Once the slave girl caught sight of him, she opened the secret door, and in he went to the Lady Badar al-Budur.

And Scheherazade noticed that dawn was approaching and stopped telling her story. When the next night arrived, however, she received the king's permission to continue her tale and said,

"Listen carefully," Aladdin said to his wife. "I want you to get dressed in your very best garments and cast off all show of melancholy. In addition, when the accursed Moor comes to visit you, you're to welcome him and greet him with a smiling face and invite him to dine with you. Make him think that you've forgotten Aladdin your beloved and your father as well, and that you've fallen tremendously in love with him. At one point, you're to ask for some wine. Make sure that it's red, and pledge yourself to him. After you've given him two or three cups full and he's grown careless, you're to drop this powder into his cup and fill it with wine. As soon as he drinks it, he'll fall down senseless as though he were dead."

"It will be very difficult for me to do all this," said the princess. "However, I know I must do it if we're to escape this vile ·magician who's tormented me by this abduction. It's both lawful and right to kill this villain."

Then Aladdin ate and drank with his wife to placate his hunger, and immediately afterward he left the pavilion. Then the Lady Badar al-Budur summoned her slave girls, who dressed her in her finest raiment, adorned her, and sprayed her with perfume. Just as they were finished, the Moor entered her apartment, and he was most pleased to see her in this condition, and even more when, contrary to her former behavior, she greeted him with a smiling face. All this made his love and lust for her increase. Then she took him by his hand, and seating him beside her, said, "My darling, if you are willing, I would like you to come and dine with me tonight. I have mourned long enough, and even if I continued to do so for a thousand or two thousand years, Aladdin could not return to me from the tomb, for I believe what you said yesterday, that my father had him slain in sorrow over the separation from me. So you needn't wonder why I've changed so much from one day to the next. I have thought about everything and decided to accept you as my friend and lover and as Aladdin's successor, especially since I have no other man except you. Therefore, I want you to dine with me tonight, and we can drink wine and enjoy each other's company. I'd particularly like to taste some of your African wine, since I've heard that it is much better than the wine we drink in China."

Although Lady Badar al-Budur's change was sudden, she managed to convince the Moor that she had abandoned all hope of seeing Aladdin, and in his ecstasy, he said, "Your wish is my command, my lady. I have a cask of our native wine at home that I've carefully kept stored deep in the ground for eight years, and I'll go now and fetch whatever we shall need and return to you as soon as I can."

But since the princess wanted to tease him and excite him even more, she said, "My darling, don't leave me alone. Send one of your eunuchs to fetch the wine. Remain seated next to me so that I may enjoy your company."

"My lady," he replied, "nobody knows where the cask is buried except me, and I won't be away too long."

After saying this, the Moor left, and after a short time, he brought back as much wine as they needed. Thereupon, the princess said to him, "You've gone to great pains to please me, my beloved, and I apologize."

"Not at all, my dearest," said the Moor. "It is an honor to serve you."

The Lady Badar al-Budur sat down at the table with him, and they began eating. Soon the princess requested the wine, and a slave girl filled her cup and then the Moor's. So she drank to his long life and his secret wishes, and he also drank to her life. Since the princess had a great gift in making eloquent speeches, she began to make all sorts of toasts to him and beguiled him by addressing him in the sweetest terms full of hidden meaning. Unable to see through her deception, the Moor thought that her actions resulted from her true inclination for him and did not suspect that she was setting a trap. So his longing for her increased, and out of love for her, his head began to swim, and the world seemed as if it were nothing in his eyes. When they came to the end of the dinner, and the wine had gotten the better of him, the princess realized that she had him at her mercy and said, "There is a custom in our country, but I don't know whether you do the same thing in yours."

"What is it?" asked the Moor.

So she said to him, "At the end of dinner, each lover takes the cup of the other beloved and drinks it."

Thereupon she took his cup and filled it with wine for herself. Then she poured the wine into hers, mixed with the drug, and asked a slave girl to give it to him. Now she had instructed the slave girl what she was to do, and all the slave girls and the eunuchs in the pavilion longed for the sorcerer's death and supported the princess's plan. Accordingly, the slave girl handed him the cup, and when he saw the princess drinking from his cup and was taken in by her show of love, he imagined he was Iskandar, Lord of the Two Horns. Then she leaned over to him, swaying to and fro, put her hand within his hand, and said, "Oh my life, your cup is with me, and mine with you, and this is the way that lovers drink from each other's cup."

Then she kissed the brim, drained his cup, and then kissed the brim of her own cup for him to drink. By now he was delirious, and he wanted to follow her example. He kissed the brim, raised the cup to her, and then drank the contents down, without worrying whether there was anything harmful in it. And immediately thereafter he rolled over on his back as though he were dead, and the cup dropped from his hand. Right then and there the slave girls ran hurriedly to the secret door and opened it for their lord Aladdin, who was still disguised as a peasant. He ran up to his wife's apartment and found her still sitting at the table and facing the drugged Moor. At once he approached her, kissed her, and thanked her for all that she had done. Overjoyed by what had taken place, he said, "Please withdraw with your slave girls to the inner chamber, and leave me alone for a while so that I may think about what I have to do."

The princess went away at once with her slave girls, and Aladdin locked the door behind them. Then he walked up to the Moor, stuck his hand into the magician's breast pocket, and drew out the lamp. After doing this, he unsheathed his sword and slew the villain. Then he rubbed the lamp, and immediately the jinnee appeared and said, "At your service, my lord. What is it you want?"

"I want you to take my pavilion and transport it to China," replied Aladdin. "You are to set it down on the spot where it was standing before."

"As you command, my lord," said the marid.

Then Aladdin went to his wife, and throwing his arms around her, he kissed her, and she kissed him, and they sat in conversation while the jinnee transported the pavilion and all its contents to the designated place. Soon Aladdin ordered the slave girls to set the table, and he and the Lady Badar al-Budur began eating and drinking with great joy until they had contented themselves. Thereafter, they withdrew to the drinking room, where they caroused and kissed each other. It had been a long time since they had been able to enjoy each other, and they continued to do so until the wine rose in their heads and sleep got the better of them.

Early the next morning, Aladdin awoke and woke his wife. Then the slave girls entered and helped her get dressed, while Aladdin donned his finest raiment. The two were ecstatic about their reunion, and the princess was especially joyous and glad that day because she expected to see her beloved father.

So much for Aladdin and his wife, the Lady Badar al-Budur. Now let us return to the sultan.

After he had driven away his son-in-law, he kept mourning the loss of his daughter, and every hour of every day he would sit and weep for her as women weep because she was his one and only child. And as soon as he shook off sleep morning after morning, he would rush to the window, throw it open, and peer in the direction of Aladdin's pavilion. Then tears would stream from his eyes until his lids were red and sore.

Now on that particular day he arose at dawn, and

according to his custom, he looked out and suddenly saw a building. So he rubbed his eyes and kept looking at it curiously until he was certain that it was his son-in-law's pavilion. So he called for a horse right away, and as soon as the steed was saddled, he mounted and headed for the pavilion.

When Aladdin saw his father-in-law approaching, he went down and met him halfway. Then, taking him by the hand, he helped the sultan upstairs to his daughter's apartment. Anxious to see her father, the princess had descended and greeted him at the door of the staircase facing the ground-floor hall. Thereupon the king hugged her in his arms and kissed her, shedding tears of joy, and she did likewise, until Aladdin finally led them to the upper salon, where they took seats, and the sultan began asking her all about what had happened.

"My father," she began, "I only regained my life yesterday when I saw my husband, and it was he who set me free from a vile magician. I don't believe that there is a more treacherous man on earth than this Moor. If it had not been for my beloved, I would never have escaped him, nor would you ever have seen me again. I had been deeply grieved because I had lost you and also my husband, to whom I shall be grateful for the rest of my life for freeing me from that wicked sorcerer."

Then the princess related everything that had happened to her, how the Moor had tricked her in the disguise of a lamp-seller, how she had given him the magic lamp, and how she had laughed at the Moor when she exchanged the old lamp for the new one, how she had been transported in the pavilion to Africa, and how Aladdin had freed them with the help of the potent drug. In turn, Aladdin recounted how he had slaughtered the wizard when he had found him dead drunk, how he had taken the lamp from the sorcerer's breast pocket, and how he had ordered the jinnee to transport the pavilion back to its proper site, ending his tale with, "And if your highness has any doubt about our story, come with me and take a look at the accursed magician."

Accordingly the king went with Aladdin, and after looking at the Moor, he ordered the corpse to be carried away and burned and its ashes scattered in the air. Then he embraced Aladdin and said, "Pardon me, my son.

Indeed I was on the verge of taking your life because of the foul deeds of this damned wizard, who put you in a dangerous situation. You must excuse me for what I did, because I was deeply upset about my daughter, my only child, who is dearer to me than my kingdom. You must know the great love parents bear for their offspring."

"Your majesty," Aladdin replied, "you did nothing that went against Holy Law, and likewise, I did not sin against you. The entire trouble was caused by that Moor, the unholy magician."

Thereupon the sultan ordered the city to be decorated and commanded the herald to announce, "This day is a great holiday. There will be public celebrations for one month in honor of the return of Lady Badar al-Budur and her husband Aladdin!"

And the people obeyed and held banquets and feasts throughout the city. And that was the end of Aladdin's troubles with the Moor.

However, even though the magician's body had been burned and his ashes scattered in the air, the villain had a brother even more vile than he was and even more adept in necromancy, geomancy, and astrology. As the saying goes, they were like two peas from the same pod, and when the pod was split, each dwelled in his own part of the globe and practiced sorcery, fraud, and treachery.

Now, one day it so happened that the Moor's brother learned what had happened to him through his geomantic sandboard. After grieving awhile, he cast the sand a second time to learn how his brother had died and where. This was how he discovered that the site was Africa and that his brother had been killed by a man called Aladdin, who was now living in China. Once this sorcerer had gathered all this information, he arose right away and equipped himself for the voyage to China. After he had traveled through wilderness and over mountains and plains for many months, he reached China and the city where he hoped to find his brother's murderer. He took lodgings at the inn for foreigners, and after resting in his room for a while, he went out and wandered about the streets contemplating a way to avenge his brother's death. Soon he entered a coffee house, a fine building which stood in the marketplace, and which attracted many people to play at dice, backgammon, chess, and other games.

There he sat down and listened to those seated next to him, and they happened to be speaking about a holy woman named Fatimah, who lived outside the town in a cell where she practiced her devotions. She entered the city only two days each month, and according to the people who were talking, she had performed many holy miracles to help those in need.

"This is exactly what I was looking for," said the Moorish sorcerer to himself. "God willing, I'll be able to carry out my plans with the help of this old woman." Then the magician turned to the people who were talking about the miracles performed by the devout old woman and said to one of them, "Friend, I heard you talking about the virtues of a certain holy woman named Fatimah. Could you tell me who she is and where she lives?"

"Remarkable!" exclaimed the man. "How come you've never heard about the miracles of the Lady Fatimah? Evidently you must be a stranger if you know nothing about her devout fasts, her asceticism, and her beautiful piety!"

"It's true, my lord," replied the Moor. "Yes, I am a stranger, and I arrived in your city only last night. And now I hope that you will tell me about the holy miracles of this virtuous woman and where she lives, for I've suffered a terrible calamity, and I'd like to visit her and request that she pray for me, so that Allah may deliver me from evil through her blessings."

In response, the man recounted the marvels of the Holy Fatimah, her piety and devout life. Then taking him by the hand, he led him outside the city and showed him the way to her abode, a cave on the top of a hill. The magician thanked him for showing him the place and returned to his khan. Now, as fate would have it, Fatimah came down to the city the very next day, and the Moor happened to leave his khan early the morning and encounter crowds of people. Since he was curious about what was going on, he went and saw the holy woman standing in the middle of a throng of people, and anyone who suffered from pain or sickness went up to her and solicited a blessing and prayer. Indeed, each and every one she touched was instantly cured from his illness. The sorcerer followed her about the city until she returned to her dwelling. Then he walked back to his khan and waited until evening, when he drank a cup of wine at a tavern. After this, he left the city and went straight to the holy woman's cave. After entering it, he saw her lying prostrate with her back on a strip of matting. So he moved forward, sat down on her stomach, drew his dagger, and began shouting at her. When she opened her eyes, she was terrified to find a Moor sitting on her belly with a dagger in his hand about to kill her. However, he said to her, "Don't utter a word! If you do, I'll slay you right this second. Now get up, and do everything I tell you to do."

Then he swore to her that if she obeyed his orders, no matter what they were, he would not kill her. After saying this, he got off her stomach and stood up, and Fatimah did likewise.

"Give me your dress," he said, "and take my garments."

So she gave him her headdress, veil, and mantilla. Then he said, "You must also use some ointment on me so that my face becomes the same color as yours."

Accordingly, she went to the back of the cave and brought out a jar of ointment, spread some of it on her palm, and smeared his face until it looked like hers. Then she hung her rosary around his neck, gave him her staff, and showed him how to walk and what to do when he entered the city. Finally, she handed him a mirror and said, "Now you look just like me."

When he gazed into the mirror, he appeared as though he were Fatimah herself. But when he had accomplished what he had wanted, he broke his word and asked for a piece of rope, which he used to strangle her. When she was dead, he hauled the corpse outside and threw it into a nearby pit. Then he went back to sleep in her cave, and when dawn arrived the next day, he went into the town and took a place under the walls of Aladdin's pavilion. Gradually the people began flocking to him, certain that he was the Holy Fatimah, and he did what she usually did. He placed his hands on those in pain and recited verses from the Koran. Soon the clamoring of the crowd was heard by the lady Badar al-Budur, who said to her slave girls, "Find out what's causing all that noise!"

So the chief eunuch went out to see what the matter was and soon returned to his mistress and said, "My lady, the commotion is being caused by the Lady Fatimah, and if you wish, I'll bring her to you so that you may obtain a blessing from her."

"Go and fetch her," said the princess. "I've heard about her miracles and virtues for some time now, and I'd very much like to meet her and get a blessing from her."

The eunuch went out and brought in the Moor disguised in Fatimah's clothing. When the magician stood before the Lady Badar al-Budur, he began to bless her right away with a string of prayers. Everyone was completely convinced that it was the holy woman herself. So the princess arose and saluted him and had him take a seat by her side.

"My lady Fatimah," she said, "It would be an honor if you would always stay here so that I could receive your blessings and learn how to follow your pious and good example."

Though this invitation was exactly what he had wanted, the sorcerer felt it would be best for the deception if he played hard to get. So he replied, "My lady, I'm a poor religious woman who dwells in a cave. People like myself are not fit to live in the palaces of kings."

But the princess replied, "Don't you worry in the least. I'll give you a separate apartment in the pavilion, and you'll be able to worship as you please. Nobody will disturb you, and it will be better place to pray to Allah than your cave."

"As you wish, my lady," said the Moor. "I'll accept your offer, for the commands of royalty are not to be opposed. My only wish is that I may be able to eat, drink, and sit in my own chamber that will be entirely private. I don't desire anything special except a bit of bread and some water that one of your slave girls could perhaps carry to me every day. If I happen to need food, I would prefer to eat it in my own room."

Of course, the reason the accursed magician said all this was to avert discovery at mealtimes, when he would have had to raise his kerchief, and his beard and moustache would have given him away.

"Oh Lady Fatimah," the princess replied. "There is nothing to worry about. Everything will be just as you desire. Now, please rise, so that I can show you the apartment."

Lady Badar al-Budur conducted the sorcerer to a separate apartment in the pavilion that she had kindly promised him for a home. Then she said, "Lady Fatimah, you can have your privacy here and live in comfort, and we shall name this place after you."

The Moor acknowledged her kindness and prayed for her. Then the princess showed him the jeweled dome with its twenty-four windows and asked him what he thought of the marvelous pavilion.

"By Allah, my daughter," said the magician, "it is wonderful, and there is probably nothing like it in the entire universe. However, it appears to be lacking one thing that would enhance its beauty."

"What is it?" asked the princess. "Please tell me, for I want it to be absolutely perfect."

"The only thing it needs," said the Moor, "is the egg of the bird Rukh hanging from the middle of the dome. If this were done, there would be absolutely nothing like this pavilion in the world."

"What is this bird?" the princess asked. "Where can we find her egg?"

"My lady, the Rukh is a gigantic bird," the sorcerer replied. "It is so powerful that it can carry off camels and elephants in its claws. It is found mainly on Mount Kaf, and the architect who built this pavilion is capable of bringing you one of its eggs."

Then they stopped their conversation, since it was noontime and when the servants set the table, the Lady Badar al-Budur invited the accursed Moor to eat with her, but he refused, and the princess had his meal carried to his room, where he ate by himself.

Now, when it turned evening, Aladdin returned from the hunt and greeted his wife by embracing and kissing her. However, when he looked her in the face, he noticed that she was somewhat sad and did not smile. So he asked her, "Has anything happened to you, my darling? Tell me what's troubling you."

"Nothing whatsoever," she replied. "But, my beloved, I had thought that our pavilion was absolutely perfect and did not lack a thing. But that is not entirely the case, Aladdin. I think that if there were a Rukh's egg that hung from the jeweled dome, there would be nothing like it in the universe."

"Is this all that's been bothering you?" Aladdin asked. "It's the easiest thing in the world for me to fix. So cheer up. All you have to do is to tell me when you want something, and I'll fetch it instantly, even if it's hidden in the bowels of the earth."

And Scheherazade noticed that dawn was approaching and stopped telling her story. When the next night arrived, however, she received the king's permission to continue her tale and said,

After making sure that his wife had regained her good spirits, Aladdin withdrew to his chamber, where he took the lamp and rubbed it. Immediately the jinnee appeared and said, "Ask whatever you want."

"I want you to fetch me the egg of the bird Rukh," Aladdin replied. "And I want you to hang it from the dome of my pavilion."

But when the marid heard these words, his face became fierce, and he shouted with a mighty and frightful voice, "You ungrateful soul! Isn't it enough that I and all the slaves of the lamp are always at your service? Yet now, you also demand that I bring you our mistress just for your pleasure and hang her up in the dome of the pavilion for the enjoyment of you and your wife. By Allah, you and she deserve to be reduced to ashes this very moment and to be scattered in the air. But since you two are not aware of the crime you have committed and its consequences, I'll pardon you. Innocent as you are, you can't help what you've done. The crime is due to that sorcerer, the brother of the Moorish magician, who is living here and pretending to be the Holy Fatimah. He put on her clothes and disguised himself as her after murdering her in her cave. Indeed, he came here to kill you out of revenge for his brother, and it is he who persuaded your wife to make this request to me."

After saying all this, the jinnee vanished. Yet, Aladdin was still trembling after hearing the marid shout at him, and he felt completely bewildered. But gradually he recovered his senses and went into his wife's apartment. There he pretended to have a headache, for he knew how famous Fatimah was for healing all sorts of pains like that. When the Lady Badar al-Budur saw him sitting with his hand on his head and complaining about the pain, she asked him what the matter was, and he replied, "I don't know why, but I've got a terrible ache in my head."

Thereupon she ordered that the Holy Fatimah be summoned immediately so that she could put her hand on his head.

"Who is this Fatimah?" Aladdin asked.

So she informed him that it was the Holy Fatimah, for whom she had provided a home in the pavilion. Meanwhile a slave girl had gone to fetch the accursed Moor, and when the villain appeared, Aladdin stood up and, acting as though he knew nothing about the magician's deception, he saluted him as though he were the real Fatimah. He kissed the hem of his sleeve, welcomed him, and treated him with honor.

"My Lady Fatimah," Aladdin said, "I would appreciate it if you would do me a favor. I am well aware that you are adept at curing pains, and I am now suffering from a terrible headache."

The accursed Moor could hardly believe his ears, since this was exactly what he had wanted. So he approached Aladdin to place his hand upon his head and heal his ache. As he did this, the other hand was under his gown holding a dagger and ready to kill him. But Aladdin was watching him carefully and waited patiently until the Moor revealed the dagger. Then, with a powerful grip, he wrenched the dagger from his grasp and plunged it deep into his heart. When the Lady Badar al-Budur saw him do this, she shrieked, "Why have you shed this holy woman's blood? Have you no fear of Allah? Don't you know that the Holy Fatimah's miracles are known throughout the world?"

"But I haven't killed Fatimah," Aladdin replied. "I've only killed Fatimah's murderer, the brother of that vile Moor who abducted you through his magic and transported my pavilion to Africa. His damned brother came to our city and planned our downfall. He murdered Fatimah and assumed her identity in order to avenge his brother's death. If you don't believe me, come over here and take a look at the person I have slain."

Thereupon Aladdin drew the Moor's veil aside, and the Lady Badar al-Budur saw a man with a full beard.

Realizing that her husband was telling the truth, she said, "My beloved, this is the second time that I've placed your life in danger!"

"No harm's been done," replied Aladdin. "Besides, your eyes are blessing enough for all the risks I've taken, and I'll joyfully take on anything that comes with being married to you."

Hearing these words, the princess embraced him and said, "My darling, I can't believe you've done all this out of your love for me! I never knew how much you loved me. But don't think that I take your affection for granted."

So Aladdin kissed her and held her close, and they could feel their love for each other grow stronger.

Now, just at that moment, the sultan appeared, and they told him about everything that had happened and showed him the corpse of the sorcerer. Consequently, the king commanded the body to be burned and the ashes to be scattered in the air, just as he had done with the wizard's brother.

Thereafter, Aladdin lived with his wife, the Lady Badar al-Budur, in happiness and joy, and he survived all the dangers that he later encountered. After a while, when the sultan died, Aladdin ascended the throne. During his reign he treated his subjects with justice and wisdom so that everyone loved him. And he lived with his wife in bliss and serenity until the Destroyer of delights and the Severer of societies came and visited him.

No sooner had Scheherazade concluded her tale than she said, "And yet, oh king, this tale is no more wondrous than the remarkable story of 'Julnar the Mermaid and her Son Badar Basim of Persia.' "

Julnar the Mermaid and Her Son Badar Basim of Persia

Many years ago there was once a mighty monarch in the land of Ajam called King Shahriman, who lived in Khorasan. He owned a hundred concubines, but none of them had blessed him by giving birth to a child. As time passed, he began to lament the fact that he was without an heir, and there would be nobody to inherit his kingdom as he had inherited it from his father and forebears. One day, as he was grieving about this, one of his mamelukes came to him and said, "My lord, there is a merchant at the door with a slave girl, who is more beautiful than any woman I've ever seen before."

"Send them in," the king said.

After they had entered, Shahriman saw that the girl had a marvelous figure and was wrapped in a silk veil lined with gold. When the merchant uncovered her face, the place was illuminated by her beauty, and her seven tresses hung down to her anklets in lovelocks. She had coal-black eyes, heavy lips, a slender waist, and luscious thighs. Just the sight of her could heal all maladies and quench the fire of hearts longing for love. Indeed, the king was amazed by her beauty and loveliness, and grace, and said to the merchant, "Oh sheikh, how much for this maiden?"

"My lord," answered the merchant, "I bought her for two thousand dinars from a merchant who owned her before I did. Since then I have traveled with her for three years, and she has cost me another three thousand gold pieces up to the time of my arrival here. Despite all these expenses, she is a gift from me to you."

As a reward for this gesture, the king presented him

with a splendid robe of honor and ten thousand ducats, whereupon the merchant kissed his hands, thanked him for his generosity, and went his way. Afterward the king gave the damsel to the slave girls and said, "Go and bathe her. Then adorn her and furnish her with a bower, where she is to reside." In addition, he ordered his chamberlains to bring her everything she requested and to shut her doors after they left.

And Scheherazade noticed that dawn was approaching and stopped telling her story. When the next night arrived, however, she received the king's permission to continue her tale and said,

Now, the king's capital was called the White City and was located on the seashore. Therefore, the chamber in which the damsel was installed had windows that overlooked the sea. When Shahriman eventually went to visit her there, she did not speak to him, nor did she take any notice of him.

"It would seem that she's been with people who never taught her any manners," he said. Then he looked at the damsel and marveled again at her beauty, loveliness, and grace. Indeed, she had a face like the rondure of the full moon or the radiant sun shining on a clear day. And he praised Almighty Allah for having produced such a splendid creature, and he walked up to her and sat down by her side. Then he pressed her to his bosom, and after seating her on his thighs, he sucked the dew of her lips, which he found sweeter than honey. Soon after this he called for trays spread with all kinds of the richest viands, and while he ate, he also fed her by mouthfuls until she had had enough. All the while she did not speak a single word. Even when the king began to talk to her and asked her name, she remained silent and did not utter a syllable or give him an answer. Only her incomparable beauty saved her from his majesty's wrath. "Glory be to God, the Creator of this girl!" he said to himself. "She would be perfectly charming if she would only speak! But perfection belongs only to Allah the Most High." And he asked the slave girls whether she had spoken, and they said, "From the time of her arrival until now she has not uttered one word, nor has she even addressed us."

Then he summoned some of his women and concubines and ordered them to sing to her and make merry so that perhaps she might speak. Accordingly they played all sorts of instruments and games before her so that all the people present enjoyed themselves except the damsel, who looked at them in silence and neither laughed nor spoke. The king became extremely distressed because of this, and he dismissed the women and the rest of the company. When everyone was gone, he took off his clothes and disrobed her with his own hand. When he looked at her body, he saw that it was as smooth as a silver ingot, and his love for her was aroused. So he lay down next to her and began making love. Soon he took her maidenhead and was pleased to find that she was a pure virgin. "By Allah," he said to himself, "it's a wonder that a girl so fair of form and face should have been left untouched and pure by the merchants!"

From then on he devoted himself entirely to her and gave up all his other concubines and favorites. Indeed, he spent one whole year with her as if it were a single day. Still, she did not speak one word, until one morning he said to her, "Oh love of my life, my passion for you is great, and I have forsaken all my slave girls, concubines, and favorites, and I have made you my entire world and had patience with you for one whole year. So I now beseech Almighty Allah to do me a favor and soften your heart so that you'll speak to me. Or, if you are mute, tell me by some sign so that I'll give up hope of ever hearing you speak. My only prayer is that the Lord will grant me a son through you so that there will be an heir to the kingdom after me. May Allah bless you, and if you love me, you'll now give me a reply."

The damsel bowed her head awhile in thought. Eventually she raised it and smiled at him, and it seemed to him as if the rays of the sun had filled the chamber. Then she said, "Oh magnanimous lord and valorous lion, Allah has answered your prayer, for I am with child by you, and the time of my delivery is near at hand, although I am not sure whether the baby will be a boy or girl. But one thing is certain: if I had not become pregnant by you, I would not have spoken one word to you."

When the king heard her talk, his face shone with joy and gladness, and he kissed her head and hands out of delight. "Praise the Lord!" he said. "Almighty Allah has granted all my wishes—your speech and a child!"

Then he got up, left her chamber, and seated himself on his throne. In his ecstasy he ordered his vizier to distribute a hundred thousand dinars to the poor and needy and widows as a way of showing his gratitude to Allah Almighty. The minister did as he was commanded, and then the king returned to the damsel, embraced her, and said, "Oh my lady, my queen, your slave desires to know why you were silent so long. You spent one whole year with me, and yet you did not speak to me until this day. Why?"

"Listen to me carefully, my lord," she replied, "for I want you to know that I am a wretched exile and broken-hearted. My mother, my family, and my brother are far away from me."

When the king heard her words, he knew how she felt and said, "There's no more need for you to feel so wretched, for I swear to you my kingdom and goods and all that I possess are at your service, and I have also become your husband. But as for your separation from your mother, brother, and family, I understand your sorrow, but just tell me where they are, and I will send for them and fetch them here."

"Gracious king, you must listen to the rest of my story," she answered. "First, let me tell you that my name is Julnar the Mermaid, and that my father was a descendant of the kings of the High Seas. When he died, he left us his realm, but while we were still upset and mourning him, one of the other kings arose against us and took over our realm. I have a brother called Salih, and my mother is also a woman of the sea. While all this was happening, I had a falling out with my brother and swore that I would throw myself into the hands of a man of the land. So I left the sea and sat down on the edge of an island in the moonshine, and a passerby found me. He took me to his house and tried to make love to me, but I struck him on the head so hard that he almost died. Once he recovered, he took me away and sold me to the merchant from whom you bought me. This merchant was a good man—virtuous, pious, loyal, and generous. If it were not for the fact that you fell in love with me and promoted me over all your concubines, I would not have remained with you a single hour. Rather, I would have sprung into the sea from this window and gone to my mother and family. Now, however, I've become ashamed to travel to them, since I am carrying your child. They would consider this to be sinful and would no longer regard me with esteem, even if I were to tell them that a king had bought me with his gold, given me his property, and preferred me over all his wives. —This then is my story."

And Scheherazade noticed that dawn was approaching and stopped telling her story. When the next night arrived, however, she received the king's permission to continue her tale and said,

Then the king thanked Julnar for telling him her story, kissed her on her forehead, and said, "By Allah, oh lady and light of my eyes, I can't bear to be separated from you for more than one hour. If you were ever to leave me, I would die immediately. What are we to do?"

"My lord," she replied, "the time of my delivery is near at hand, and my family must be present so that they can tend me. You see, the women of the land do not know how women of the sea give birth to children, nor do the daughters of the ocean know the ways of the daughters of the earth. When my people come, we will all be reconciled to one another."

"But how do people of the sea walk about in the water and breathe?" asked the king.

"We walk in the water and breathe as you do here on ground," she said, "thanks to the names engraved on the ring of Solomon David-son. But now, listen to me, when I call for my kith and kin to come here, I'll tell them how you bought me with gold and have treated me with kindness and benevolence. It will be important for you to show them that you have a magnificent realm and that you're a mighty king."

"My lady," he said, "do whatever you think is appropriate, and you can rely on me to carry out your commands."

Then the damsel continued telling him about her life. "Yes," she said, "we walk in the sea and perceive everything that is in the water. We even behold the sun, moon, stars, and sky, as though they were on the surface of the earth. But this does not bother us. There are many types of people in the high seas and various forms and creatures on land, but the differences are not all that great."

The king was astounded by her words, and then she pulled two small pieces of Comorin lign aloes from her bosom, and after kindling a fire in a chafing dish, she took some of the lign aloes and threw them into the fire. Right after that she whistled loudly and said something that the king could not understand. Suddenly a great deal of smoke arose, and she said to the king, "My lord, get up and hide yourself in a closet so that I may show you my brother, mother, and family without them seeing you. I have decided to bring them here, and you will soon see a wondrous thing and marvel at the strange creatures and forms that Allah Almighty has created."

So he quickly entered a closet and began watching what she would do. And indeed, she continued her incantations until the sea began to foam and froth, and all at once a handsome young man arose from it. He was as bright as the full moon with a handsome white brow, ruddy cheeks, and teeth like pearls. Moreover, he was very much like his sister in looks. After him came an ancient dame with speckled gray hair and five maidens, radiant moons, who resembled Julnar a great deal. The king watched them as they walked on the face of the water until they drew near Julnar's window and saw her. Once they recognized her, they entered the chamber through the window, and she rose to greet them with joy and gladness. Indeed, they embraced and wept profusely until one of them said, "Oh Julnar, how could you leave us four years and not tell us where you were? By Allah, we've been extremely upset since our separation, and we haven't been able to enjoy food or drink. No, not for one day. We have longed so much for you that we've not been able to stop weeping!"

Then Julnar began kissing the hands of her mother, brother, and relatives, and they sat with her awhile asking her to tell them what had happened to her and what she was doing there.

"When I left you," Julnar began, "I emerged from the sea and sat down on the shore of an island, where a man found me and sold me to a merchant, who brought me to this city and sold me for ten thousand dinars to the king of this country. Now, this king has treated me with great honor and given up all his concubines, women, and favorites for my sake. Moreover, he has devoted all this time and energy into looking after my welfare."

"Praise be to Allah, who has reunited us with you," said her brother. "But now, my sister, it's time for you to come back with us to our country and people."

When the king heard these words, he almost went out of his mind, fearing that Julnar might agree with her brother and he would not be able to stop her. He loved her passionately and was extremely afraid of losing her.

"By Allah," Julnar replied, "the mortal who bought me is the lord of this city, and he is a mighty king and a wise, good, and generous man. Moreover, he has a great deal of wealth and does not have an heir to his throne. He has treated me with honor, done all sorts of favors for me, and has never spoken one unkind word to me. He does nothing without my advice, and I have the best of all possible worlds with him. Furthermore, if I were to leave him, he would perish, for he cannot endure to be separated from me for more than one hour. Indeed, if I left him, I, too, would die because I love him so much. Even if my father were alive, I could not have a better life than the life I presently lead with this great and glorious monarch. And right now, to tell you the truth, I am carrying his child, and praise be to Allah, who has made me a daughter of the kings of the sea, and my husband the mightiest of kings of the land. Indeed, Allah has compensated me for whatever I lost."

And Scheherazade noticed that dawn was approaching and stopped telling her story. When the next night arrived, however, she received the king's permission to continue her tale and said,

Julnar paused for a moment and then continued explaining her situation to her brother and family. "As I mentioned before, this king does not have an heir, and so I have prayed to Allah to bless me with a son who would inherit everything that belonged to this mighty lord's realm."

Now, when her brother and family heard her speech, they understood her situation much better and responded, "Oh Julnar, you know how much we respect and love you. You are the dearest of creatures, and we only want you to lead a life without travail or trouble. Therefore, if you are suffering in any way, we want you to come with us to our land and folk. But if you are happy here and are honored the way you should be, we would not want to take you away or do anything against your wishes."

"By Allah," she said, "I have all the comfort, solace, and honor I need here."

When the king heard what she said, his heart was set at rest, and he thanked her silently for everything. His love for her grew immensely, and he now knew that she loved him as he loved her and desired to remain with him, and that he would get to see his child.

Then Julnar ordered her women to set the table with all sorts of viands, which had been cooked in the kitchen under her supervision, and fruit and sweetmeats. When that was done, she and her kinsfolk sat down and ate. But soon they said to her, "Julnar, we have never met your lord, and yet we have entered his house without his permission or knowledge. You have praised his excellent qualities and have set his food before us, which we have eaten. Yet, we have not enjoyed his company or seen him." So they all stopped eating and were angry with her. Suddenly fire spouted from their mouths, and the king was scared out of his wits.

But Julnar arose, and after calming them, she went to the closet where the king was hidden, she said, "My lord, have you seen and heard how I praised you to my people and have you noted that they would like to take me back to my land?"

"I heard and saw everything," he said. "May the Lord reward you for what you have said and done! By Allah, until this blessed moment I did not know how much you loved me!"

"My lord," she replied, "what is the best reward for kindness but kindness! You have been most generous with me and have treated me with love and respect. So, how could my heart be content to leave you, especially after you have been so good to me? But now I would like you to show how courteous you are. Please welcome my family and become friends with them. Thanks to my praise of you, my brother, mother, and cousins already love you and refuse to depart for their home until they have met you."

"As you wish," said the king. "Indeed, this has been my very own desire as well."

Upon saying this he arose, went over to them, and greeted them warmly. In turn, they stood up and received him with utmost respect. Then he sat down and ate with them, and he entertained them in his palace for the next thirty days, at which point they desired to return home. So they took leave of the king and queen, and after he showed them all possible honors, they departed for home. Some time after this Julnar gave birth to a boy, and he looked as radiant as the full moon. Of course, the king was beside himself with joy, for he had been longing to have an heir for many years. Soon they celebrated the event for seven days and decorated the entire city. Everyone was filled with joy, and on the seventh day Julnar's mother, Queen Farashah, her brother, and her cousins arrived, for they had learned about her giving birth to a son.

And Scheherazade noticed that dawn was approaching and stopped telling her story. When the next night arrived, however, she received the king's permission to continue her tale and said,

The king was most happy about their visit, and told them, "I promised not to give my son a name until you arrived and could know what he was to be called." So they named him Badar Basim, and all agreed that this was a fine name. Then they showed the child to his Uncle Salih, who took him in his arms and began to walk all around the room with him. Soon he left the palace with him and took him down to the ocean until he was hidden from the king's sight. Now, when Shahriman saw him take his son and disappear with him into the depths of the ocean, he gave the child up for lost and began weeping. But Julnar said to him, "Don't worry. There is no need to grieve for your son, for I love my child more than you, and he is with my brother. Therefore, you don't have to be afraid of the sea or of his drowning. If my brother had thought that the little one would be harmed, he would not have done this. Don't worry, he'll soon bring your son safely back to you."

After an hour went by and the ocean sea became turbulent, King Salih emerged and left the water. When he came up to them with the child lying quiet and his face as radiant as the full moon, he said to the king, "Perhaps you were afraid your son would be harmed when I plunged into the sea with him?"

"Yes," he said, "I was afraid and even thought that he wouldn't come back."

"My lord," Salih replied, "we penciled his eyes with an eye powder that we know and recited the names engraved on the ring of Solomon David-son over him, for this is what we generally do with our newborn children. Now you'll never have to fear his drowning or suffocation in all the oceans of the world. Just as you walk on land, we walk in the sea, and he, too, has our gift."

Then he pulled an engraved and sealed box from his pocket, and after he broke the seals and emptied it, all sorts of jacinths and other jewels fell out. In addition, there were three hundred emeralds and other gems as big as ostrich eggs that glistened more brightly than the sun and moon.

"Your majesty," said Salih, "these jewels and jacinths are a present from me to you. The reason we never brought you a gift before this is that we never knew where Julnar was residing, nor did we have any trace of her. But now that we know she is united with you and we have all become part of the same family, we have brought you this present, and every once in a while we shall bring you more of the same. These jewels and jacinths are like pebbles on the beach for us, and we know how good and bad they can be, and we know all about their power and where to find them."

When the king saw these jewels, he was completely amazed and dazzled. "By Allah," he said, "just one single gem of these jewels is worth my entire realm!" Then he thanked Salih the Merman, and turning toward Queen Julnar, he said, "I am abashed before your brother, for he has treated me most generously and bestowed this splendid gift on me."

So she, too, thanked him for his deed, and Salih replied to the king, "My lord, it is we who are obliged to you, for you have treated our sister with kindness, and we have entered your palace and eaten your food. Therefore, even if we stood on our heads in serving you, it would be nothing but a scant gesture for what you deserve."

The king thanked him warmly, and the merman and mermaids remained with him for forty days, at the end of which time Salih arose and kissed the ground before his brother-in-law, who asked, "What can I do for you, Salih?"

"Your majesty, you have done more than enough for us, and we only crave your permission to depart, for we long for our people and country. We shall never forget you, our sister, or our nephew and shall always be there to serve you. By Allah, it is not easy to part from you, because you have been so kind to us, but what can we do? We were reared in the sea, and we cannot get accustomed to the land."

When the king heard these words, he arose and said farewell to Salih, his mother, and his cousins, and they all wept together. Soon they said to him, "We must be off, but we won't forsake you, for we plan to visit you as often as possible."

Then they departed, and after descending into the sea, they disappeared from sight.

And Scheherazade noticed that dawn was approaching and stopped telling her story. When the next night arrived, however, she received the king's permission to continue her tale and said,

After this King Shahriman showed Julnar even more kindness and honored her with even more respect than before. Their son grew up and flourished, while his maternal uncle, grandma, and cousins visited the king whenever they could and stayed with him a month or two months at a time. The boy became more and more handsome and lovely as years went by, and when he reached the age of fifteen he had a grand physique. Moreover, he learned how to write and read the Koran and studied history, syntax, and lexicography. He became an expert in archery, spear-throwing, horsemanship, and whatever else it was fitting for the son of a king to learn. Everyone in the city, man, woman, and child, talked continually about the boy's charms, for he was perfectly handsome and pleasant. And, indeed, the king loved him more than anything else, and one day he summoned his vizier, emirs, chief officers of state, and grandees of his realm and made them take an oath that they would make Badar Basim their new king. In turn, they gladly pledged their loyalty, for the monarch was liberal to his lieges, diplomatic, and fair, and he always thought of his people first. The next day Shahriman mounted with his troops, emirs, and lords and went into the city to announce what they had done. Then they began their return to the palace, and as they approached it, the king dismounted to wait upon his son, who remained on his horse. The king and all the emirs and nobles carried the saddle cloth of honor before him, until they came to the vestibule of the palace, where the prince got off his horse, and his father and the emirs embraced him and seated him on the royal throne. While they stood before him, Badar Basim began to hold court and to judge the people, rewarding the just and punishing the unjust, and he continued doing so until noon, when he descended the throne and went to his mother, Julnar the Mermaid, with the crown on his head as if he were the moon. When she saw him with the king standing before him, she rose, and after kissing him, she rejoiced in his becoming sultan and wished him and his sire long lives and victory over their foes. Badar Basim sat with his mother and rested until the hour of midafternoon prayer, when he mounted his horse and went to the Maydan plain preceded by the emirs, and there he played at arms with his father and his lords until nightfall. After that he returned to the palace preceded by his entourage.

Badar Basim continued riding out every day to the tilting ground, and he continued judging the people in a just manner for one whole year. At the end of that time he went out hunting and made the rounds of the cities and countries under his rule, guaranteeing the people his protection and security as it was fitting for kings to do. Gradually he established a wonderful reputation among the people because of his valor and sense of justice.

Now one day it so happened that the old king fell ill, and when the sickness became worse and he knew that

he was near death, he called his son and commended his
mother and subjects to his care and ordered all the emirs
and nobles once more to swear allegiance to the prince.
After that he lingered a few days, and then Allah merci-
fully granted him his death. His son and widow and all
the emirs, ministers, and lords mourned over him, and
they built him a tomb and buried him in it. They continued mourning for one whole month until Salih, his mother,
and cousins arrived and offered their condolences to the
grieving young king. Then they said to Julnar, "Though
the king is dead, he has left this noble and peerless
youth, and he who has left such a valorous and radiant
son is therefore still with us."

*And Scheherazade noticed that dawn was approaching
and stopped telling her tale. When the next night arrived,
however, she received the king's permission to continue
her tale and said,*

So the nobles and ministers of the empire went to see
King Badar Basim, and they said to him, "Your majesty,
there is no harm in mourning for the late sovereign, but
it is not fitting to mourn too long. Only women carry on
like that, and we ask you not to occupy your heart and
our hearts with mourning anymore. Remember, insofar
as he has left you behind him, he is still with us."

Then they comforted him, provided him with distrac-
tions, and took him to the Hammam bath. When he
came out of the bath, he donned a rich robe lined with
gold and embroidered with jewels and jacinths. After
placing the royal crown in his head, he sat down on his
throne and regulated the affairs of the folk by ruling
wisely and justly so that his people loved him and showed
him great affection. He continued doing this for one
whole year, while every now and then his kinsfolk of the
sea visited him, and his life was pleasant, and he saw
things clearly.

Now one night it so happened that his Uncle Salih
came to visit Julnar, and after she greeted him, she
asked, "How are you and my mother and cousins?"

"They are fine and doing well," he replied. "The only
thing they lack is the sight of your face."

Then she set some food before him, and he ate. After

the meal they talked about King Badar Basim and all his
remarkable charms and skills. Now Badar was lying on
some pillows nearby, and since he heard that his mother
and uncle were talking about him, he pretended to be
asleep and listened to their conversation. Soon Salih said
to his sister, "Your son is now seventeen years old and is
unmarried, and I wouldn't want anything to happen to
him without his having an heir to the throne. So I'd like
him to marry soon, and indeed, I'd like him to marry a
princess of the sea, who would be his match in beauty
and loveliness."

"Whom do you have in mind?" she asked. "Tell me
their names, for I know them all."

So Salih proceeded to name them to her, one by one,
but as each princess was named, Julnar said, "I don't like
her for my son. I'll only marry him to a princess who is
his equal in beauty, wit, piety, good breeding, magna-
nimity, rank, and lineage."

"I've named all the daughters of the kings of the sea to
you," said Salih, "and I don't know any more than the
hundred I've mentioned. Of course, there is someone . . .
But wait now, sister, and make sure that your son's
asleep."

So she felt Badar to see if he was asleep, and he did
not move. Consequently, she said to Salih, "Don't worry.
I'm sure he's asleep. Now tell me what you have to say
and why you wanted me to make sure that he was
sleeping."

"Well, to tell the truth," he said, "There is a mermaid
who would be a perfect match for your son. But I'm
afraid to mention her name when he's awake. She is so
remarkable, and if he were to fall in love with her and we
were unable to win her, it would cause great trouble for
us and the nobles of the realm."

When Julnar heard these words, she insisted, "Tell me
all about her and her name. If I judge her worthy of
Badar, I'll demand her in marriage from her father, even
if I have to spend all that I possess for her. Tell me all
about her, and don't worry, for my son's sound asleep."

So Salih said, "By Allah, my sister, no woman is
worthy of your son except the Princess Jauharah, daughter of King Al-Samandal, for she is his match in beauty,
loveliness, and brilliance. You won't find a sweeter gift

on land or on sea than this princess, for she has rosy
cheeks, a brow as white as a flower, sparkling teeth, dark
black eyes, wide hips, a slender waist, and exquisite legs.
When she moves about and turns, she puts the gazelles to
shame. When she unveils her face, she outshines the sun
and moon, and anyone who glances at her is immediately
captivated. Ah, she has such sweet lips and such a soft
manner!"

Now, when Julnar heard what Salih had to say, she
replied, "All that you've said is true, my brother! By
Allah, I've seen her many times, and she was my companion when we were little, but since then I've heard
very little about her, nor have I set eyes on her for
eighteen years. By Allah, none is worthy of my son but
her!"

While they were talking, Badar heard everything from
first to last, and he fell in love with the Princess Jauharah
just on hearsay. Pretending to be asleep, he felt the fire
of love being kindled in his heart because of her, and he
was drowned in a sea without shore or bottom.

*And Scheherazade noticed that dawn was approaching
and stopped telling her story. When the next night arrived,
however, she received the king's permission to continue
her tale and said,*

Then Salih said to his sister, "There is, however, one
problem: there is no greater fool among the kings of sea
than her father, nor one with a more violent temper than
he! So don't tell your son the name of the girl until we
demand her hand in marriage from her father. If he
consents, we shall praise Allah Almighty, and if he re-
fuses us, we won't say a word about it and seek some
other match."

"That is sound advice," Julnar said, and they stopped
talking, but Badar spent the night with a heart on fire for
Princess Jauharah. However, he concealed his love and
did not speak to his mother or uncle about it. Now, when
morning came, the king and his uncle went to the
Hammam bath and washed. Then they went back to the
palace, drank wine, and ate. After the meal they washed
their hands, and Salih rose and said to his nephew and
sister, "With your permission, I would like to go to my

mother and my folk, for I've been with you some days, and my kinfolk have been missing me."

But Badar Basim said to him, "Please spend the day with us and then depart." After Salih consented, the king continued, "Come, my uncle, let us go into the garden."

So they walked around the garden for a while until the king lay down under a shady tree with the intention of resting and sleeping, but he remembered his uncle's description of the beautiful Princess Jauharah and began shedding tears and sighing. When his uncle saw the tears, he smacked his hand on the ground and exclaimed, "By Allah, you heard your mother and me talking about Princess Jauharah last night!"

"Yes, my uncle," Badar Basim replied, "I fell in love with her through hearsay. Indeed, my heart has swollen with love, and I feel that I'm going to burst! I cannot live without her!"

"Let us return to your mother," Salih said, "and tell her how you feel. Then I'll ask her permission to take you with me and seek the princess's hand in marriage from her father. I'm afraid to take you without her leave, because she would be very angry with me. Indeed, she'd be right to be angry, because I'd be the cause of your departure. Moreover, the city would be left without a king, and there would be no one to govern the citizens and look after their affairs. Then the kingdom would be upset, and the people would no longer recognize you as their king."

But Badar Basim responded, "Uncle, if I return to my mother and ask for her advice in this matter, I know she won't grant me permission to depart. Therefore, I refuse to consult her." And he began weeping and added, "Let's just go, and we'll tell her everything when we return."

When Salih heard what his nephew wanted to do, he became confused and said, "May Allah help me!" However, he realized how determined his nephew was to go, whether his mother would grant him permission or not, and so he drew from his finger a ring with certain names of Allah the Most High engraved on it and gave it to him. "Put this on your finger," he said, "and it will keep you safe from drowning and other dangers, especially from the mischief of sea beasts and large fish."

So King Badar Basim took the ring and set it on his finger. Then they dove into the deep sea.

And Scheherazade noticed that dawn was approaching and stopped telling her story. When the next night arrived, however, she received the king's permission to continue her tale and said,

After diving into the deep, Salih and his nephew King Badar Basim journeyed until they came to Salih's palace, where they found Badar's grandmother seated with her kinsfolk. When the old queen saw Badar, she rose, embraced him, kissed him on his forehead, and said, "My blessings! And how is your mother?"

"She is well and happy," he replied, "and she sends you and her cousins her greetings."

Then Salih related to his mother what had happened between him and his sister and how Badar had fallen in love with the Princess Jauharah. He concluded his story by saying, "And Badar has come with the sole intention of marrying the princess."

Upon hearing this, the old queen was extremely angry with her son and most disturbed. "Oh Salih," she said, "it was wrong of you to name the princess in front of your nephew, especially since you know that her father is stupid and violent and is unwilling to give his daughter to anyone. All the monarchs of the high seas have sought her hand, and he has rejected every single one of them and argued, 'You are no match for her in beauty, loveliness, or anything else!' Therefore, I'm afraid to demand her hand in marriage from him. If he rejects us as he has rejected all the others, we shall be brokenhearted."

"Mother," Salih said, "what's there to do? The fact is that Badar is determined to marry her even if he has to give his whole kingdom for her. And he's also told me that if he cannot wed her, he'll die of love for her. To tell the truth, he is handsome and wealthier than she is. His father was king of all the Persians, and as his successor, no one is worthier of Jauharah than Badar. Therefore, I propose to carry a gift of jacinths and jewels to her father befitting his dignity and request her hand in marriage for Badar. If he objects and says that he is a king, I shall point out that our man is also a king and son of a king.

Or if he objects and says his daughter is beautiful, I shall point out that our man is more handsome than she is beautiful. Or if he objects and says his realm is vast, I shall point out that our man's realm is vaster and that he has many more troops and guards. I'll do anything I can to further the cause of my sister's son, even if it costs my life. In truth, I'm responsible for all this, and since I'm the one who plunged him into the ocean of her love, then with the help of Almighty Allah, I intend to help him marry her!"

"Do as you want," said his mother, "but beware of saying anything impolite to her father. You know how stupid and violent he is! I'm just afraid he might do you some mischief, for he has no respect for anyone."

"I'll remember your advice," Salih said, and he got up and left the room with his nephew. Then he took two bags full of gems such as rubies, emeralds, and other jewels and gave them to his servants to carry. Afterward he set out with Badar Basim for the palace of Al-Samandal. When they arrived there, he sought an audience with the king, and after being admitted, he kissed the ground before him and saluted him with a respectful salaam. The king rose and honored him with a seat, and after he was seated, the king said, "May you be blessed for visiting us. We have not had the pleasure of your company for a long time, Salih! What brings you to us? Tell me your errand, so I may help you fulfill it."

Thereupon Salih arose, kissed the ground a second time, and said, "I have come on an errand to you, my magnanimous liege lord and valiant lion, whose good qualities have been made known by caravans far and wide, and whose reputation for beneficence, clemency, graciousness, and generosity has been spread to all climes and countries." After making this address, Salih opened the bags of jewels, displayed their contents before Al-Samandal, and said, "I hope you will accept this gift and do me the favor of healing my heart."

And Scheherazade noticed that dawn was approaching and stopped telling her story. When the next night arrived, however, she received the king's permission to continue her tale and said,

* * *

Then King Al-Samandal asked, "Why have you given me this gift? Tell me your story and what is entailed. If it is within my power to help you accomplish your goal, I'll do what I must to save you toil and trouble. But if I'm unable to assist you, you will understand that Allah never compels anyone to exceed his power."

After listening to the king, Salih rose, kissed the ground three times, and said, "Your majesty, that which I desire is well within your power to grant. I do not intend to impose upon you, nor have I been demented by the jinn that I would ask the impossible of you. For as one of our sages has said, 'If you desire to have your wish granted, never ask what cannot be readily attained.' So, I have come to ask you, oh king, and may Allah bless you with long life, for something that is within your power to grant."

The king replied, "Ask what you would like and tell me what you are seeking."

Then Salih said, "Your majesty, I have come as a suitor, seeking that unique pearl the Princess Jauharah, daughter of our lord the king, and I beseech you not to disappoint me."

Now, when the king heard this, he laughed so hard that he fell over on his back. After mocking Salih like this, he stood up and said, "Oh Salih, I thought you were a young man with a good head on your shoulders. What's happened to your senses that you've been urged to seek this monstrous thing? Why are you endangering yourself by seeking to marry a daughter of kings, lords of cities and climates? Tell me, are you so lordly that you can aspire to such eminence? Have you lost your mind and thus feel free to offend me with this request?"

"By Allah," replied Salih, "I am not seeking her for myself, and even if I did, I am her match, and even more than her match, for you know that my father was king of the kings of sea despite the fact that you are king right now. No, I am seeking her for King Badar Basim, lord of the lands of the Persians and son of King Shahriman, whose power you know. If you maintain that you are a great and mighty king, well then, let me tell you that King Badar is greater. And if you maintain that your daughter's beauty is incomparable, well then, let me tell you that King Badar is more handsome and comes from a

better rank and lineage. Indeed, he is the champion of
the people of his day. Therefore, if you grant my request,
your majesty, you will setting up a perfect match. But if
you deal arrogantly with us, you'll pay for being unjust.
Moreover, you know that the Princess Jauharah needs to
be wedded and bedded one day, for the sage says, a girl's
lot is either grace of marriage or the grave. Consequently,
if you intend to marry her, my sister's son is more worthy
of her than any man alive."

Now, when King Al-Samandal heard Salih's words, he
became extremely furious. He almost lost his head, and
his soul almost exploded from his body because of his rage.
"Oh dog!" he cried. "How dare you name my daughter and
address me as you have in front of my court assembled
here? And how dare you say that the son of your sister
Julnar is a match for her? Who are you and who is this
sister of yours and her son and who was his father that
you dare to speak to me this way? You're all nothing but
dogs in comparison to my daughter!" Then he called out to
his guards and barked, "Off with that scoundrel's head!"

So they drew their swords and approached Salih, but
he fled and made for the palace gate, where he saw his
kinsfolk and servants on horseback armed from head to
foot in iron and close-knitted mail coats and carrying
spears and glittering swords. And when they saw Salih
come running out of the palace—they had been sent by
his mother just in case—they asked him what had happened, and he told them what to do. Of course, they all
knew that King Al-Samandal had a violent temper and
was a fool to boot. So they dismounted, drew their swords,
and entered the audience hall, where they found King
Al-Samandal seated on his throne and unaware of their
coming. He was still fuming because of Salih, and they
caught him and his entourage unprepared. Then, when
he saw them, he cried out, "Woe to you! Off with the
heads of these dogs!" But before the hour had gone by,
Al-Samandal's party was put to rout, and Salih and his
kinsmen seized the king and bound him.

*And Scheherazade noticed that dawn was approaching
and stopped telling her story. When the next night arrived,
however, she received the king's permission to continue
her tale and said,*

* * *

Right after the struggle began, Princess Jauharah awoke and discovered that her father had been taken captive and his guards slain. So she fled the palace to a certain island and climbed up a high tree and hid herself in the top. Now, when the two parties had clashed, Badar met some of King Al-Samandal's pages in flight and asked them what had happened. When he heard that the king was a prisoner, Badar became anxious, for he felt that he had caused all this turmoil, and that the guards would soon be after him. Therefore, he took to flight and ran without knowing where he was going. As destiny would have it, he landed on the very same island where the princess had taken refuge, and he came to the very tree which she had climbed. It was there that he threw himself down like a dead man, hoping to rest and not knowing that there is no rest for the pursued. Indeed, nobody knows what fate has in store for him. As he lay down, he raised his eyes, and his glance met the eyes of the princess in the treetop. As he gazed at her, he thought she was like the moon rising in the east, and he cried out, "Glory to Him who created that perfect form! By Allah, if my sentiments are true, it is Jauharah, daughter of King Al-Samandal! I believe that when she heard of our clash with her father, she fled to this island and hid herself in this treetop. But even if it isn't the princess herself, then it's a woman even more divine than she is." Then he reflected about his situation and said to himself, "I'll get up and seize her and ask her who she is. If she is indeed who I think she is, I'll ask her personally to marry me and win my wish."

So he stood up and called to her, "Oh end of all desire, who are you, and who brought you here?"

She looked at Badar Basim, and discovering that he was like the full moon when it shines through a black cloud, so slender in shape and so sweet a smile, she answered, "Oh fair one, I am Princess Jauharah, daughter of the King Al-Samandal, and I took refuge in this place because Salih and his host came to blows with my sire. They slew his troops and took him and some of his men prisoner. Therefore, I had to flee out of fear for my life, especially since I don't know what has happened to my father."

When King Badar Basim heard these words, he was astounded by this strange coincidence and thought to himself, "Undoubtedly I've won my wish, since her father is now a prisoner." Then he looked at Jauharah and said to her, "Come down, my lady, for I have fallen totally in love with you, and your eyes have captivated me. To tell you the truth, the battle that was fought today was because of me and you, for I am King Badar Basim, lord of the Persians, and Salih is my mother's brother, and it was he who came to request your hand in marriage for me. As for me, I left my kingdom for your sake, and our meeting here is a unique coincidence. Therefore, I beg you to come down to me, and let us two go to your father's palace so that I may beseech my Uncle Salih to release your father and so that I can make you my lawful wife."

When Jauharah heard these words, she said to herself, "It was because of this miserable scoundrel, then, that everything has happened! Because of him my father's been taken prisoner, his chamberlains and other officers have been slain, and I've been forced to flee the palace and take refuge on this island! And now, if I don't think of something fast to defend myself, he'll possess me and do what he wants with me. He's in love, and whenever a man's in love, anything he does is excusable." So she beguiled him with charming words and sweet speeches, while he was unaware that she was plotting something perfidious against him. And at one point she asked, "My lord and light of my eyes, tell me, are you truly King Badar Basim, son of Queen Julnar?"

And Scheherazade noticed that dawn was approaching and stopped telling her story. When the next night arrived, however, she received the king's permission to continue her tale and said,

When Badar heard her question, he replied, "Yes, my lady."

"Well, then," she replied, "may Allah turn His back on my father and take away his kingdom from him! May Allah let him suffer and drive him into exile! I say all this because he could not have found a more handsome or virtuous man to be my suitor. By Allah, he is not very smart or discerning!" Then she added, "Despite all this, oh king, please do not punish him for what he's done. If you have just a drop of the immense love I feel for you, then you'll do this for me. Indeed, I've fallen into the net of your love and have become your captive. The love that was in you has been transferred to me, and there is a little left in you and a vast amount in me!"

After saying all this, she slid down the tree and walked over to him. Then she drew him to her bosom and began kissing him, causing his passion and desire for her to increase and making him feel that she was definitely in love with him and he could trust her. Returning her kisses and caresses, he said to her, "By Allah, my uncle did not know the least thing about your charms!"

Then Jauharah pressed him even closer to her bosom, uttered some words that he did not understand, and suddenly spat on his face. "I command you to change your form! Change and become a bird! Yes, it's a bird you shall become!"

No sooner had she spoken than King Badar Basim found himself transformed into a beautiful white bird with a red bill and red legs, and he stood there in astonishment.

Now, Jauharah had one of her slave girls by the name of Marsinah with her, and she called her and said, "If it weren't for the fact that I fear for the life of my father, who is his uncle's prisoner, I would kill him! May Allah never reward him! He is the one who has caused all his misfortune. Yes, all this trouble is due to his stubbornness! So, I want you to bring him to the Thirsty Island and leave him there to die!"

So Marsinah left the island and brought him to another one with numerous trees, fruit, and streams, and after she deposited him there, she returned to her mistress and reported that she had left him on the Thirsty Island.

In the meantime, Salih had begun searching for Jauharah after capturing the king and killing his guards. However, since he could not find her, he returned to his palace and asked his mother, "Where is Badar?"

"By Allah," she replied, "I don't know where he is. When he learned that you and King Al-Samandal had come to blows and that the fighting had led to slaughter, he became frightened and fled."

When Salih heard this, he grieved for his nephew and said, "Mother, I've been too careless with King Badar, and I'm afraid that he might perish or meet one of King Al-Samandal's soldiers or his daughter, Jauharah. If that were to happen, Julnar would never forgive me, especially since I took her son without her permission."

Then he sent out his guards and scouts throughout the sea and other places to look for Badar, but they could not discover where he was. When they returned and told King Salih, his concern increased, and he was most distressed because of Badar.

Now, Julnar the Mermaid had been long expecting their return, but they had disappeared after going into the garden, and she had no news of them. Therefore, when many days of fruitless waiting had gone by, she arose, went down into the sea, and returned to her mother, who embraced her when she arrived. Then she asked her mother about King Badar Basim and her uncle, and the old queen replied, "To tell you the truth, he came here with his uncle, who took jewels and jacinths to King Al-Samandal and demanded his daughter for Badar. However, when the king did not consent, a violent battle ensued, and Allah helped your brother capture the king and slay his guards. Meanwhile, your son feared for his life and fled, and we have not had any news of him since then."

Then Julnar inquired about her brother, Salih, and her mother told her, "He has taken over King Al-Samandal's throne and has sent messengers and scouts in every direction to search for your son and Princess Jauharah."

When Julnar heard her mother's story, she mourned for her son and was extremely angry with her brother, Salih, for having taken her son and gone down into the sea without her permission. And she said, "Mother, I fear for our realm, for I came here without telling anyone, and I'm afraid that if I stay here too long, there will be chaos in the kingdom, and the throne will be usurped. Therefore, I think it's best if I return and govern the kingdom until my son's affair is settled here, if it pleases Allah. But I want you to look after him, for if he should be harmed in any way, I would die, since he is the joy of my life and the light of my world."

"I'll gladly do this, my daughter," she replied, "and

with love. We have already suffered a great deal because of his absence."

Then the old queen sent out messengers to search for her grandson, while Julnar returned to her kingdom, weeping and heavy-hearted, and indeed, she could no longer take delight in the world.

And Scheherazade noticed that dawn was approaching and stopped telling her story. When the next night arrived, however, she received the king's permission to continue her tale and said,

With regard to King Badar Basim, he dwelled as an enchanted bird on the island, eating its fruit and drinking its water, and did not know where to go or how to fly. Then one day, a fowler came to the island to catch some birds, for this was how he earned his living. When he caught sight of King Badar Basim in his form of a beautiful white bird with red bill and legs, he was captivated and said to himself, "What a wonderful bird! I've never seen anything as beautiful in my life." So he cast his net over Badar and took him to the town with the intention of selling him for a high price. On his way, one of the townspeople approached him and asked, "How much for that bird, fowler?"

"What will you do with him if you buy him?" responded the fowler.

"I'll cut his throat and eat him," said the man.

"Who could have the heart to kill this bird and eat him?" said the fowler. "I intend to give him to our king as a present, and he'll give me more than you would give me. Moreover, I'm sure he won't kill him but enjoy himself by gazing at the bird's beauty and grace. Honestly, in all my life, ever since I've been a fowler, I've never seen such a marvelous bird. In short, I won't sell him to you!"

Then he carried the bird to the king's palace, and when the king saw the bird from his window, he was pleased by his beauty and grace and by his unusual coloring. So he sent one of his eunuchs, who asked the fowler whether he would sell the bird.

"No," he replied. "The bird is a gift from me to the king."

So the eunuch carried the bird to the king and told him what the man had said. Thus the king took the bird and gave the fowler ten dinars, whereupon he kissed the ground and went his way. Then the eunuch carried the bird to a room in the palace and placed him in a fine cage with something to eat and drink and hung the cage up. When the king finished holding court, he said to the eunuch, "Where is the bird? Bring it to me so that I may gaze upon it. By Allah, it's the most beautiful bird I've ever seen!"

So the eunuch brought the cage and set it between the hands of the king, who looked and noticed that the food was untouched. "By Allah," the king said, "we must find the right food to nourish it!"

Then he called for food, and they set the table for the king to eat and let the bird out of the cage. Now, when the bird saw the meat, fruit, and sweetmeats, he began eating everything that was on the trays, while the sovereign and all the bystanders were amazed, and the king said to his attendants, "In all my life I've never seen a bird eat the way this one does!"

Then he sent a eunuch to fetch his wife so that she might enjoy watching the bird, and the eunuch said to her, "My lady, the king desires your presence so that you might enjoy watching a bird that he has bought. When we set it on the table, it ate everything that was on the trays. So please come and take pleasure in this wonderful sight!"

Upon hearing these words, she rushed to the king's chamber, but when she caught sight of the bird, she veiled her face and turned to leave. The king stood up immediately and asked her, "Why have you veiled your face when there is nobody in our presence except the women and eunuchs who wait on you and your husband?"

"Oh king," she said, "this bird is not a bird, but a man just like yourself."

"You're lying," he responded. "Or you're jesting. How can this bird be a man?"

"I'm not jesting," she contended. "I'm telling the truth. This bird is King Badar Basim, son of King Shahriman, lord of the land of the Persians, and his mother is Julnar the Mermaid."

*   *   *

And Scheherazade noticed that dawn was approaching and stopped telling her story. When the next night arrived, however, she received the king's permission to continue her tale and said,

"How was he turned into a bird?" the king asked.

"Princess Jauharah has enchanted him," she said and told him all that had happened to King Badar Basim from first to last.

The king was amazed by his wife's story and implored her to free Badar from this enchantment (for she was the most notable enchantress of her age) and to put an end to his torment. "May Almighty Allah cut off Jauharah's hand for doing this!" he said. "What a foul witch! She's nothing but a treacherous and cunning creature!"

Then the queen said, "You're to say to him, 'Oh Badar Basim, enter that closet over there!' "

So the king ordered him to enter the closet, and he went in obediently. After that the queen veiled her face, took a cup of water in her hand, and entered the closet, where she pronounced some incomprehensible words and ended with, "By virtue of these mighty names and holy verses and by the majesty of Allah Almighty, Creator of heaven and earth, you are to abandon this form and return to the shape in which the Lord created you!"

No sooner had she ended her words than the bird trembled once and became a man. Then he opened the closet door, and the king saw before him the most handsome youth on the face of the earth. And when King Badar Basim found himself restored to his own shape, he cried, "There is no god but *the* God. Glory be to the Creator of all creatures and the Provider of their provisions."

Then he kissed the king's hand and wished him long life, and the king kissed his head and said to him, "Oh Badar Basim, tell me your story from beginning to end."

So he told the king his entire tale and did not forget a thing, and the king was amazed by it and said, "Allah has saved you from the spell, but what do you intend to do now?"

"Your majesty," Badar replied, "I need your help and generosity, and I am requesting a ship with a company of your servants and all that is necessary for a voyage. I have been away from my kingdom a long time, and I'm worried that my kingdom might be usurped. Moreover, I fear that my mother may be dead from grief over my disappearance, for she does not know whether I am dead or alive."

"Your wish is my command," said the king after listening to this polite and touching speech. So he provided Badar with a ship and all that was needed for a voyage along with a company of his servants. After taking leave of the king, Badar Basim set sail, and for ten days he had a favorable wind, but on the eleventh, the ocean became turbulent. The ship rose and fell, and the sailors were unable to control it. So they drifted at the mercy of the waves, until the vessel came near a rock and crashed on it. All on board were drowned, except King Badar Basim, who got on one of the planks of the ship. For three whole days Badar was driven on the plank by the rough sea, and he had no notion about where he was going.

But on the fourth day, the plank drifted to a shore, where he sighted a white city built on a peninsula that jutted out into the sea. It was a magnificent city with high towers and lofty walls against which the waves beat. When Badar Basim saw this, he rejoiced, for he was almost dead of hunger and thirst. So he stood up and wanted to wade to the beach, but a herd of wild horses and mules came charging at him and prevented him from marching on the sand. So he swam around to the back of the city, where he waded to shore. After entering the place, he could not find a single soul and was astounded. "I wish I knew who ruled over this city," he said to himself. "And where did all those horses and mules come from that prevented me from landing?" He began walking and was pondering the situation when he came upon an old grocer. So he saluted him, and the grocer returned his salaam and asked him, "Where have you come from, my handsome youth, and what has brought you to this city?"

Badar told him his story, and the old man was amazed by it and said, "Did you see anything along the way?"

"To tell the truth," Badar replied, "I was astounded to find the city empty."

"My son," said the sheikh, "come into my shop or else you will perish from hunger."

So Badar went into his shop and sat down, whereupon

the old man brought him some food and said, "Glory be to Allah Almighty, who has preserved you from that she-devil!"

King Badar Basim was tremendously frightened by the grocer's words, but he ate his fill and washed his hands. Then he glanced at his host and said to him, "My lord, what is the meaning of your words? Truly, you've made me afraid of this city and its people."

"You must know, my son," replied the grocer, "that this is the City of the Magicians, and its queen is like a she-satan, a sorceress and a mighty enchantress. Oh, she is extremely crafty and treacherous! All those horses and mules you encountered were once sons of Adam, just like you and me. They were also strangers, for whoever enters this city, especially young men like yourself, this miscreant witch takes him and houses him for forty days. After that time is up, she enchants him, and he becomes a mule or a horse like those animals you saw on the seashore."

And Scheherazade noticed that dawn was approaching and stopped telling her story. When the next night arrived, however, she received the king's permission to continue her tale and said,

After the grocer paused for a moment, he continued his story by saying to Badar, "When you intended to land, they were worried that you would be transformed like themselves. So they tried to warn you by signs not to land, fearing that she would do the same thing to you that she's done to them. She took control of this city by sorcery, and her name is Queen Lab, which in Arabic means Almanac of the Sun."

When Badar Basim heard the old man's story, he was extremely frightened and trembled like a reed in the wind and said to himself, "No sooner am I freed from one enchantment than destiny sets another snare for me!" And he began reflecting about his predicament and everything that had happened to him. When the old man looked at him and realized how terrified he was, he said, "My son, come and sit at the threshold of the shop and look at the people and how they dress and act. Don't be afraid, for the queen and the entire city love me and will not annoy or trouble me."

So King Badar Basim went to the threshold and looked at the people who passed by the shop. When the people caught sight of him, they approached the grocer and said to him, "Is this young man your prisoner? Did you just capture him?"

"He is my brother's son," the old man replied. "I heard that his father had died, and so I sent for him so that I might comfort him."

"Truly, he is a handsome young man," they said, "but aren't you afraid that Queen Lab will turn on you and use some treacherous means to take him away from you? For she loves handsome young men."

"The queen will not go against my orders," the sheikh said, "for she loves me, and when she finds out that he is my brother's son, she will not molest him or trouble me on his account."

Then King Badar Basim stayed with the grocer for some months, and the old man became extremely fond of him. One day, as the grocer sat outside his shop, as was his custom, a thousand eunuchs with drawn swords and clad in various kinds of raiment with jeweled belts approached him on Arabian steeds. They saluted the grocer as they passed his shop, and soon they were followed by a thousand damsels like moons clad in silk and satin clothes lined with gold and embroidered with jewels of all kinds, and spears were slung over their shoulders. In their midst rode Queen Lab in all her majesty mounted on a marvelous mare with a golden saddle lined with jewels and jacinths. As the damsels rode by the shop, they, too, saluted the grocer, but Queen Lab came right up to him, because she had caught sight of King Badar Basim sitting in the shop as if he were a full moon. She was amazed by his handsome and lovely features and fell passionately in love with him. Her desire for him was so great that she dismounted and took a seat next to Badar and said to the old man, "Where does this handsome young man come from?"

"He's my brother's son," the sheikh replied, "and he's just arrived here."

"Let him stay with me tonight so that I may talk with him," she said.

"Only if you promise not to enchant him," he responded.

"But of course," she said.

"Swear it to me," he insisted.

So she swore to him that she would not do him any harm or enchant him. Then she commanded that a fine horse with a gold bridle and harness be brought over, and she gave the old man a thousand dinars and said, "These are for your daily expenses."

Then she led Badar Basim away on the horse, while all the people felt sorry for him and said, "By Allah, this handsome young man does not deserve to be bewitched by that wretched sorceress!"

Now King Badar Basim heard all they said, but he kept silent and left his fate in the hands of Allah Almighty.

And Scheherazade noticed that dawn was approaching and stopped telling her story. When the next night arrived, however, she received the king's permission to continue her tale and said,

When they arrived at the palace gate, the emirs, eunuchs, and noblemen dismounted, and the queen ordered her chamberlains to dismiss her officers and grandees, who kissed the ground and went away. Meanwhile she entered the palace with Badar Basim and her eunuchs and women. Never before in his life had he seen a place like that. The palace was built of gold, and in its midst was a large pond surrounded by a vast garden that had all kinds of birds warbling in sweet and melodious voices. Everywhere he looked he saw magnificent things and cried out, "Glory to God for providing such a marvelous estate!" The queen sat down at a latticed window overlooking the garden on an ivory couch next to a bed, and King Badar Basim seated himself by her side. She kissed him and pressed him to her breast, and soon thereafter she ordered her women to bring a tray of food. So they brought a gold tray lined with pearls and jewels, and on the tray were all kinds of viands.

Both the queen and Badar ate until they were satisfied, and then they washed their hands. Once again the waiting women came, and this time it was with gold and silver flagons and all kinds of flowers and dishes of dried fruit. Next the queen summoned the singing women, ten maidens as beautiful as the moon, and they all began playing different instruments. Queen Lab poured a cup to the brim, and after drinking off the top, she filled another and passed it to King Badar Basim, who took it and drank, and they kept drinking until they were satisfied. Then she ordered the damsels to sing, and they sang various kinds of songs until it seemed to Badar that the palace was dancing with joy. He was filled with ecstasy and felt so relieved that he forgot his outcast state and said to himself, "Truly, this queen is young and beautiful, and I'll never leave her, for her kingdom is vaster than my kingdom, and she is more beautiful than Princess Jauharah." So he resumed drinking until the evening, and they both became drunk, while the singers kept making music. Then Queen Lab, who was quite intoxicated, rose from her seat and lay down on a bed. After dismissing her women, she called to Badar Basim to come and sleep by her side. So he lay down beside her and enjoyed her till the morning.

And Scheherazade noticed that dawn was approaching and stopped telling her story. When the next night arrived, however, she received the king's permission to continue her tale and said,

When the queen awoke, she went to the Hammam bath in the palace with King Badar, and they bathed together and were purified. After that she clad him in the finest raiment and called for wine. After drinking the wine, the queen took Badar by the hand, and they sat down to eat and then washed their hands. Then the damsels fetched the fruit, flower, and confections, and they kept eating and drinking until the evening while the singing girls sang various songs. They continued this routine for forty days, at the end of which time the queen asked him, "Oh Badar Basim, tell me whether it is more pleasant to be at my place or at your uncle's shop."

"By Allah," he replied, "this is much more pleasant, for my uncle is but a poor man, who sells pots of herbs."

She laughed at his words, and the two of them lay together and enjoyed one another until the morning. Then Badar awoke from his sleep and did not find Queen Lab by his side. "If only I knew where she went!" he said to himself. And indeed he was troubled by her absence and puzzled by her disappearance, for she stayed away a long time and did not return. So he got dressed and went looking for her, and when he did not find her, he said to himself, "Perhaps she went to the garden." Thereupon he went into the garden and came to a stream, where he saw a white female bird, and on the bank of the stream was a tree full of birds of different colors, and Badar stood and watched the birds without them noticing him.

All of a sudden a black bird flew down upon the white female bird and began billing her in pigeon fashion. Then he leapt on her and trod her three consecutive times, after which the bird changed and became a woman, and Badar saw that it was Queen Lab! All at once it became clear to him that the black bird was a man, who had been transformed through magic. Moreover, it was clear that she was enamored of him and had transformed herself into a bird so that he could enjoy her. Consequently, Badar was overcome with jealousy and was angry with the queen because of the black bird.

Then he returned to his place and lay down on the couch, and after an hour or so she came back to him and began kissing and playing with him. However, since he was furious with her, he did not say a word to her. Nevertheless, she knew what he was feeling and was certain that he had witnessed what had happened to her when she had been a white bird, but she decided not to talk about it. After he had fulfilled her needs, he said to her, "Queen, I would like your permission to go to my uncle's shop, for I miss him and haven't seen him for forty days."

She replied, "You may go, but don't stay away very long from me, for I cannot stand to be parted from you more than an hour."

"As you wish," he said, and after mounting his steed, he rode to the shop of the grocer, who welcomed him with an embrace and asked him, "How are things going with the queen?"

"I was very happy until this past night," he replied, and he told him what had happened in the garden with the black bird.

Now, when the old man heard his story, he said, "Beware of her, for the birds on the trees were all young men and strangers whom she loved and turned into birds through magic. That black bird you saw was one of her mamelukes, whom she loved with great passion, until he cast his eyes upon one of her women. Consequently, she changed him into a black bird."

And Scheherazade noticed that dawn was approaching and stopped telling her tale. When the next night arrived, however, she received the king's permission to continue her tale and said,

Then the grocer added, "Whenever she lusts after him, she transforms herself into a bird so that he may enjoy her, for she still loves him with passion. Now that she has realized that you've discovered her relationship with the black bird, she will plot something evil against you, for she does not love you as much as she loves the mameluke. But no harm will come to you so long as I protect you. Therefore, you have nothing to fear, for I am a Moslem by the name of Abdallah, and there is no one who knows as much magic as I do in this day and age. However, I don't make use of my magical skills unless I am forced to do so. Many a time I have undermined the sorcery of that wicked queen and saved people from her, and I'm not worried about her, because she cannot harm me. In fact, she's even afraid of me, as are all the people of the city, who are magicians like her and serve the fire, but not the Omnipotent Sire. So I want you to come to me tomorrow and tell me all that she does, for tonight she will begin to look for a way to destroy you, and if you tell me all that you see tonight, I'll be able to tell you what mischief she's planning so that you'll be able to save yourself."

Then Badar said farewell to the sheikh and returned to the queen, who was awaiting him. When she saw him, she rose and welcomed him. Then she ordered the meal, and after they had had enough and washed their hands, they drank some wine until half the night was spent drinking and he was drunk and lost his head. When she saw him like this, she said, "By Allah and whatever you worship, if I ask you a question, will you answer me correctly and truthfully?"

And since he was drunk, he answered, "Yes, my lady."

"My lord and light of my eyes," she said, "when you awoke last night and did not find me, you kept looking for me until you saw me in the garden in the form of a white bird, and you also saw the black bird leap on me and tread me. Now I'll tell you the truth about this. That black bird was one of my mamelukes, whom I loved with a great passion. But one day he cast his eyes upon one of my slave girls, causing me to become jealous, and so I transformed him through a magic spell into a black bird and slew her. But now I cannot live without him for a single hour. So whenever I lust after him I change myself into a bird and go to him so that he can leap on top of me and enjoy me as you witnessed. Aren't you therefore furious with me because of this, even though I love you more than ever and have devoted myself to you?"

Being drunk, he answered, "You are right about my anger, for I am jealous of your love for the black bird."

After hearing this, she embraced him and kissed him and displayed a great deal of love for him. Then she lay down to sleep, and he was next to her. Soon, about midnight, she rose from the couch, and Badar Basim was awake, but he pretended he was asleep and watched stealthily to see what she would do. Indeed, she began taking something red out of a red bag, and she planted it in the middle of the chamber. Then it became like a running stream, and she took a handful of barley, strewed it on the ground, and watered it with water from the stream. All at once it became wheat, which she gathered and ground into flour. Finally, she set it aside, returned to bed, and lay down next to Badar.

The next morning he arose, washed his face, and asked her permission to visit the sheikh. She consented, and he went to Abdallah and told him what had happened. The old man laughed and said, "By Allah, this evil witch is plotting some mischief against you. But you have no need to be afraid of her!" Then he gave him a pound of parched corn and said to him, "Take this with you, and when she sees you with it, she'll ask what it is and what you intend to do with it. You're to answer, 'It's always good to have an abundant supply of good things.' Then eat it, and she'll bring out her own parched grain and say to you, 'Eat some of this sawik.' You are to pretend to eat some of it, but eat the parched corn instead. Be certain that you don't eat so much as a grain of hers, for if you do, her spells will have power over you, and she will enchant you and transform you into a bird or animal. If you don't eat her grains, her magic will be powerless, and nothing will happen to you. Once she realizes this, she will be exceedingly ashamed of herself and say to you, 'I really didn't want to enchant you. I was only jesting.' She'll make a great display of love and affection, but this will all be hypocritical. Nevertheless, you are also to make a great display of love and say to her, 'My lady and light of my eyes, eat some of this parched barley and see how delicious it is.' And if she eats some, even a grain, take some water in your hand and throw it in her face and say, 'Change your human form!' and give her whatever form you want. Then leave her and come to me, and I'll tell you what to do."

So Badar Basim took leave of him, and after returning to the palace, he went into see the queen, who said, "Welcome, and may you be in a good mood." And she rose and kissed him. "You've been away a long time, my lord."

"I've been with my uncle," he replied, "and he gave me some of this sawik to eat."

"We have better than that," she said. Then she placed his parched sawik in one plate and hers in another and said to him, "Eat this. It's better than yours."

So he pretended to eat it, and when she thought he had eaten it, she took some water in her hand, sprinkled him with it, and said, "Change your form, you miserable scoundrel, and become a stinking mule with one eye!"

But he did not change, and when she realized this, she went up to him, kissed him on the forehead, and said, "Oh my beloved, I was only jesting with you. Don't be angry with me because of it."

"Oh my lady," he said, "I'm not angry with you. No, I'm convinced that you love me, but why don't you eat some of my parched barley."

So she ate a mouthful of Abdallah's sawik, and no sooner had it settled in her stomach than she had convulsions, and King Badar Basim took some water in his hand, threw it at her, and said, "Change your form, and become a dapple mule!"

No sooner had he spoken than she found herself changed

into a mule, whereupon tears rolled down her cheeks, and she began to rub her muzzle against his feet. Then he wanted to bridle her, but she would not take the bit. So he left her, and after returning to the grocer, he told him what had happened. Abdallah brought out a bridle for him and told him to rein her with it. So he went back to the palace, and when she saw him, she came up to him, and he set the bit in her mouth, mounted her, and rode forth to the sheikh. When the old man saw her, he rose and said to her, "May Almighty Allah punish you for your sins, you wicked woman!" Then he said to Badar, "My son, there's no sense in your remaining in this city any longer. So ride her and travel wherever you want. But beware that you do not give the bridle to anyone else."

King Badar thanked him and said farewell. Then he journeyed for three days until he drew near another city, and there he met an old gray-headed man, who asked him, "Where are you coming from, my son?"

"From the city of this witch," replied Badar.

And the old man said, "Please be my guest tonight."

He consented and went with him along the way, until they met an old woman, who wept when she saw the mule, and said, "There is no god but *the* God! Truly, this mule resembles my son's dead mule, and his heart continues to long for this mule. So, please, my lord, sell it to me!"

"By Allah," he replied, "I cannot sell her."

But she cried, "Please don't refuse my request! My son will surely die if I don't buy this mule."

And she kept imploring him until he exclaimed, "I will only sell the mule for a thousand dinars," thinking to himself that this woman would never have a thousand dinars. However, she took out a purse containing a thousand ducats from her apron, and when Badar saw the purse, he said, "Mother, I was only jesting with you. I cannot sell the mule."

But the old man looked at him and said, "My son, in this city nobody may lie, and whoever lies they put to death."

And Scheherazade noticed that dawn was approaching and stopped telling her story. When the next night arrived,

*however, she received the king's permission to continue
her tale and said,*

So King Badar Basim had to get off the mule, and
when he delivered it to the old woman, she drew the bit
from its mouth, took some water in her hand, sprinkled
the mule, and said, "Oh daughter, change your form,
and become what you were once before!"

All at once Queen Lab was restored to her original
form, and the two women embraced and kissed each
other. The old woman was no one else but the queen's
mother, and Badar knew that he had been tricked and
wanted to flee. But the old woman whistled loudly, and
her call was obeyed by a jinnee as large as a mountain.
Upon seeing this jinnee, Badar was terrified and could
not budge from his spot. Then the old woman mounted
the jinnee's back, placing her daughter behind her and
Badar before her, and the ifrit flew off with them. Within
an hour they were in the palace of Queen Lab, who sat
down on her throne and said to Badar, "Now that I have
returned to my palace, you are a dead man! I've gotten
what I wanted, and soon I'll show you what I'm going to
do with you and that old man the grocer! I've done
numerous favors for him, and yet he offends me. Surely,
you would not have been able to trick me without his
help."

Then she took water, sprinkled him with it, and said,
"Change your form and become a stinking bird, the
foulest of all the birds," and she set him in a cage and
deprived him of food and drink. However, one of her
waiting women could not bear her cruelty and gave him
food and water without her knowledge.

One day, this same woman slipped out of the palace
without Queen Lab seeing this, and she went to the old
grocer and told him, "Queen Lab intends to bring an end
to your nephew's life," and she recounted everything that
had happened.

The sheikh thanked her and said, "She leaves me no
choice. Now I must take the city from her and make you
the queen in her place." Then he whistled loudly, and a
jinnee with four wings appeared before him. "Take this
damsel," the sheikh said to the ifrit, "and carry her to
the city of Julnar the Mermaid and her mother, Farashah,

for the two are the most powerful magicians on the face of the earth." Then he turned to the damsel and said, "When you arrive there, tell them that King Badar Basim is Queen Lab's captive."

After he finished speaking, the ifrit picked up the damsel and flew with her to the terrace roof of Queen Julnar's palace, where he deposited her. Then she descended the stairs, and after entering the queen's chamber, she kissed the ground and told the queen what had happened to her son from first to last. Thereupon, Julnar arose, thanked her, and treated her with honor. Afterward she had the drums beat throughout the city and informed her lieges and lords about the good news about Badar. Then she and her mother, Farashah, and her brother, Salih, assembled all the tribes of the jinn and all the troops of the high sea, for the kings of the jinn obeyed them ever since Salih had taken King Al-Samandal prisoner. Soon they all flew up in the air, landed on the city of Queen Lab, sacked the town and palace, and slew all the unbelievers in the twinkling of an eye. Then Julnar said to the damsel, "Where is my son?"

And the slave girl brought the cage and pointed to the bird inside it. "This is your son," she declared.

So Julnar took him out of the cage, sprinkled some water on him, and said, "Return to your proper form!" No sooner had she spoken these words than Badar became a man as he was before. Upon seeing him as he once was, his mother embraced him and began weeping. Moreover, his Uncle Salih, his grandmother, and his cousins kissed his hands and feet. Then Julnar sent for Sheikh Abdallah and thanked him for the kindness that he had shown her son. Finally, Julnar married Abdallah to the damsel who had helped save Badar and made him king of the city. Moreover, she summoned the survivors of the city, who were all Moslems, and made them swear an oath of loyalty to Abdallah. Indeed, they all obeyed and pledged their allegiance. Afterward, Julnar and her company said farewell to Abdallah and returned to their own capital, where crowds of people came out to meet them with drums. Then they decorated the city, and for three days they celebrated the return of King Badar Basim with immense joy. After the celebration was over,

Badar said to his mother, "The only thing left is for me to marry."

"You're right, my son," Julnar replied, "but wait until we find the right princess for you."

And his grandmother Farashah and his cousins said, "Badar, we will help you fulfill your desire by searching for the damsel most suited for you."

Then each one of them arose and journeyed forth in foreign lands, while Julnar sent out her waiting women on the backs of jinnees, ordering them not to leave a city without looking at all the beautiful girls in it. But when Badar saw all the trouble they were taking in this matter, he said to Julnar, "Mother, please stop, for no one will satisfy me except Jauharah, daughter of King Al-Samandal. Indeed, like her name, she is a jewel!"

"I agree with you, my son," said Julnar, and she immediately ordered King Al-Samandal to be summoned to her. As soon as he was present, she sent for Badar Basim, and when Al-Samandal saw him, he stood up and saluted him. Thereupon, King Badar Basim requested his daughter's hand in marriage.

"You have my permission, and I shall place her at your disposal," said King Al-Samandal, and he sent some of his suite to search for her. When they found her, they told her that her sire was in the hands of King Badar Basim, and she returned with them through the air. As soon as the princess saw her father, she went up to him and threw her arms around his neck. Then, looking at her, he said, "My daughter, I want you to know that I have given you in wedlock to the magnanimous and valiant King Badar Basim, son of Queen Julnar the Mermaid. Indeed, he is the most beneficent of the people of his day, the most powerful, the most exalted, and the most noble. He is clearly your match, and you are clearly his."

"I shall not oppose you, my sire," she said. "Do as you wish, for sorrow and spite have come to an end, and I agree to be his wife."

So they summoned the kazi and the witnesses, who drew up the marriage contract between King Badar Basim and the Princess Jauharah, and the citizens decorated the city, rejoiced, and beat the drums. Amnesty was given to all the prisoners in the jails, while the king gave generously to the widows, orphans, and poor and bestowed robes of honor on the lords of the realm, the emirs, and the nobles. For ten days there were wedding feasts and banquets from morning until night, and at the end of that time they displayed the bride in nine different dresses before King Badar Basim, who bestowed an honorable robe on King Al-Samandal and sent him back to his country and people. And they did not stop leading a most pleasurable life nor enjoying fine food, drink, and luxury until the Destroyer of delights and the Sunderer of societies came upon them. This is the end of their story, and may Allah have mercy on them all!

No sooner had Scheherazade concluded her tale than she said, "And yet, oh king, this tale is no more wondrous than the tale about the thief of Alexandria and the police chief."

The Tale About the Thief of Alexandria and the Chief of Police

Once upon a time there was a chief of police in Alexandria called Husam al-Din, the sharp Scimitar of the Faith. Now one night, as he was sitting at his desk, a trooper came running into his office and said, "My lord, I entered your city this very night, and soon after I went to sleep at a certain khan, I awoke to find my saddlebags sliced open and a purse with a thousand gold pieces missing!"

No sooner had he finished speaking than the chief summoned all his officers and ordered them to seize all the people in the khan and throw them into jail. The next morning, he had rods and whips brought to his office, and after sending for the prisoners, he intended to have them flogged until someone confessed to the theft in the presence of the owner. Just then, however, a man broke through the crowd of people at his office and went straight to the chief.

"Stop!" he cried out. "Let these people go! They've been falsely accused. It was I who robbed this trooper. Look, here's the purse I stole from his saddlebags."

Upon saying this, he pulled out the purse from his sleeve and laid it before Husam al-Din, who said to the soldier, "Take your money, and put it away. You no longer have any grounds to lodge a complaint against these people of the khan."

Thereupon, the people of the khan and all those present began praising the thief and blessing him. However, he said, "Please stop. It doesn't take much skill to bring the purse to the chief in person. But it does take a great deal of skill to take it a second time from this trooper."

"And how did you manage to do that?" asked the chief.

And the robber replied, "My lord, I was standing in the money changer's shop at Cairo, when I saw this soldier receive the gold in change and put it into this purse. So I followed him from street to street but did not find the right opportunity to steal it. Then he left Cairo, and I followed from town to town, plotting along the way to rob him without avail, until I entered this city, where I dogged him to the khan. There I took my lodgings next to him and waited until he fell asleep. Then I went up to him quietly, and I slit open his saddlebags with this knife and took the purse just as I am taking it now."

No sooner had he spoken those words than he stretched out his hand and grabbed the purse from the trooper in front of the chief, and everyone thought that he was merely demonstrating how he had committed the theft. But, all at once, he broke into a run and sprang into a nearby river. The chief of police shouted to his officers, "Stop that thief!" And his men ran after him. But before they could doff their clothes and descend the steps of the river, he had made it to the other side. Of course, they continued searching for him, but there was no way they could find him, for he was able to escape through the back streets and lanes of Alexandria.

So the officers returned without the purse, and the chief of police said to the trooper, "I can't do anything for you now. The people are innocent, and your money was returned to you. But you weren't wise enough to protect it from the thief."

Consequently, the trooper was compelled to leave without his money, while the people were delivered from his hands and those of the chief of police. And all this had the blessing of Almighty Allah.

No sooner had Scheherazade concluded her story than she said, "And yet, oh king, this tale is no more wondrous than the tale of Prince Behram and the Princess Al-Datma."

Prince Behram and the
Princess Al-Datma

There was once a king's daughter called Al-Datma who, in her time, had no equal in beauty and grace. In addition to her lovely looks, she was brilliant and feisty and took great pleasure in ravishing the wits of the male sex. In fact, she used to boast, "There is nobody who can match me in anything." And the fact is that she was most accomplished in horsemanship and martial exercises, and all those things a cavalier should know.

Given her qualities, numerous princes sought her hand in marriage, but she rejected them all. Instead, she proclaimed, "No man shall marry me unless he defeats me with his lance and sword in fair battle. He who succeeds I will gladly wed. But if I overcome him, I will take his horse, clothes, and arms and brand his head with the following words: 'This is the freedman of Al-Datma.'"

Now the sons of kings flocked to her from every quarter far and near, but she prevailed and put them to shame, stripping them of their arms and branding them with fire. Soon, a son of the king of Persia named Behram ibn Taji heard about her and journeyed from afar to her father's court. He brought men and horses with him and a great deal of wealth and royal treasures. When he drew near the city, he sent her father a rich present, and the king came out to meet him and bestowed great honors on him. Then the king's son sent a message to him through his vizier and requested his daughter's hand in marriage. However, the king answered, "With regard to my daughter Al-Datma, I have no power over her, for she has sworn by her soul to marry no one but him who defeats her in the listed field."

254

"I journeyed here from my father's court with no other purpose but this," the prince declared. "I came here to woo her and to form an alliance with you."

"Then you shall meet her tomorrow," said the king.

So the next day he sent for his daughter, who got ready for battle by donning her armor of war. Since the people of the kingdom had heard about the coming joust, they flocked from all sides to the field. Soon the princess rode into the lists, armed head to toe with her visor down, and the Persian king's son came out to meet her, equipped in the fairest of fashions. Then they charged at each other and fought a long time, wheeling and sparring, advancing and retreating, and the princess realized that he had more courage and skill than she had ever encountered before. Indeed, she began to fear that he might put her to shame before the bystanders and defeat her. Consequently, she decided to trick him, and raising her visor, she showed her face, which appeared more radiant than the full moon, and when he saw it, he was bewildered by her beauty. His strength failed, and his spirit faltered. When she perceived this moment of weakness, she attacked and knocked him from his saddle. Consequently, he became like a sparrow in the clutches of an eagle. Amazed and confused, he did not know what was happening to him when she took his steed, clothes, and armor. Then, after branding him with fire, she let him go his way.

When he recovered from his stupor, he spent several days without food, drink, or sleep. Indeed, love had gripped his heart. Finally, he decided to send a letter to his father via a messenger, informing him that he could not return home until he had won the princess or died for want of her. When his sire received the letter, he was extremely distressed about his son and wanted to rescue him by sending troops and soldiers. However, his ministers dissuaded him from this action and advised him to be patient. So he prayed to Almighty Allah for guidance.

In the meantime, the prince thought of different ways to attain his goal, and soon he decided to disguise himself as a decrepit old man. So he put a white beard over his own black one and went to the garden where the princess used to walk most of the days. Here he sought out the gardener and said to him, "I'm a stranger from a country far away, and from my youth onward I've been a gardener, and nobody is more skilled than I am in the grafting of trees and cultivating fruit, flowers, and vines."

When the gardener heard this, he was extremely pleased and led him into the garden, where he let him do his work. So the prince began to tend the garden and improved the Persian waterwheels and the irrigation channels. One day, as he was occupied with some work, he saw some slaves enter the garden leading mules and carrying carpets and vessels, and he asked them what they were doing there.

"The princess wants to spend an enjoyable afternoon here," they answered.

When he heard these words, he rushed to his lodging and fetched some jewels and ornaments he had brought with him from home. After returning to the garden, he sat down and spread some of the valuable items before him while shaking and pretending to be a very old man.

And Scheherazade noticed that dawn was approaching and stopped telling her story. When the next night arrived, however, she received the king's permission to continue her tale and said,

In fact, the prince made it seem as if he were extremely decrepit and senile. After an hour or so a company of damsels and eunuchs entered the garden with the princess, who looked just like the radiant moon among the stars. They ran about the garden, plucking fruits and enjoying themselves, until they caught sight of the prince disguised as an old man sitting under one of the trees. The man's hands and feet were trembling from old age, and he had spread a great many precious jewels and regal ornaments before him. Of course, they were astounded by this and asked him what he was doing there with the jewels.

"I want to use these trinkets," he said, "to buy me a wife from among the lot of you."

They all laughed at him and said, "If one of us marries you, what will you do with her?"

"I'll give her one kiss," he replied, "and then divorce her."

"If that's the case," said the princess, "I'll give this damsel to you for your wife."

So he rose, leaned on his staff, staggered toward the damsel, and gave her a kiss. Right after that he gave her the jewels and ornaments, whereupon she rejoiced and they all went on their way laughing at him.

The next day they came again to the garden, and they found him seated in the same place with more jewels and ornaments than before spread before him.

"Oh sheikh," they asked him, "what are you going to do with all this jewelry?"

"I want to wed one of you again," he answered, "just as I did yesterday."

So the princess said, "I'll marry you to this damsel."

And the prince went up to her, kissed her, and gave her the jewels, and they all went their way.

After seeing how generous the old man was to her slave girls, the princess said to herself, "I have more right to these fine things than my slaves, and there's surely no danger involved in this game." So when morning arrived, she went down by herself into the garden dressed as one of her own damsels, and she appeared all alone before the prince and said to him, "Old man, the king's daughter has sent me to you so that you can marry me."

When he looked at her, he knew who she was. So he answered, "With all my heart and love," and he gave her the finest and costliest of jewels and ornaments. Then he rose to kiss her, and since she was not on her guard and thought she had nothing to fear, he grabbed hold of her with his strong hands and threw her down on the ground, where he deprived her of her maidenhead. Then he pulled the beard from his face and said, "Do you recognize me?"

"Who are you?"

"I am Behram, The King of Persia's son," he replied. "I've changed myself and have become a stranger to my people, all for your sake. And I have lavished my treasures for your love."

She rose from him in silence and did not say a word to him. Indeed, she was dazed by what had happened and felt that it was best to be silent, especially since she did not want to be shamed. All the while she was thinking to herself, "If I kill myself, it will be senseless, and if I have him put to death, there's nothing that I'd really gain. The best thing for me to do is to elope with him to his own country."

So, after leaving him in the garden, she gathered together her money and treasures and sent him a message informing him what she intended to do and telling him to get ready to depart with his possessions and whatever else he needed. Then they set a rendezvous for their departure.

At the appointed time they mounted racehorses and set out under cover of darkness, and by the next morning they had traveled a great distance. They kept traveling at a fast pace until they drew near his father's capital in Persia, and when his father heard about his son's coming, he rode out to meet him with his troops and was full of joy.

After a few days went by, the king of Persia sent a splendid present to the princess's father along with a letter to the effect that his daughter was with him and requested her wedding outfit. Al-Datma's father greeted the messenger with a happy heart (for he thought he had lost his daughter and had been grieving for her). In response to the king's letter, he summoned the kazi and the witnesses and drew up a marriage contract between his daughter and the prince of Persia. In addition, he bestowed robes of honor on the envoys from the king of Persia and sent his daughter her marriage equipage. After the official wedding took place, Prince Behram lived with her until death came and sundered their union.

No sooner had Scheherazade concluded her tale than she said, "And yet, oh king, this tale is no more wondrous than the tale of the three apples."

The Tale of the Three Apples

One night the Caliph Harun al-Rashid summoned his vizier Ja'afar and said to him, "I want to go down into the city and question the common folk about the conduct of those charged with carrying out my laws. If the commoners complain about any of my officers, we will dismiss them, and those they praise, we will promote."

"As you wish," replied Ja'afar.

So the caliph went with Ja'afar and the eunuch Masrur to the town and walked about the streets and markets, and as they were passing through a narrow alley, they came upon a very old man with a fishing net and crate for carrying small fish on his head. In his hand he held a staff, and he walked at a leisurely pace and chanted a song about poor people.

When the caliph heard his verses, he said to Ja'afar, "I'm sure that this man's verses are about his own sorry state." Then he approached him and asked, "Tell me, oh sheikh, what do you do for a living?"

"My lord," he answered, "I'm a fisherman with a family to support, and I've been out between midday and this time, and Allah hasn't granted me a thing to feed my family. I can't even pawn myself to buy them a supper, and I hate and am disgusted by my life and I hanker after death."

"Listen to me," said the caliph. "If you return with us to the banks of the Tigris and cast your net, I'll pay you a hundred gold pieces for whatever turns up."

The man rejoiced when he heard these words and said, "Fine with me!"

Upon arriving at the river he cast his net and waited

259

awhile. Then he hauled in the rope and dragged the net ashore, and in it was a heavy chest with a padlock on it. The caliph examined the chest and found it to be very heavy. So he gave the fisherman two hundred dinars and sent him about his business.

In the meantime, Ja'afar and Masrur carried the chest to the palace, set it down, and lit some candles. Then the caliph told them to break it open, and they found a basket of palm leaves tied with red worsted. After cutting this open, they saw a piece of carpet, which they lifted out of the chest. Then they saw a woman's mantilla folded in four, which they also pulled out, and at the bottom of the chest they came upon a young lady, fair as a silver ingot, who had been slain and cut into nineteen pieces. When the caliph gazed upon her, he cried out, "Alas!" and soon tears ran down his cheeks as he turned to Ja'afar and said, "Can we allow folk to be murdered in my realm and cast into the river? This woman is our burden and responsibility! By Allah, we must avenge her, find the murderer, and make him die the worst of deaths!" After a brief pause, he added, "Now, as surely as we are descended from the sons of Abbas, if you don't bring me the murderer so I can bring him to justice, I'll hang you at the gate of my palace, you and forty of your kith and kin by your side."

Since the caliph was furious and fuming, Ja'afar requested three days to find the murderer, and the caliph granted his request. So Ja'afar returned to his own house, full of sorrow, and said to himself, "How shall I find the man who murdered this damsel? If I bring the caliph someone other than the murderer, the Lord will hold it against me. In truth, I don't know what to do."

Ja'afar stayed in his house for three days, and on the fourth the caliph sent one of the chamberlains for him, and when Ja'afar arrived before him, he asked, "Where is the murderer of the damsel?"

"Oh, Commander of the Faithful," Ja'afar replied, "I haven't been able to find the murderer. It's never been my duty to track down murderers, and I don't even know where to begin looking."

The caliph was furious at his answer and ordered his executioners to hang his minister in front of the palace gate. Before the hanging was to take place, however, he commanded that a crier be sent to announce the execution throughout the streets of Baghdad.

The people flocked from all quarters of the city to witness the hanging of Ja'afar and his kinsmen, even though they did not know why they were to be hung. After the gallows were erected, Ja'afar and the others were made to stand underneath to be ready for the execution, but while every eye looked for the caliph's signal and the crowd wept for Ja'afar and his cousins, a young man suddenly appeared and began pushing his way through the people until he stood immediately before the vizier. He had a fair face and dressed neatly and looked like the radiant moon with bright black eyes, white brow, rosy cheeks, fluff instead of a beard, and a mole like a grain of ambergris. As the vizier looked at him, the young man said, "I've come to rescue you, my lord, for I am the man who slew the woman you found in the chest! So hang me, and let justice be done in her name!"

When Ja'afar heard the youth's confession, he rejoiced, but he was sorry for the handsome young man. Just then, while they were still talking, another man, much older, pushed forward through the crowd of people until he came to Ja'afar and the youth. After saluting the vizier, he said, "Don't believe the words of this young man, my lord! I am the one who murdered the damsel. So take her vengeance out on me. I demand this before Almighty Allah!"

"Oh vizier," the youth intervened, "this old man has become senile, and he doesn't know what he's saying. I'm the one who murdered her. So take her vengeance out on me!"

"My son," said the old man, "you're young and can still appreciate the joys of the world. I'm old and weary and have had enough of the world. I want to offer my life as a ransom for you and for the vizier and his cousins. No one murdered the damsel but me. So, by Allah, I want you to hang me right away! There's no life left in me now that hers is gone."

The vizier was astonished by this strange exchange of words, and he brought the young man and the old man before the caliph. After kissing the ground seven times, he said, "Oh Commander of the Faithful, I bring you the murderer of the damsel!"

"Where is he?" asked the caliph.

"The young man says that he's the murderer," replied the vizier, "but this old man says that he's lying, and maintains that he's the murderer. So I have brought you both of them, and they are now standing before you."

The caliph looked at the old man and the young man and asked, "Which of you killed the girl?"

The young man responded, "No one slew her but me."

The old man answered, "The truth is that I'm the murderer."

Then the caliph said to Ja'afar, "Take the two, and hang them both."

But Ja'afar replied, "It would be an injustice to do that, my lord, since one of them is certainly the murderer."

"By Allah," cried the youth, "I'm the one who slew the damsel," and he went on to describe the way she was murdered and the basket, the mantilla and the bit of carpet, and, in fact, all that the caliph had found with her.

So the caliph was sure that the young man was the murderer, and he was puzzled why he had killed the maiden. "Tell me," he said, "why have you confessed without the bastinado? What brought you here to surrender your life, and what made you say, 'Take her vengeance out on me'?"

"My lord," the youth answered, "this woman was my wife and the mother of my children. She was also my first cousin and the daughter of this old man here, my paternal uncle. When I married her, she was a virgin, and Allah blessed me with three male children by her. She loved me and served me, and I saw no evil in her, for I also loved her with a great deal of affection. Now on the first day of this month, she fell ill with a terrible sickness, and after I had the physicians attend her, she recovered but very slowly. When I wanted her to go to the Hammam bath, she said, 'There is something I long for before I go to the bath, and I have a tremendous longing for it.' 'You only need to ask,' I responded. 'What is it?' Then she said, 'I have a great craving for an apple, to smell it, and to bite a bit of it.' 'Oh,' I replied, 'Even if you had a thousand longings, I'd try to satisfy them all.' So I went straight into the city and looked for apples, but I couldn't find any. Even if they had cost a gold piece each, I would have bought them. Naturally, I was extremely disturbed by this and went home and said, 'By Allah, I haven't been able to find any.' She was most distressed by this, and since she was still very weak, her sickness increased that night, and I felt anxious and alarmed about her condition. As soon as morning dawned, I went out again and made the rounds of the gardens, one by one, but found no apples anywhere. At last I encountered an old gardener, who said to me, 'My son, this is a rare fruit in these parts and can only be found in the garden of the Commander of the Faithful at Bassorah, where the gardener keeps the apples for the caliph's table.' Troubled by my lack of success, I returned home, and my love for my wife moved me to undertake the journey to Bassorah. So I got ready and traveled two weeks back and forth and brought her three apples, which I bought from the gardener for three dinars. But when I went to my wife and set them before her, she did not take any pleasure in them and let them sit by her side, for her fever had increased, and her malady lasted ten days without abating. After that time, she began to recover her health. Therefore, I left my house and began buying and selling again at my shop. About midday a great ugly black slave, long as a lance and broad as a bench, passed by my shop holding one of the three apples and playing with it. 'Oh my good slave,' I said, 'tell me where you got that apple so that I can get one like it.' He laughed and answered, 'I got it from my mistress, for I had been absent for some time, and on my return I found her lying ill with three apples by her side, and she told me that her horned nitwit of a husband had made a journey to Bassorah and had bought them for three dinars. So I ate and drank with her and took this one from her.' When I heard these words from the slave, my lord, the world darkened before my eyes, and I stood up, locked up my shop, and went home beside myself with rage. When I looked for the apples and found only two of the three, I asked my wife, 'Where is the third apple?' Raising her head languidly, she answered, 'I have no idea.'" This reply convinced me that the slave had spoken the truth. So I took a knife, approached her from behind, and slit her throat without saying a word. Then I hewed off her head and chopped her limbs into pieces. After wrapping her in her mantilla and a rag of carpet, I hurriedly sewed up the whole, which I set in a chest, which I locked up tight. Next I loaded the chest on my mule, brought it to the Tigris, and threw it in with my own hands. When I returned to my house, I found my eldest son crying, even though he didn't know what I had done to his mother. 'Why are you crying, my boy?' I asked him, and he answered, 'I took one of the three apples which were by my mommy and went down into the lane to play with my brothers, when all of a sudden a tall black slave snatched it from my hand and said, 'Where did you get this?' And I said, 'My father traveled to Bassorah for my mother, who was ill, and he bought it along with two other apples for three ducats.' He paid no attention to my words, and I repeatedly asked him to return the apple, but he cuffed me and kicked me and went off with it. I was afraid that my mother would give me a licking because of the apple. So, out of fear for her, I went with my brother outside the city and stayed there until evening came. And, truthfully, I'm afraid of her. So, please, Father, don't tell her anything about this, or it will make her more sick.' After I heard my son's story, I knew that the slave had slandered my wife and was sure that I had wrongfully slain her. So I wept profusely, and soon my uncle came, and I told him what had happened. He sat down by my side and wept with me, and we didn't stop weeping until midnight. We've been mourning for her these last five days, bemoaning her unjust death. If it weren't for the gratuitous lying of that slave, she'd still be alive today! So you now know how and why I killed her, and I beseech you, by the honor of your ancestors, kill me right away and let justice reign, for there is no life in me anyway after her death!"

The caliph was astounded by his words and said, "By Allah, this young man deserves to be pardoned. The only one I'll hang is that foul slave! It's the only way to do something which will comfort those who have suffered, and which will please the Almighty."

And Scheherazade noticed that dawn was approaching and stopped telling her story. When the next night arrived, however, she received the king's permission to continue her tale and said,

Then the caliph turned to Ja'afar and said, "Fetch me the accursed slave, who was the sole cause of this catastrophe, and if you don't bring him to me within three days, you'll be slain in his stead."

So Ja'afar went away and began weeping, "I've already encountered death and survived, but if you fill a pitcher to the brim too often, it's bound to crack. Skill and cunning are no help here, and only He who saved my life the first time can save me again. By Allah, I won't leave my house during the next three days, and I'll let Him expose the truth as He desires." So Ja'afar stayed in his house for three days, and on the fourth day he summoned the kazi and legal witnesses, made his last will and testament, and began weeping as he took leave of his children. Soon a messenger from the caliph arrived and said to him, "The Commander of the Faithful is furious beyond belief, and he wants you to come to his palace right away. Moreover, he swears that you're sure to hang if you don't produce the slave who caused the damsel's murder."

When Ja'afar heard this, he wept even more, and his children, slaves, and friends wept with him. After he said adieu to everyone except his youngest daughter, he proceeded to bid farewell to her alone, for he loved this little one, who was a beautiful child, more than all his other children. When he pressed her to his breast and kissed her, he felt something round inside the bosom of her dress and asked her, "What are you carrying in your bosom, my dear?"

"It's an apple with the name of our lord the caliph written on it," she replied. "Rayhan, our slave, brought it to me four days ago and gave it to me, but only after I paid him two dinars for it."

When Ja'afar heard her speak of the slave and the apple, he was very happy and put his hand into the slit of his daughter's dress and drew out the apple. He recognized it immediately and cried with joy, "My trust in Allah is complete!" Then he ordered a servant to bring him the slave and said, "What a terrible thing you've done, Rayhan! Where did you get this apple?"

"By Allah, oh master," he replied, "it doesn't pay to tell lies, even if can get away with it once. Truth always pays. I didn't steal this apple from your palace, nor did I take it from the gardens of the Commander of the Faithful. The truth is that five days ago, as I was walking along one of the alleys of the city, I saw some little ones at play, and this apple was in the hand of one of them. So I snatched it from him and beat him, and he cried and said, 'Oh slave, this apple is my mother's, and she's ill. She told my father how she longed for an apple, and he traveled to Bassorah and bought her three apples for three gold pieces, and I took one of them to play with.' He wept again, but I paid no attention to what he said and brought it here, where my little lady bought it from me for two gold dinars. And this is the whole story."

When Ja'afar heard his words, he was astounded that the murder of the damsel and all the misery related to it could have been caused by his slave. He was sorry for the slave, with whom he had a good relationship, but he also rejoiced about his own escape from death. Then he took the slave's hand and led him to the caliph's palace, where he related the story from first to last, and the caliph was extremely astonished and then laughed until he fell on his back. Then he ordered that the story be recorded and made public among the people. But Ja'afar said, "You may find this adventure astonishing, Commander of the Faithful, but it is not as wondrous as the story of the Vizier Nur al-Din Ali of Egypt and his brother Shams al-Din Mohammed."

"What can be more marvelous than this adventure?" the caliph said. "Out with it!"

"My lord," Ja'afar answered, "I'll only tell it to you on the condition that you'll pardon my slave."

"If your story is indeed more wondrous than that of the three apples," the caliph said, "I'll grant you his blood, but if not, I'll definitely slay him."

So Ja'afar began in these words

The Tale of Nur al-Din Ali and His Son

In times gone by the land of Egypt was ruled by a generous and just sultan, one who loved the pious and the poor and who associated with the olema and learned men. Now, he had a vizier who was wise and experienced in the affairs and art of government. This minister, who was a very old man, had two sons like two moons, for no one had ever seen such handsome and graceful young men. The elder was called Shams al-Din Mohammed and the younger Nur al-Din Ali. Among the two, it was the younger who was more handsome and more pleasing, so that people heard about his fame in foreign countries and men flocked to Egypt just for the purpose of seeing him.

In the course of time their father, the vizier, died and was deeply missed and mourned by the sultan, who sent for his two sons, and after presenting them with robes of honor, he said to them, "Don't trouble yourselves, for you shall both replace your father and be joint ministers of Egypt."

Upon hearing this they rejoiced, kissed the ground before him, and performed the ceremonial mourning for their father one whole month. After that time was over, they became viziers, and their father's office passed into their hands, with each doing his duty for a week at a time. They lived under the same roof, and their word was one. Whenever the sultan desired to travel, they took turns attending him.

Now, it happened one night that the sultan decided to set out on a journey the next morning, and the elder, whose turn it was to accompany him, was sitting and conversing with his brother and said to him, "My brother, it's my wish that we both marry two sisters, and sleep with them on the same night, and they shall conceive on their wedding nights and bear children to us on the same day. And by Allah's will, your wife will bear you a son, and my wife will bear me a daughter. Then we'll wed them to each other, for they will be cousins."

"What dowry will you require from my son for your daughter?" Nur al-Din asked.

"I shall take three thousand dinars, three pleasure gardens, and three farms," said Shams al-Din. "It would not be fitting if the youth agreed to take less than this."

When Nur al-Din heard this demand, he replied, "Is this the kind of dowry that you would impose on my son? Don't you realize that we are brothers and both, by Allah's grace, vizers and equal in office? It's really your duty to offer your daughter to my son without a marriage settlement. Or, if one is necessary, then it should be nominal or a public gesture of some kind. Indeed, you know that the male is more valuable than the female, and our memory will be preserved by my son, not by your daughter."

"But what is she to have?" asked Shams al-Din.

"We won't be remembered among the lords of the earth through her," Nur a-Din stated. "But I see you'd like to treat me according to the saying—if you want to bluff off a buyer, keep asking him for a higher price. Or do as a man did who needed something and went to a friend for help and was answered, 'You're welcome to it, but come tomorrow and I'll give you what you need.' Whereupon the other replied in verse:

"When he who is asked a favor says 'tomorrow,'
The wise man knows 'tis vain to beg or borrow."

"Basta!" said Shams al-Din. "I see that you don't respect me, since you're placing more value on your son than on my daughter. And it's plain to see that you lack manners and understanding. Let me remind you, as your elder brother, that I decided to let you share the vizier's office out of pity, not wishing to mortify you, so that you could help me as a kind of assistant. But, by Allah, since you talk this way, I'll never marry my daughter to your son. Never, not for her weight in gold!"

When Nur al-Din heard his brother's words, he became angry and said, "And I, too, will never, never marry my son to your daughter, even if it would mean my death!"

Shams al-Din replied, "I wouldn't accept him as a husband, since he isn't even worth the tip of her toenail!

If I weren't about to travel, I would make an example of you. However, when I return, I'll show you how I can assert my dignity and vindicate my honor. But let Allah's will be done."

When Nur al-Din heard all this from his brother, he became furious and lost his head, but he hid what he felt and held his peace. The brothers spent the night far apart from one another, each fuming with anger at the other.

As soon as dawn arrived, the sultan journeyed forth in state and crossed over from Cairo to Jizah and headed for the Pyramids, accompanied by the vizier Shams al-Din, for it was his turn of duty. Meanwhile his brother, Nur al-Din, who had spent the night in rage, rose with the light and said the dawn prayer. Then he went to his treasury, took a small pair of saddlebags, and filled them with gold. All the while he recalled his brother's threats and the contempt that his brother had shown him, and he said to himself, "Travel, and you'll find new friends to replace the old ones left behind. There's no honor in staying at home." So he ordered one of his pages to saddle his Nubian mule. Now she was a dapple-gray mule with ears like reed pens and legs like columns and a back high and strong as a dome built on pillars. Her saddle was made of gold cloth and her stirrups of Indian steel. Indeed, she had trappings that could serve the Chosroës, and she was like a bride adorned for her wedding night. Moreover, Nur al-Din ordered a piece of silk to be laid on her back for a seat along with a prayer carpet, under which were his saddlebags. When this was done, he said to his pages and slaves, "I intend to go on a small trip outside the city on the road to Kalyub. I'll spend three nights away, and I don't want any of you to follow me, for there is something troubling my heart."

Then he took some provisions for the journey, mounted the mule in haste, and set out from Cairo into the open and wild countryside around it. About noon he reached the city of Bilbay, where he dismounted and stayed awhile to rest himself and his mule. After eating some of his victuals, he bought all that he needed for himself and his mule and continued on his journey. Toward nightfall he entered a town called Sa'adiyah, where he dismounted and ate some of his food. Then he spread his strip of silk on the sand and set the saddlebags under his head and slept in the open air, for he was still filled with anger. When morning arrived, he mounted and rode onward until he reached the Holy City of Jerusalem, and from there he went to Aleppo, where he dismounted at one of the caravan stops and stayed three days to rest himself and the mule and taste the air.

Determined to travel afar, he set out again, wandering without knowing where he was going. After having joined a group of couriers, he kept traveling until he reached Bassorah and did not even know what the place was. It was pitch-black when he arrived at the khan, so he spread out his prayer carpet, took down the saddlebags from the back of the mule, and told the doorkeeper to walk her about, and the porter did as he was requested to do.

Now it so happened that the vizier of Bassorah, a very old man, was sitting at the lattice window of his mansion opposite the khan, and he saw the porter walking the mule up and down. He was struck by her priceless trappings and thought her a nice beast suited for viziers or even for royalty. The more he looked, the more he was perplexed, and he finally said to one of his pages, "Bring me the porter over there."

The page went and returned with the porter, who kissed the ground, and the minister asked him, "Who is the owner of that mule you're walking, and what kind of man is he?"

"My lord," he answered, "the owner of this mule is a handsome young man, very pleasant but also grave and dignified. Undoubtedly he is one of the sons of the merchants."

When the vizier heard the porter's words, he arose right away, mounted his horse, rode over to the khan, and entered it to see Nur al-Din. As the minister advanced toward him, Nur al-Din stood up and greeted him. The vizier welcomed him to Bassorah, embraced him, made him sit by his side, and asked, "My son, where have you come from, and what are you doing here?"

"My lord," Nuir al-Din replied, "I've come from Cairo, where my father was the vizier, but he has died," and he continued to inform him of all that had happened to him from beginning to end, whereupon he added, "And now

I'm determined never to return home until I have seen all the cities and countries of the world."

When the vizier heard this, he said to him, "My son, don't let yourself be carried away by your emotions, or you'll become your own worst enemy. It makes no sense to wander aimlessly. Many regions are just wastelands, and I fear that fortune may turn against you." Then he had the saddlebags, the silk, and the prayer carpets loaded on the mule and brought Nur al-Din to his own house, where he lodged him in a pleasant place, treated him honorably, and indulged him, for he was extremely fond of him. After a while the vizier said to him, "Here I am, a man rich in years, but I have no sons. Fortunately, Allah has blessed me with a daughter who can match you in her beauty. Now, I've rejected all her suitors, men of rank and substance, but my affection for you has become deep, and I would like you to become her husband. If you accept, I'll go with you to the sultan of Bassorah and tell him that you are my nephew, the son of my brother. I'll arrange it so that you will be appointed vizier in my place so that I may keep the house, for I am stricken in years and have become weary."

When Nur al-Din heard the vizier's words, he bowed his head in modesty and said, "As you wish."

At this the vizier rejoiced and ordered his servants to prepare a feast and decorate the great assembly hall in which they were accustomed to celebrate the marriages of emirs and nobles. Then he assembled the notables of the realm, the merchants of Bassorah, and his friends, and when they all stood before him, he said, "I had a brother who was a vizier in the land of Egypt, and Allah Almighty blessed him with two sons, while to me, as you all well know, He gave a daughter. My brother requested that I wed my daughter to one of his sons, and I agreed. Since my daughter is now of the age to marry, he sent me one of his sons, the young man now present, to whom I intend to marry her. So I'm drawing up the contract and celebrating the night of unveiling with due ceremony, for he is nearer and dearer to me than a stranger. After the wedding, if it pleases him, he will dwell with me, or if he prefers, I will enable him to travel with his wife to his father's home."

Upon hearing this, everyone rejoiced and was pleased

by the vizier's choice of the bridegroom. Consequently, the vizier sent for the kazi and legal witnesses, and they wrote out the marriage contract, after which the slaves sprayed the guests with incense and served them with sherbet. Then they sprinkled them with rose water, and the people went their ways. Afterward the vizier ordered his servants to take Nur al-Din to the Hammam bath and sent him a suit of his own best raiment along with napkins, towels, bowls, perfume burners, and everything else that was necessary. When Nir al-Din came out of the bath and donned the garments, he was just like the full moon on the fourteenth night. Thereupon he mounted his mule and went straight to the vizier's palace, where he dismounted and went in to see the minister and kissed his hands, and the vizier bade him welcome.

And Scheherazade noticed that dawn was approaching and stopped telling her story. When the next night arrived, however, she received the king's permission to continue her tale and said,

After welcoming him, the vizier said, "Arise and go and see your wife tonight. Tomorrow I'll bring you to the sultan, and I pray that Allah will bless you and look after your welfare."

So Nur al-Din left him and went to his wife, the vizier's daughter. So much for Nur al-Din at present.

In the meantime, his elder brother, Shams al-Din, was absent with the sultan a long time, and when he returned from his journey, he did not find his brother, and he asked his servants and slaves where he was.

"On the day of your departure with the sultan," they replied, "your brother had his mule groomed and outfitted as if for a state procession. Then he mounted it and told us that he was going toward Kalyub and would be absent three days, for his heart was disturbed, and he didn't want any one of us to follow him. Well, ever since he left, we've had no news of him."

Shams al-Din was greatly troubled by the sudden disappearance of his brother and grieved at his loss. "This is only because I chided and upbraided him the night before my departure with the sultan," he said to himself.

"Most likely his feelings were hurt, and he decided to go off traveling, but I must send after him."

Then he went to the sultan and acquainted him with what had happened. Next he wrote letters and sent dispatches carried by couriers to his deputies in every province. But during the twenty days of Shams al-Din's absence, Nur al-Din had traveled far and had reached Bassorah. So after a diligent search the messengers failed to come up with any news of him and returned to Cairo. As a result, Shams al-Din despaired of finding his brother and said, "In truth, I exceeded the bounds of propriety in regard to the marriage of our children. If only I had not done that! All this comes from my carelessness and stupidity!"

Soon after this he sought the hand of the daughter of a Cairo merchant, drew up the marriage contract, and celebrated a splendid wedding with her. And so it happened that he slept with his wife on the very same night that Nur al-Din also slept with his wife, the daughter of the vizier of Bassorah. Of course, all this was in accordance with the will of Almighty Allah so that He might determine the destiny of His creatures. Furthermore, everything turned out as the brothers had said it would, for their two wives became pregnant by them on the same night, and both gave birth on the same day: the wife of Shams al-Din, vizier of Egypt, had a daughter, whose beauty was unmatched in Cairo; the wife of Nur al-Din had a handsome son, whose looks were incomparable in his time. They named the boy Badar al-Din Hasan, and his grandfather, the vizier of Bassorah, rejoiced when he was born, and on the seventh day after his birth, he held a banquet with entertainment that would have befitted the birth of a prince's son. Then he took Nur al-Din to the sultan, and his son-in-law kissed the ground in homage. In response, the sultan rose up to honor them and asked the vizier who the young man was. And the minister answered, "This is my brother's son," and related his tale from first to last.

"Well, how is it that he's your nephew," the sultan asked, "and we've never heard of him before this?"

"My lord," the vizier responded, "I had a brother who was a vizier in the land of Egypt, and he died and left behind two sons. The eldest took his father's place, and

the younger, whom you see before you, came to me, for
I had sworn that I would not marry my daughter to
anyone but him. So, when he came, I married her to
him. Now he is young, and I am old. My hearing has
become weak, and my judgment is easily fooled. Therefore, I would like to request, my lord, that you let him
take my place, for he is my brother's son and my daughter's wife. Moreover, he is fit to become a vizier, since he
is a wise and cunning young man."

The sultan looked at Nur al-Din and took a liking to
him. So he established him in the office of the vizier, and
he presented him with a splendid robe of honor and a
mule from his private stables. In addition, he gave him a
salary, stipends, and supplies. Nur al-Din kissed the sultan's hand and went home with his father-in-law in a
most joyous mood.

"All this follows on the heels of the boy Hasan's birth!"
he said.

The next day he presented himself before the sultan
and kissed the ground. Then the sultan asked him to sit
down in the vizier's seat. So he sat down and began to
address the business of his office. He went into the cases
of the lieges and their suits, as is the custom of the
ministers, while the sultan watched him and admired his
wit, good sense, judgment, and insight. Indeed, he became deeply fond of him and took him into his confi-
dence. When the divan was dismissed, Nur al-Din returned
to his house and related what had happened to his father-
in-law, who rejoiced. From then on Nur al-Din continued
to serve as vizier, and the sultan sought his company day
and night. Moreover, he increased his stipends and supplies until Nur al-Din's means were ample, and he became the owner of ships that made trading voyages at his
command. He also possessed numerous mamelukes and
blackamoor slaves, and he had many estates developed
and set up Persian wheels and planted gardens. When his
son, Hasan, was four, the old vizier died, and Nur al-Din
arranged for a sumptuous funeral ceremony for his father-
in-law before he was laid to dust. Then he concerned
himself with the education of his son, and when the
strong and healthy boy turned seven, he brought him a
fakih, a doctor of law and religion, to teach him in his
own house. Indeed, he charged the fakih to give him a

good education and instruct him in politeness and good manners. So the tutor made the boy read and retain all kinds of useful knowledge as well as learn the Koran by heart. At the same time he continued to grow handsome and strong.

Over the years the professor brought him up in his father's palace teaching him reading, writing, and ciphering along with theology and belles lettres. Indeed, he never left the house and grounds, since he was fully occupied there. Then, on a certain day, his father clad him in his best clothes, mounted him on one of the finest mules, and went with him to the sultan. When the sultan gazed at Badar al-Din Hasan, he marveled at how handsome he was and took a great liking to him. As for the people in the city, they were so struck by his handsome features when he first passed before them that they sat down on the road to wait for his return so that they might gaze again at his graceful and lovely features. The sultan treated the lad with special favor and said to his father, "Oh vizier, you must bring him to me every day."

"As you wish," replied Nur al-Din.

Then the vizier returned home with his son and continued to bring him to court until he reached the age of twenty. At that time his father became sick and, after sending for Badar al-Din Hasan, he said, "I want you to know, my son, that the world of the present is but a house of mortality, while that of the future is a house of eternity. Before I die, I want to bequeath certain tasks to you, and I want you to pay attention to what I say and take my words to heart." Then he gave him last instructions about the best way to deal with his neighbors and his affairs. After all was said, he recalled his brother, his home, and his native land and wept over his separation from those he had first loved. As he wiped away his tears, he turned to his son and said to him, "Before I proceed to my last requests and commands, I want you to know that I have a brother, your uncle, who is called Shams al-Din, the vizier of Cairo. Many years ago I left him against his will. Now, take a sheet of paper and write down what I tell you."

Badar al-Din took a sheet of paper and did as his father requested, and he wrote down the full account of what had happened to his father from the day of his dispute with his brother twenty years ago to the very present. At the end, Nur al-Din added, "And this is written at my dictation, and may Almighty Allah be with him when I am gone!" Then he signed the paper, folded it, sealed it, and said, "My son, guard this paper with utmost care, for it will enable you to establish your origin, rank, and lineage, and if anything adverse happens to you, set out for Cairo, ask for your uncle, and show him this paper. Then tell him that I died a stranger far from my own people and full of yearning to see him and them."

So Badar al-Din Hasan took the document, and after wrapping it up in a piece of waxed cloth, he sewed it like a talisman between the inner and outer cloth of his skullcap and wound his light turban around it. And he began to weep about his father and his untimely separation from him, for he was but a young man. Then Nur al-Din lapsed into a swoon that prefigured his death. Soon, however, he recovered a little and said, "Oh Hasan, my son, listen now to my five last commands. The first is that you should not be overly intimate with anyone or too familiar, otherwise you will not be safe from his mischief. Security lies in seclusion of thought and a certain distance from the company of your compatriots. The second command is that you should not deal harshly with anyone, otherwise fortune might deal harshly with you. In this world fortune is with you one day and against you the next. All worldly goods are but a loan to be repaid. The third command is that you should learn to be silent in society, and let the faults of others make you aware of your own faults. Safety dwells in silence. The fourth command, my son, is that you should be aware of indulging in too much wine, for wine is the head of all obstinance and a fine solvent of human brains. So shun, and again I say, shun mixing strong liquor. The fifth command is that you should take good care of your wealth, and if you do so, it will take good care of you. Guard your money, and it will guard you. Do not waste your capital, otherwise you might be forced to go begging from the meanest of mankind. Save your dirhams, and consider them the best salve for the wounds of the world."

Nur al-Din continued to advise his son in this way until his hour came, and sighing one last sob, he died. Then the voice of mourning rose high in his house, and the sultan and all the nobles grieved for him and buried him. However, his son did not stop lamenting his loss for two months, during which time he never mounted a horse, attended the divan, or presented himself before the sultan. At last the sultan became so furious with him that he replaced him as vizier with one of his chamberlains and gave orders to seize and set seals on all Nur al-Din's houses, goods, and domains. So the new vizier went forth with a mighty posse of chamberlains, courtiers, watchmen, and a host of idlers to carry out the sultan's command and to seize Badar al-Din Hasan and bring him before the sultan, who would deal with him as he deemed fit.

Now, among the crowd of followers was a mameluke of the deceased vizier, and when he heard the sultan's order, he rode his horse full-speed to the house of Badar al-Din Hasan, for he could not endure to see the degradation of his old master's son. The mameluke found Badar al-Din Hasan sitting at the gate with his head hung down, mourning the loss of his father, as was his custom. So he dismounted, kissed his hand, and said, "My lord, hurry and get away before everything's laid to waste!"

When Hasan heard this, he trembled and asked, "What's the matter?"

"The sultan is angry at you," the man said, "and he's issued a warrant for your arrest. The evildoers are hard on my heels. So flee for your life!"

Upon hearing these words, Hasan's heart was ignited, his rosy cheeks turned pale, and he asked the slave, "Is there any time for me to get some of my things from the house that I may need during my exile?"

But the slave replied, "My lord, get up at once and save yourself! Leave this house while there's still time!"

So Badar al-Din covered his head with the skirt of his garment and went forth on foot until he stood outside the city where he heard the people saying, "The sultan's sent his new vizier to the house of the old one to seal his property and to seize his son, Badar al-Din Hasan, and bring him to the palace, where he's to be put to death."

"Alas! Such a handsome and lovely man!" they cried.

When he heard this, he fled at hazard and did not stop running until destiny drove him to the cemetery where his father was buried. So he entered and walked among the graves until he reached his father's sepulcher, where he sat down and let the skirt of his long robe fall from his head. While he was sitting by his father's tomb, a Jew suddenly came toward him, and he seemed to be a shroff with a pair of saddlebags containing a great deal of gold. After the Jew stopped and kissed his hand, he said, "Where are you going, my lord? It's late in the day. Indeed, you are lightly clad, and I read signs of trouble in your face."

"I had been asleep this past hour," answered Hasan, "when my father appeared to me and chided me for not having visited his tomb. So I awoke trembling and came straight here. Otherwise, the day would have gone by without my having visited him, and this would have been very grievous to me."

"Oh my lord," the Jew replied, "your father had many merchantmen at sea, and since some of them are now due to arrive, I would like to buy the cargo of the first ship that comes into port with this thousand dinars of gold."

"You have my consent," said Hasan, whereupon the Jew took out a bag full of gold and counted out a thousand sequins, which he gave to Hasan, the son of the vizier, and said, "Write a bill of sale for me and seal it."

So Hasan took a pen and paper and wrote these words in duplicate: "The writer, Hasan Badar al-Din, son of Vizier Nur al-Din, has sold to Isaac the Jew all the cargo of the first of his father's ships that comes into port for a thousand dinars, and he has received the payment for the goods in advance." And after the Jew took one copy, he put it into his pouch and went away. But Hasan began weeping as he thought of the dignity and prosperity that had once been his. Soon night fell, and he leaned his head against his father's grave and was overcome by sleep. He continued to slumber until the moon rose and his head slipped from the tomb so that he lay on his back with his limbs outstretched and his face shining bright in the moonlight. Now the cemetery was haunted day and night by jinnees who were of the true believers, and soon a jinniyah came out and saw Hasan asleep. She marveled at how handsome he was and cried, "Glory to God! This youth can be none other than one of the Wuldan of

Paradise." Then she flew high into the air, as was her custom, and she met an ifrit, who was also flying about. After he greeted her, she asked him, "Where are you coming from?"

"From Cairo," he replied.

"Do you want to come with me and gaze upon the beauty of a youth who is sleeping in that cemetery down there?" she inquired.

"Yes," he responded.

And so they flew until they landed at the tomb, where she showed him Hasan and remarked, "Did you ever in your born days see something like this?"

The jinnee looked at him and exclaimed, "Praise be to Him that has no equal! But, my sister, shall I tell you what I've seen this day?"

"What's that?" she replied.

"I have seen the counterpart of this youth in the land of Egypt," he said. "She is the daughter of the Vizier Shams al-Din, and she's a model of beauty and loveliness. When she reached the age of nineteen, the sultan of Egypt heard about her, and after sending for her father, he said to him, 'Hear me, oh vizier, I've been told that you have a daughter, and I want to request her hand in marriage.' The vizier replied, 'My lord, please accept my excuses and have compassion with me, for you know that my brother, who was my partner, disappeared from us many years ago, and we don't know where he is. He departed because of a quarrel we had while we were sitting together and talking of wives and children to come. Indeed, we had some sharp words with one another, and he went off extremely angry at me. But I swore that I would marry my daughter to no one but his son, and I took this oath on the day that my daughter was born nineteen years ago. Now, recently I've learned that my brother died at Bassorah, where he had married the daughter of the vizier, and she had given birth to a son. Consequently, I won't and can't marry my daughter to anyone but him in memory of my brother. I recorded the date of my marriage and the conception of my wife and the birth of my daughter, and from her horoscope I've found that her name is linked with that of her cousin. May I also remind my lord that he has the pick of numerous damsels in his kingdom.' Upon hearing his vizier's answer, the king became extremely furious and cried, 'When the likes of me asks for a damsel in marriage from the likes of you, it must be considered an honor! Yet you reject me and put me off with insipid excuses! Now by my life I intend to marry her to the most vile of my men to spite you!' In the palace was a horsegroom, a gobbo, with a hump on his breast and a hunch to his back, and the sultan sent for him and had him betrothed to the daughter of the vizier against his will. Then he arranged for a spectacular wedding procession for him. The hunchback is to sleep with his bride this very night. I have just now flown from Cairo, where I left the hunchback at the door of the Hammam bath among the sultan's white slaves, who were waving lit torches about him. As for the minister's daughter, she is sitting among her nurses and attendants, weeping and wailing, for they have forbidden her father to come near her. Never have I seen, my sister, a more hideous creature than this hunchback, while the young lady looks just like this young man. Indeed, she is even fairer than he."

And Scheherazade noticed that dawn was approaching and stopped telling her story. When the next night arrived, however, she received the king's permission to continue her tale and said,

After the jinnee had told the jinniyah how the sultan had caused the wedding contract to be drawn up between the hunchbacked groom and the lovely young lady, who was heartbroken out of sorrow, and how she was the fairest of Allah's creatures and even more beautiful than this youth, the jinniyah exclaimed, "You're lying! There's no one as handsome as this youth!"

But the ifrit insisted that he was telling the truth and added, "By Allah, this damsel is definitely fairer than this youth. Nevertheless, he's the only one who deserves her, for they resemble each other like brother and sister or at least like cousins. In any case, she's wasted on that hunchback!"

"Brother, I have an idea!" the jinniyah replied. "Let's lift him up and carry him to Cairo so that we can compare him with the damsel and determine which of the two is the fairer."

"Your idea is a good one," he answered. "This way we'll get right to the bottom of the matter, and I myself will carry him." So he raised Hasan from the ground and flew with him like a bird soaring through the air while the jinniyah kept close by his side at equal speed. Finally, they landed with him in Cairo, set him down on a stone bench, and woke him. Gradually he realized that he was no longer at his father's tomb in Bassorah, and after looking right and left he saw that he was in a strange place. Indeed, he would have cried out, but the ifrit gave him a cuff which persuaded him to keep quiet. Then he brought Hasan rich raiment with which he clothed him, and after giving him a lighted torch, he said, "I want you to know that I've brought you here with the intention of doing you a good turn for the love of Allah. So take this torch and mix with the people at the Hammam door. Then walk on with them without stopping until you reach the house of the wedding festivities. Then you're to go boldly forward and enter the great salon. Don't be afraid of anyone, but take a place at the right of the hunchback bridegroom. Whenever any of the nurses, maids, or singing girls come up to you, put your hand into your pocket, which you will find filled with gold. Take the gold out and throw it to them. You don't have to worry about losing your money, for your pouch will remain full. Give liberally and fear nothing, but place your trust in Him who created you, for this is not your own strength but that of Almighty Allah."

When Badar al-Din Hasan heard the ifrit's words, he said to himself, "If only I knew what all this means, and what's causing all this kindness!" Without further wondering, however, he began to mix with the people and moved on with the bridal procession until he came to the bath, where he found the hunchback already on horseback. Then he pushed his way into the crowd, and he was truthfully a handsome specimen of a man, dressed in the finest apparel with tarbush, turban, and a long-sleeved robe lined with gold. Whenever the singing girls stopped to receive money from people, he put his hand into his pocket, took out a handful of gold, and threw it on the tambourine until he filled it with gold pieces. The singers were amazed by his generosity, and the people were astounded by his handsome features, grace, and splendid

dress. Now Hasan continued doing this until he reached
the mansion of the vizier, who was his uncle. There the
chamberlains drove the people back and forbade them to
go any further. But the singing girls and maids said, "By
Allah, we won't enter unless this young man is allowed to
enter with us, for he has given us a long life with his
generosity, and we won't display the bride unless he is
present."

Consequently, Hasan was allowed to enter the bridal
hall with them, and they made him sit down, defying the
evil glances of the hunchbacked groom. The wives of the
nobles, viziers, chamberlains, and courtiers stood in a
double line, each holding a large torch. All of them wore
thin face veils, and the two rows extended from the
bride's throne to the head of the hall next to the chamber
from where the bride was to come forth. When the ladies
saw Badar al-Din Hasan and noticed his handsome features and lovely face that shone like the new moon, their
hearts went out to him, and the singing girls said to all
present, "That handsome man gave us nothing but gold
coins. So don't hesitate to serve him and comply with his
requests, no matter what he asks."

Then all the women crowded around Hasan with their
torches, gazed at his handsome features, and admired his
loveliness. One and all would gladly have lain on his
bosom an hour if not a year. They were so excited that
they let their veils fall from their faces and said, "Happy
is she who belongs to this youth or to whom he belongs!"
And they began cursing the crooked groom and the sultan, who was the cause of the hunchback's marriage to
the vizier's beautiful daughter. As often as they blessed
Badar al-Din Hasan, they damned the hunchback and
said, "Truly, this youth and no one else deserves our
bride. May Allah's curse land on the head of the hideous
hunchback and on the sultan who commanded the marriage!" Then the singing girls beat their tambourines and
announced the bride's appearance with joy.

The vizier's daughter entered with her attendants, who
had made her look her best, for they had put perfume
and incense on her and adorned her hair. Moreover, they
had dressed her in raiment and ornaments that suited the
mighty Chosroë kings. The most notable part of her
dress was a loose robe worn over her other garments: it

was embroidered with golden figures of wild beasts, birds whose eyes and beaks were made of gems, and claws of red rubies and green beryl. Her neck was graced with a necklace of Yamani work worth thousands of gold pieces, and the settings for the gems were great round jewels the like of which has never been owned by an emperor or Tobba king. Indeed, the bride resembled the full moon when at its fullest on the fourteenth night, and as she walked through the hall, she was like one of the houris of heaven!

Now the ladies surrounded her like clustering stars, and she shone among them like the moon when it eats up the clouds. When the bride emerged with her graceful swaying, Badar al-Din Hasan was sitting in full gaze of the people, and her hunchbacked bridegroom stood up to meet and receive her. However, she turned away from the horrid creature and walked forward until she stood before her cousin Hasan, the son of her uncle. There-upon, the people laughed, but when they saw her at-tracted toward Badar al-Din, they made a mighty clamor, and the singing women shouted their loudest. Then he put his hand into his pocket, and after pulling out a handful of gold, he cast it into their tambourines, causing the girls to rejoice and say, "If we had our wish, this bride would be yours."

Upon hearing this, he smiled, and the people came around him, torches in hand, while the gobbo bride-groom was left sitting alone like a tailless baboon. In-deed, every time they lit a candle for him, it went out willy-nilly. So he was left in darkness and silence and could see nothing but himself. When Badar al-Din saw the bridegroom sitting alone in the dark and all the wedding guests with their torches and candles crowding around himself, he was bewildered, but he also rejoiced and felt an inner delight. He longed to greet the bride and gazed intently at her face, which was radiant with light. Then her attendants took off her veil and displayed her in the first bridal dress, which was made of scarlet satin. As Hasan looked at her, his eyes were dazzled, and his wits, dazed. She moved to and fro, swaying with graceful gait, and she turned the heads of all the guests, women as well as men. Then her attendants changed that dress and displayed her in a robe of azure. When she reappeared, it was like the full moon when it rises over the horizon. Her hair was coal-black; her cheeks, delicately fair; and her white teeth showed through her sweet smiles as her firm breasts rose and crowned her most soft sides and round waist. Next they changed her garments for some other dress. Veiling her face in her lush hair, they loosened her lovelocks that were so dark and long that their darkness and length outdid the darkest nights. After that her attendants displayed her in the fourth bridal dress, and she came forward shining like the rising sun and swayed to and fro with lovely grace and supple ease like a gazelle. And she struck all hearts with the arrows of her eyelashes. In her fifth dress she appeared as the very light of loveliness, like a wand of waving willow. Her locks which hung like scorpions along her cheeks were curled, and her neck was bowed in blandishment, and her lips quivered as she walked. Following this dress her attendants adorned her with a green one, and she shamed the brown spear in her slender straightness. Her radiant face dimmed the brightest beams of the full moon, and she outdid the bending branches in gentle movement and flexile grace. Her loveliness exalted the beauties of the earth's four quarters, and she broke men's hearts with her remarkable appearance. Finally, her attendants displayed her in the seventh dress with a color between safflower and saffron. Thus they showed the bride in her seven dresses before Badar al-Din, completely neglecting the gobbo, who sat moping alone. And when she opened her eyes, she said, "Oh Allah, make this man my bridegroom, and deliver me from the evil of this hunchbacked groom."

As soon as this part of the ceremony had come to an end, the wedding guests were dismissed, and everyone left with the exception of Hasan and the hunchback. Meanwhile the servants led the bride into an inner room to change her garb and get her ready for the bridegroom. Thereupon, the hunchback came up to Badar al-Din Hasan and said, "My lord, you have cheered us tonight with your good company and overwhelmed us with your kindness and courtesy, but now it's time to go."

"In Allah's name," he replied, "so be it!"

He rose and went to the door, where he was met by the jinnee, who said, "Stay right here, Badar al-Din, and when the hunchback leaves to go to the toilet, you're to go immediately to the alcove and sit down. When the bride comes, you're to say to her, 'It's me who is your husband, for the king devised this trick because he was afraid of the evil eye, and he whom you saw is only a syce, a groom, one of our stablemen.' Then walk boldly up to her and unveil her face."

While Hasan was still talking with the ifrit, the groom suddenly left the hall and entered the toilet, where he sat down on the stool. No sooner had he done this than the jinnee came out of the water tank in the form of a mouse and began to squeak.

"What's the matter with you?" asked the hunchback.

But the mouse grew until it became a pitch-black cat and let forth a "Meow! Meow!" Then it grew more and more until it became a dog and barked, "Bow-wow! Bow-wow!"

When the hunchback saw this, he became frightened and exclaimed, "Get out of here, you evil spirit!"

But the dog grew and swelled until it became an ass that brayed and snorted in his face, "Heehaw! Heehaw!"

Thereupon the hunchback quaked and cried, "Help! People, help!"

But the ass grew and became as big as a buffalo and wailed and spoke with the voice of the sons of Adam, "Woe to you, you hunchback, you stinkard, you filthiest of grooms!"

Upon hearing this, the groom was seized with a colic, and he sat down on the toilet bowl in his clothes with his teeth chattering.

"Is the world so tiny," asked the ifrit, "that the only person you can find to marry is my lady love?" Since the hunchback did not respond, the jinnee continued, "Answer me, or you'll become dust!"

"By Allah," said the gobbo, "Oh King of the Buffaloes, this is not my fault! They forced me to wed her, and honestly I didn't know that she had a lover among the buffaloes. So now I repent, first before Allah and then before you."

"I swear to you," said the jinnee, "that if you leave this place or utter a word before sunrise, I'll surely wring your neck. When the sun rises, I want you to go your way and never return to this house again." After saying this, the ifrit took the gobbo and set him head downward and feet upward in the slit of the privy. Then he declared, "I'm going to leave you here, but I'll be on the lookout for you until sunrise, and if you stir before then, I'll grab you by the feet and bash out your brains against the wall. So watch out for your life!"

In the meantime, Badar al-Din had made his way to the alcove and was sitting there when the bride came in. She was attended by a very old woman, who stood at the door and said, "My lord, arise and take what God has given to you."

The old woman went away, and the bride, Sitt al-Husan, otherwise called the Lady of Beauty, entered the inner part of the alcove brokenhearted and saying to herself, "By Allah, I'll never abandon myself to him. No, not even if he were to take my life!" But as she came to the far end of the alcove, she saw Badar al-Din Hasan, and she said, "My dear, are you still sitting here? By Allah, I had been wishing that you were my bridegroom, or at very least, that you and the hunchbacked horse groom were partners and shared me."

"Oh beautiful lady," he replied, "why should the syce have you, and why should he share you?"

"Who *is* my husband, you or he?"

"Sitt al-Husan," he answered, "we have not done this for mere fun, but only as a trick to ward off the evil eye. You see, when the attendants, singers, and wedding guests saw your beauty being displayed to me, they became afraid of fascination, and your father hired the horse groom for ten dinars to take the evil eye off us. And now the hunchback has received his pay, he has gone his way."

When the Lady of Beauty heard these words, she smiled and laughed pleasantly. Then she whispered to him, "By Allah, you have quenched a fire that was torturing me, and now, my dark-haired darling, take me to you and press me against your chest." Then she stripped off her outer garment, and she threw open her chemise from the neck downward and showed her womb and the rondure of her hips. When Badar al-Din saw this glorious sight, his desires were aroused, and he got up, took off his clothes, wrapped the purse of gold that contained the thousand dinars from the Jew in his bag trousers, and laid them under the edge of the bed. Then he took off his turban, placed it on top of his clothes, and had nothing on except his skullcap and fine shirt of blue silk laced with gold. Thereupon, the Lady of Beauty embraced him, and he took her into his arms, set her legs around his waist, and aimed his cannon point-blank at the spot where it would batter down the bulwark of maidenhead and lay it to waste. And he found her a pearl unpierced and a filly unridden by men except himself. So he took her virginity and enjoyed her youth in his virility, and soon he withdrew sword from sheath. Then he returned to the fray right away, and when the battle and the siege were finished, there had been some fifteen assaults, and she conceived through him that very night. Afterward he placed his hand under her head, and she did the same, and they embraced and fell asleep in each other's arms.

As soon as the jinnee saw the two asleep, he said to the jinniyah, "Arise and slip under the youth, and let us carry him back to his place before dawn overtakes us, for day is near."

So she came forward and, after getting under him as he lay asleep, she lifted him, clad only in his fine blue shirt, and left the other garments under the bed. Once they were in the air, the jinnee joined them, and they kept flying until they realized that dawn was upon them, and they had only reached the halfway mark. Then Allah had his angelic host shoot the jinnee down with a shooting star, and he was consumed. But the jinniyah managed to escape, and she descended with Badar al-Din to the place where the jinnee was burned. After seeing what had happened to the jinnee, she decided not to carry Badar back to Bassorah, fearing that he might come to some harm.

Now, by the order of Him who determines all things, they arrived at Damascus in Syria, and the jinniyah set her burden down at one of the city gates and flew away. When the gates were opened, the people came forth and saw a handsome youth with no other clothes but his blue shirt of gold-embroidered silk and skullcap. He was lying on the ground drowned in sleep after his hard labor that night. So the people looked at him and said, "Oh lucky her who has spent the night with this young man! But he should have put on his garments afterward."

"They're a sorry lot, those sons of great families!"
someone said. "Most likely he came out of a tavern and
the wine went to his head. So he probably forgot where
he was heading and strayed until he came to the gate of
the city. Finding it shut, he lay down and went to bye-bye
land!"

While the people were bandying guesses about him,
the morning breeze suddenly blew upon Badar al-Din,
and raising his shirt to his middle, it revealed a stomach
and navel with something below it. His legs and thighs
were as clear as crystal and smooth as cream, and the
people cried, "By Allah, he's a pretty fellow!"

And as they cried out, Badar al-Din awoke and found
himself lying at a city gate with a crowd gathered around
him. Of course, he was greatly surprised by this and
asked, "Where am I, good people? Why have you gathered around me?"

"We found you lying here asleep during the call to
dawn prayer," they said, "and this is all we know. But
where did you spend last night?"

"By Allah, good people," he replied, "I spent last
night in Cairo."

"You've surely been eating hashish," said somebody.

"He's a fool," said another.

"He's a fathead," a third commented.

And a fourth asked him, "Are you out of your mind?
How can you spend the night in Cairo and wake in the
morning at the gate of Damascus?"

"By Allah, my good people," Hasan cried, "I'm not
lying to you. Truthfully, I spent last night in Cairo, and
before that, yesterday afternoon, I was in Bassorah."

"Well, well," remarked someone.

"Ho! Ho!" commented another.

"So! So!" said a third.

And a fourth exclaimed, "This young man is possessed
by the jinnees!"

So they clapped their hands at him and said to one
another, "Alas, such a pity, for he's so young. By Allah,
he's a madman, and madness has no respect of anyone,
no matter who the person is!"

Then they said to him, "Collect yourself, and be sensible! How could you have been in Bassorah yesterday and

in Cairo last night, and wake up in Damascus this morning?"

But he persisted, "Indeed, I was a bridegroom in Cairo last night."

"Perhaps you were dreaming and saw all this in your sleep," they replied.

So Hasan pondered this for a while and said, "By Allah, this was no dream. Nor does it seem to have been a vision. I'm certain I was in Cairo. They displayed the bride before me in the presence of a third person, the hunchback groom, who was sitting nearby. By Allah, my brothers, this was not a dream, and if it were a dream, where is the bag of gold I was carrying with me, and where are my turban, my robe, and my trousers?"

Then he rose and entered the city meandering through the streets and bazaar, while the people followed him and jeered at him, "Madman! Madman!" until he was beside himself with rage and took refuge in a cook's shop. Now this cook was one of those who had been a trifle too cunning in his youth, that is, he was a rogue and a thief, but Allah had made him repent and turn from his evil ways. This is why he had opened a shop, and all the people of Damascus lived in fear of him because he could still be bold and mischievous. Consequently, when the crowd saw the youth enter his shop, they became afraid and went their ways. The cook looked at Badar al-Din, and, noting how handsome he was, he immediately took a great liking to him and asked, "Where have you come from, young man? Tell me your tale at once."

So Hasan told him all that had happened to him from beginning to end, and the cook said, "You undoubtedly realize how marvelous your story is. Therefore, I advise you to conceal what has happened to you until Allah takes care of the evil forces working against you. In the meantime, since I have no children, I'll adopt you."

"As you wish, uncle," Badar al-Din replied.

Accordingly, the cook went to the bazaar and bought a fine suit of clothes for him and made him put it on. Then he brought him to the kazi and formally declared that he was his son. So Badar al-Din Hasan became known in Damascus as the cook's son, and he stayed there for quite a long time.

With regard to his cousin, the Lady of Beauty, she

awoke in the morning and missed Badar al-Din Hasan, but she thought that he had gone to the privy and expected him to return in an hour or so. However, it was her father, Shams al-Din Mohammed, vizier of Egypt, who came to see her. Now, he was rather upset because of the harsh way that the sultan had treated him by forcing him to marry his daughter to the lowest of the sultan's menials, who, to boot, was a hunchback. Indeed, he said to himself, "I'll slay this daughter of mine if she yielded to that lump of a groom of her own free will." So he went to the door of the bride's private chamber and said, "Ho! Sitt al-Husan!"

She answered, "Here I am! Here I am, my lord!" and she came out unsteadily after the pains and pleasures of the night. She kissed her father's hands, her beautiful face glowing even brighter than usual for having lain in the arms of her cousin. When her father saw her in such condition, he asked, "You should be cursed for rejoicing after having slept with that horse groom!"

And Sitt al-Husan smiled sweetly and answered, "By Allah, don't mock me. I had enough of that yesterday when people laughed at me and joined me with that groom fellow, who is not even fit to carry my husband's shoes or slippers! My lord, never in my life have I spent a night so sweet as last night. So, don't mock me by reminding me of the gobbo!"

When her father heard her words, he was filled with anger, and his eyes glared at her so that only the whites showed, and he cried, "Shame upon you! What are you saying? It was the hunchbacked groom who spent the night with you!"

"By Allah," replied the Lady of Beauty, "don't trouble me about the gobbo. May Allah damn his father! And stop jesting with me! You know yourself that this groom was only hired for ten dinars and went his way after taking his wages. As for me, I entered the bridal chamber after the singers had displayed me to my true bridegroom, and I found him sitting there. It was the same young man who had crossed their hands with gold and had turned all the paupers at the wedding into rich people. And I spent the night on the breast of this lovely man, a most lively darling with his black eyes and full eyebrows."

When her father heard these words, the light before his face became night, and he cried out, "You whore! What's this you're telling me? Where are your brains?"

"Father," she responded, "you're breaking my heart! Why are you being so hard on me? Indeed, my husband, who took my virginity, has just gone to the privy, and I feel that he's made me pregnant."

The vizier was astounded by these words. So he turned from the door and went into the privy, where he found the hunchbacked horse groom with his head in the hole and his heels in the air. Confused by this sight, he said to himself, "Why it's none other than that rascal the hunchback!" So he called to him, "Ho, hunchback!"

The hunchback responded with a murmur and gulp, thinking it was the jinnee who was speaking to him. Therefore, the vizier shouted at him and said, "Speak out, or I'll cut off your head with this sword!"

"By Allah, oh Sheikh of the Jinnees," he replied, "ever since you put me in this place, I've not lifted my head. So take pity upon me, and treat me kindly!"

When the vizier heard these words, he asked, "What are you saying? I'm the bride's father, not a jinnee."

"Enough of this! You've practically been the death of me!" answered the hunchback. "Get out of here before he finds you here. Couldn't you have married me to someone else instead of the lady love of buffaloes and the beloved of jinnees? Allah curse her and curse him who married me to her and who has caused me such misery!"

And Scheherazade noticed that dawn was approaching and stopped telling her story. When the next night arrived, however, she received the king's permission to continue her tale and said,

Then the vizier said to him, "Get up and out of this place!"

"Do you think I'm crazy?" responded the hunchback. "I won't leave here without the permission of the ifrit, whose last words to me were: 'When the sun rises, get up and go your way.' So, has the sun risen or not? I won't budge from this place if it hasn't!"

"Who brought you here?" asked the vizier.

"I came here last night to answer a call of nature," said the hunchback, "and suddenly a mouse came out of the water and squeaked at me. The next thing I knew it swelled and grew until it was as big as a buffalo and uttered threats to me that I fully understood! Then he left me here and went away. May Allah curse the bride and him who married me to her!"

The vizier walked up to him and lifted his head out of the cesspool hole, and the hunchback ran out of the privy for dear life and did not bother to check whether the sun had risen or not. Indeed, he headed straight for the sultan and told him everything that had happened to him. In the meantime, the vizier returned to the door of the bride's private chamber, very worried about her, and he said to her, "Daughter, explain this strange matter to me!"

"It's simple," she answered. "The bridegroom to whom they displayed me last night lay with me all night and took my virginity, so that now I am with child by him. He is my husband, and if you don't believe me, his turban, dagger, and trousers are beneath the bed along with something wrapped up in them."

When her father heard this, he entered the private chamber and found the turban which had been left there by Badar al-Din Hasan, and he took it in his hand, turned it over, and said, "This is the turban worn by viziers. The only difference is that it's made of Mosul material." So he opened it, and, finding what seemed to be an amulet sewn up in the fez, he unsewed the lining and took it out. Then he lifted up the trousers that contained the purse of the thousand gold pieces. After opening the purse, he found the written receipt of the Jew made out to Badar al-Din Hasan, son of Nur al-Din, the Egyptian, and the thousand dinars were also there. No sooner had Shams al-Din read this than he uttered a loud cry and fell to the ground in a faint. As soon as he revived and understood the gist of the matter, he was astonished and said, "This must be the will of Allah the Almighty! Do you want to know, daughter, who it was who took your virginity?"

"Yes, of course," she replied.

"Truly, it was your cousin, the son of my brother, and this thousand dinars is your dowry. Praise be to Allah! If only I knew how all this has come about!" Then he opened the amulet that had been sewn in the lining of the turban and found a piece of paper in the handwriting of his deceased brother. When he saw the handwriting, he kissed it again and again, and he wept over his dead brother. Then he read the scroll and discovered the recorded dates of his brother's marriage with the daughter of the vizier of Bassorah, the night that he took her virginity, and the birth of Badar al-Din Hasan, and all his brother's doings up to the day of his death. He was greatly astounded by all this and shook with joy. Then he compared the dates with his own marriage, the taking of his wife's virginity, and the birth of their daughter, Sitt al-Husan, and he found that they matched perfectly with those of his brothers. Then he took the document, went with it to the sultan, and told him everything that had happened from first to last. Indeed, the sultan was so impressed by the wondrous events that he ordered them to be recorded at once.

Now the vizier stayed with his daughter expecting his brother's son to return, but he did not appear. So the vizier waited a second day, a third, and so on until the seventh day, but there was no news of him. So he said, "By Allah, I'm going to do something that's never been done before!" And he took pen and ink and drew a plan of the whole house on a sheet of paper. He showed the whereabouts of the private chamber with the curtain in such a place and the furniture in another and so on until he had noted everything that was in the room. Then he folded up the sketch and ordered all the furniture to be collected along with Badar al-Din's garments, the turban, robe, and purse. Afterward he had everything taken to his house, where he locked them up with a padlock on which he set his seal. Finally he declared that the lock was not to be opened until his nephew, Badar al-Din Hasan, returned.

After nine months passed, the vizier's daughter gave birth to a son as radiant as the full moon, the image of his father in beauty, loveliness, shape, and grace. Once the umbilical cord was cut and his eyelids penciled with charcoal to strengthen his eyes, they named him Ajib the Wonderful and gave him to the nurses and governesses. His early years passed rapidly, and when he became seven, his grandfather sent him to school and ordered the master to teach him the Koran and to educate him well. He remained at the school four years until he began to bully his schoolmates and abuse them.

"Who among you is like me?" he cried. "I'm the son of the vizier of Egypt!"

Finally, the other boys went to the assistant master to complain about how harshly Ajib had been treating them, and he said to them, "I'll tell you something you can do to him so that he'll stop coming to school. When he enters tomorrow, sit down around him, and one of you is to say to the other, 'By Allah, nobody is allowed to play this game unless he tells us the names of his mama and his papa, for he who doesn't know the names of his mother and father is a bastard, a son of adultery, and he won't be permitted to play with us.'"

When morning dawned, the boys went to school, and they flocked around Ajib and said, "Let's play a game, and no one can join unless he tells us the name of his mother and father." And everyone agreed. Then one of them cried out, "My name's Majid, and my mommy's name is Alawiyah, and my daddy's Izz al-Din." Another spoke up, followed by a third, until it was Ajib's turn, and he said, "My name's Ajib, and my mother's is Sitt al-Husan, and my father's Shams al-Din, the vizier of Cairo."

"By Allah," they cried out, "the vizier's not your true father!"

"Yes, the vizier is my father!" Ajib responded.

Then the boys all laughed and clapped their hands at him and cried out, "He doesn't know who his papa is! Get away from us! Nobody can play our game unless he knows his father's name."

Thereupon, they ran around him, laughed at him, and derided him. So he became choked up with tears, and his feelings were hurt. Then the assistant master said to him, "We know that the vizier is your grandfather, the father of your mother, Sitt al-Husan, and not your father. But neither you nor we know your father, for the sultan married your mother to the hunchbacked horse groom. Supposedly a jinnee came and slept with her, but nobody knows your father for sure. So stop bragging about yourself and mocking the little ones at the school until you know whether you have a legal father. Until then you'll pass among them as a child of adultery. Even a huckster's son knows his own father, but you only know your grandfather and not your father. So, be sensible and don't brag or exaggerate anymore!"

When Ajib heard these insulting words from the assistant master and the schoolboys and understood their reproach, he left the school at once and ran to his mother. But he was crying so bitterly that his tears prevented him from speaking for a while. When she heard his sobs and saw his tears, her heart felt as though it were on fire for him, and she said, "My son, why are you weeping? May Allah keep the tears from your eyes. Tell me what has happened to you."

So he told her all that he had heard from the boys and the assistant master and ended by asking, "And who is my father?"

"Your father is the vizier of Egypt," she replied.

"Don't lie to me!" he answered. "The vizier is your father, not mine! Who's my father? If you don't tell me the truth, I'll kill myself with this dagger."

When his mother heard him speak about his father, she recalled her cousin, the bridal night, and all that happened then, and she wept. Then she wailed and shrieked loudly, and her son did the same. All at once the vizier came in, and he was extremely upset by the way they were lamenting.

"Why are you crying?" he asked.

So the Lady of Beauty told him what had happened between her son and his schoolmates, and he also began to weep, since he recalled what had occurred between him and his brother and what had happened to his daughter and how he had failed to solve the mystery of her giving birth to Ajib. Then he got up and went straight to the sultan and told his tale, after which he asked his permission to travel to Bassorah and inquire about his brother's son. In addition, he requested that the sultan write him letters, authorizing him to take Badar al-Din into his custody, no matter where he might be. And he wept before the king, who took pity on him and wrote royal letters to his deputies in different cities and countries. So now the vizier rejoiced and prayed that Allah might help him. After taking leave of his sovereign, the vizier returned to his house, where he equipped himself, his daughter, and grandson Ajib with all the necessary things for a long journey. Then they set out and traveled three days until they arrived at Damascus, where the vizier set up camp on the open space called Al-Hasa. After pitching the tents, he said to his servants, "We'll stop here for two days."

So his servants went into town on several occasions to sell and buy this and that. They also went to the Hammam bath and visited the cathedral mosque of the Banu Umayyah, the Ommiades, which has nothing like it in the world. Ajib also went with his attendant eunuch to enjoy the city, and the servant followed with a staff of almond wood so heavy that if he struck a camel with it the beast would never rise again. When the people of Damascus saw Ajib's handsome features and perfect grace (for he was a marvel of comeliness and loveliness, softer than the cool breeze of the north, sweeter than the fresh water that the thirsty man drinks, and more pleasant than the good health that everyone desires), many followed him, while others ran on before him and sat alongside the road until he came by so that they could gaze at him. Then, as destiny had decreed, the eunuch stopped opposite the shop of Ajib's father, Badar al-Din Hasan, whose beard had grown long and thick and who had matured during the twelve years that had passed. During that time the cook had died, and Hasan of Bassorah had inherited his goods and shop, for he had been formally adopted before the kazi and witnesses. Now, when his son and the eunuch happened to stop near his shop, he gazed at Ajib with a throbbing heart and was drawn to him through blood and natural affection. Since he had just finished making a conserve of pomegranate grains with sugar, he called to his son, Ajib, and said, "My lord, you've overwhelmed my heart, and I would feel honored if you would grace my house and ease my soul by joining me in a repast of meat."

Then his eyes streamed with tears that he could not prevent, for he thought about all that he had gone through and all that he had become. When Ajib heard his father's words, his heart also yearned to be with him, and he looked at the eunuch and said, "To tell the truth, my good guard, my heart goes out to this cook. He is like one that has a son far away from him. So let us enter and warm his heart by accepting his hospitality. Perhaps, if we do so, Allah may reunite me with my father."

When the eunuch heard these words, he cried, "By Allah, what a thing to do! Shall the sons of viziers be seen eating in a common cook's shop? Indeed, I've kept the folk off you with my staff so they won't even dare look at you. And now I won't permit you to enter this shop at all."

When Hasan of Bassorah heard this speech, he was astounded and turned to the eunuch with tears pouring down his cheeks, and Ajib said, "Truly, my heart loves him!"

But the eunuch responded, "Stop this talk! I won't let you go in."

Thereupon, Hasan turned to the eunuch and said, "Worthy sir, why won't you warm my soul by entering my shop? Oh, you who are like a chestnut, dark but inside white of heart! Discreet and polite, angels would vie for your service."

The eunuch was pleased by these words, and so he took Ajib by the hand and went into the cook's shop. Then Hasan offered them saucers with pomegranate grains wonderfully coated with almonds and sugar and said, "You have honored me with your company. Please eat, and may you have good health and happiness!"

In response, Ajib said to his father, "Sit down and eat with us so that Allah might perhaps unite us with the man we long for."

"My son," said Hasan, "have you suffered the loss of a loved one in your tender years?"

"Indeed, I have," answered Ajib. "My heart burns for the loss of a beloved who is none other than my father. This is why I and my grandfather have gone out to search the world for him. It's such a pity that we haven't found him, for I long to meet him!" Then he wept a great deal, and his father also wept upon seeing him weep and also on account of his own bereavement, for he recalled his long separation from his mother and dear friends. And the eunuch was moved to compassion. Then they ate together until they were satisfied, and Ajib and the slave rose and left the shop. Immediately Hasan felt as though his soul had left his body and had gone with them, even

though he did not know that Ajib was his son. Since he
did not want to lose sight of the boy, he locked up his
shop and hurried after them. And he walked so fast that
he caught up with them before they had gone through the
west gate. Now the eunuch turned toward him and said,
"What's the matter with you?"

"When you left me," Badar al-Din replied, "it seemed
as though my soul had gone with you, and since I had
some business outside the city gate, I thought I might
keep you company until I took care of my affairs."

The eunuch was angry and said to Ajib, "This is just
what I had feared! We ate that unlucky mouthful (which
we are bound to respect), and now this fellow is following us from place to place, for the vulgar can do nothing
but vulgar things."

Upon seeing the cook behind them, Ajib's face red-
dened with anger, and he said to the servant, "Let him
walk the highway of the Moslems, but when we turn off
to go to our tents and he's still following us, we'll send
him packing!" Then he bowed his head and moved on
with the eunuch walking behind him. But Hasan was not
daunted, and he followed them to the plain Al-Hasa, and
as they drew near, Ajib became very angry, fearing that
the eunuch might tell his grandfather what had happened. His indignation was particularly great because his
grandfather might learn that the cook had followed them
after they had entered the cook's shop. So he turned and
looked at Hasan of Bassorah and found his eyes fixed on
his own, for the father had become a body without a
soul, and it seemed to Ajib that his eyes were treacherous or that he was some lewd fellow. So his rage increased and, stooping down, he picked up a stone weighing
half a pound and threw it at his father. It struck him on
the forehead, cutting it open from eyebrow to eyebrow
and causing the blood to stream down. Then Hasan fell
to the ground in a swoon while Ajib and the eunuch
made for the tents. When Hasan came to himself, he
wiped away the blood, tore off a strip from his turban,
and bandaged his head. Then he began reprimanding
himself and said, "I shouldn't have shut my shop and
followed the boy! It wasn't right. Now he probably thinks
that I'm some evil-minded fellow."

Then he returned to his place, where he opened up the

shop and proceeded to sell his sweetmeats as usual. However, he yearned to see his mother in Bassorah and wept when he thought about her. In the meantime, the vizier stayed in Damascus three days and then traveled to Emesa, making inquiries about Hasan along the way. From there he journeyed to Bassorah by way of Hamah, Aleppo, Diyar Bakr, Maridin, and Mosul. As soon as he secured lodgings there, he presented himself to the sultan, who treated him with high honor and respect due to his rank. When the sultan asked him the reason for his coming to Bassorah, the vizier told him all about his past and that the minister Nur al-Din was his brother. Upon hearing this, the sultan exclaimed, "May Allah have mercy on him!" Then he added, "My good sahib, he was my vizier for fifteen years, and I loved him very much. Then he died leaving a son who dwelled here for only one month after his father's death. Since that time, he's disappeared, and nobody has had any news of him. But his mother, who is the daughter of my former minister, is still with us."

When Shams al-Din heard that his nephew's mother was alive and well, he rejoiced and said, "Oh king, I would very much like to meet her."

The sultan gave him permission right away to visit her, and so he went to the mansion of his brother, Nur al-Din, where he cast sorrowful glances at all the things in and around it and kissed the threshold. Then he began weeping as he thought about his brother and how he had died in a strange land far away from kith and kin and friends. As he passed through the gate into a courtyard, he found a vaulted doorway built of hardest syenite with an inlay of different kinds of multicolored marble. After walking though this doorway, he wandered about the house and saw the name of his brother, Nur al-Din, written in gold upon the walls. So he went up to the inscription and kissed it and wept while thinking of how he had been separated from his brother and how he had now lost him forever. Then he walked on until he came to the apartment of the mother of Badar al-Din.

From the time of her son Badar al-Din's disappearance, his mother had never stopped weeping for him. And when the years grew long and lonely, she had a tomb of marble built in the middle of the salon, and she used to weep for him day and night and always slept close by. When the vizier drew near her apartment, he heard her voice and stood behind the door while she addressed the sepulcher. As she was talking, he entered and greeted her. Then he informed her that he was her husband's brother and told her the entire story of what had happened between them. In addition, he related to her how her son Badar al-Din Hasan had spent a whole night with his daughter ten years ago but had disappeared in the morning, and he ended by saying, "My daughter gave birth to a boy through your son, and your grandson is with me."

When she heard the news that her boy Badar al-Din was still alive, and when she saw her brother-in-law, she arose and threw herself at his feet and kissed them. Then the vizier sent for Ajib, and his grandmother stood up, embraced him, and wept. But Shams al-Din said, "This is no time for weeping. This is the time to get you ready for a journey to Eygpt. Let us hope that Allah will reunite you and me with your son and my nephew."

"As you wish," she said and immediately began to gather together her baggage, jewels, equipment, and slave girls for the trip while the vizier went to take his leave from the sultan of Bassorah, who requested that he carry presents and rare items from him to the sultan of Egypt. Then he set out at once on the homeward journey and came to Damascus, where he stayed at the same place. After pitching tents, he said to his company, "We'll stay here one week to buy presents and rare things for the sultan."

Now Ajib remembered what had happened before and said to the eunuch, "I want some amusement. Come, let us go down to the great bazaar of Damascus and see what's become of the cook whose sweetmeats we ate and whose head we broke, for he was indeed kind to us and we treated him badly."

"As you wish," the eunuch answered.

So they left the tents, and Ajib was drawn toward his father. After passing through the city gate, they walked through the streets until they reached the cook's shop, where they found Hasan of Bassorah standing at the door. It was near the time of the midafternoon prayer, and it so happened that he had just finished making a

confection of pomegranate grains. When Ajib and the
eunuch drew near him, Ajib's heart pounded with yearning, and when he noticed the scar from the stone that he
had thrown had darkened on Hasan's brow, he said to
him, "Peace be with you! I want you to know that my
heart goes out to you!"

But when Badar al-Din looked at his son, his heart
fluttered, and he bowed his head and remained speechless. Then he raised his head humbly toward the boy and
said, "Heal my broken heart and eat some of my sweetmeats. By Allah, I cannot look at you without my heart
fluttering. Indeed, I should not have followed you that
other time, but I couldn't control myself."

"By Allah," answered Ajib, "you certainly do care for
us! We ate a mouthful the last time we were in your
house, and you made us repent it, for you almost dis-
graced us by following us. So now we won't eat here
unless you promise us not to go out and trail us like a
dog. Otherwise, we won't visit you again during our
present stay. We'll be here one whole week, for my
grandfather wants to buy certain presents for the sultan."

"I promise to do just as you wish," said Hasan.

So Ajib and the eunuch entered the shop, and his
father set a saucer with pomegranate grains before them.

"Sit down and eat with us," Ajib said. "Let us hope
that Allah will dispel our sorrows."

Hasan was exceedingly happy and sat down and ate
with them, but his eyes kept gazing fixedly on Ajib's
face. Finally, the boy said to him, "You're becoming a
nuisance. Stop staring at my face!"

But Hasan kept feeding Ajib morsels of the pomegranate grains, as well as the eunuch, and they ate until they
were satisfied and could eat no more. Then they all got
up, and the cook poured water on their hands. After
loosening a silken waist shawl, he dried their hands and
sprinkled them with rose water from a bottle he had with
him. Then he went out and soon returned with a goglet
of sherbet flavored with rose water, scented with musk,
and cooled with snow. He set this before them and said,
"Complete your kindness to me!"

So Ajib took the goglet, drank from it, and passed it to
the eunuch. And it went round until their stomachs were
full, and they were content with a larger meal than they

were accustomed to eat. Then they went away and walked
hurriedly to their tents, and Ajib went in to see his
grandmother, who kissed him, and thinking of her son,
Badar al-Din Hasan, she groaned aloud and wept. Then
she asked Ajib, "My son, where have you been?"

And he answered, "In the city of Damascus."

Thereupon she arose and set before him a bit of scone
and a saucer with conserve of pomegranate grains, which
was sweetened too much, and she said to the eunuch,
"Sit down with your master!"

And the servant said to himself, "By Allah, we don't
have any desire to eat right now. I can't stand the sight of
food." But he sat down, and so did Ajib, although his
stomach was full of what he had already eaten and drunk.
Nevertheless, he took a bit of the bread and dipped it in
the pomegranate conserve and started eating, but he
found it too sweet and said, "Uggh! What's this terrible
stuff?"

"Oh, my son," cried his grandmother, "don't you like
my cooking? I made this myself, and no one can cook it
as nicely as I can except for your father, Badar al-Din
Hasan."

"By Allah, my lady," Ajib answered, "this dish tastes
terrible, especially when you compare it to the pomegranate grains made by the cook in Bassorah. His dish
has such a wonderful smell that it opens the way to your
heart, and the taste makes a man want to eat it forever.
Your dish can't match his in the least."

When his grandmother heard his words, she became
extremely angry and looked at the servant.

*And Scheherazade noticed that dawn was approaching
and stopped telling her story. When the next night arrived,
however, she received the king's permission to continue
her tale and said,*

"You will pay for this!" the grandmother said to the
servant. "Do you think it's right to spoil my grandson
and take him into common cook shops?"

The eunuch was frightened and denied taking Ajib
there. "We didn't go into the shop," he said. "We only
passed by it."

"By Allah," cried Ajib, "we *did* go in, and we ate till

it came out of our nostrils, and the dish was better than grandmother's dish!"

Then his grandmother rose and went to her brother-in-law, who was incensed by the eunuch's actions. Consequently, he sent for him and asked, "Why did you take my grandson into a common cook's shop?"

Since he was frightened, the eunuch answered, "We did not go in."

But Ajib said, "We *did* go inside and ate the pomegranate grains until we were full. And the cook also gave us iced and sugared sherbet to drink."

Upon hearing this, the vizier's indignation increased, and he continued questioning the castrato, who kept denying everything. Then the vizier said, "If you're speaking the truth, I want you to sit down and eat in front of us."

So the eunuch sat down and tried to eat. However, there was nothing he could do but throw away the mouthful.

"My lord," he cried, "I've been full since yesterday!"

Now the vizier knew that the eunuch had eaten at the cook's shop and ordered his slaves to give him a beating. So they began giving him a sound thrashing until he pleaded for mercy. "Master, please tell them to stop beating me, and I'll tell you the truth."

The vizier ordered his slaves to stop and said, "Now tell the truth!"

"Well," said the eunuch, "we really did enter the cook's shop, and he served us pomegranate grains. By Allah, I never ate anything as delicious as that in my life, and I must admit that this stuff before me has a nasty taste."

The eunuch's words made the grandmother very angry, and she said, "I've heard enough! Now you must go back to the cook and bring me a saucer of his pomegranate grains and show it to your master. Then he'll be able to judge which tastes better, mine or his."

"I'll do as you say," the eunuch replied.

The grandmother gave him a saucer and half a dinar, and he returned to the shop and said, "Oh sheikh of all cooks, we've made a wager in my lord's house concerning your abilities as a cook. Someone has made pomegranate grains there, too, and we want to compare it to half a dinar's worth of yours. So give me a saucerful and make sure it's your best, for I've already been given a full meal of a beating with sticks on account of your cooking, and I don't want them to make me eat more of that kind."

Hasan laughed and answered, "By Allah, no one can prepare this dish as it should be prepared except for me and my mother, and she's in a country quite far from here."

Then he ladled out a saucerful, and after finishing it off with musk and rose water, he sealed it in a cloth and gave it to the eunuch, who hurried back to his master. No sooner did Badar al-Din's mother taste it and examine the excellent way it had been cooked than she knew who it had prepared it. All at once she uttered a loud scream and fell down in a faint. The vizier was most startled by this and sprinkled rose water on her. After a while she recovered and said, "If my son is still alive, then it was he who prepared this conserve of pomegranate grains and nobody else! This cook must be my very own son, Badar al-Din Hasan. There is no doubt in my mind, nor can there be any mistake, for only he and I know how to prepare pomegranate grains this way, and I taught him."

When the vizier heard her words, he rejoiced and said, "How I long to see my brother's son! We've waited so long for this meeting, and only Allah can help us bring it about." Then he arose without delay, went to his servants, and said, "I want fifty of you to go to the cook's shop with sticks and staffs. You're to demolish it, tie his arms behind him with his own turban, and say, 'It was you who made that stinking mess of pomegranate grains!' and drag him here with force but without doing him any harm."

And they replied, "You can count on us to carry out your command."

Then the vizier rode off to the palace right away and met with the viceroy of Damascus and showed him the sultan's orders. After careful perusal, the viceroy kissed the letter and asked, "Who is this offender of yours?"

"A man who is a cook," said the vizier.

So the viceroy sent his guards to the shop at once, and they found it demolished and broken into pieces, for while the vizier had gone to the castle, his men had carried out his command. Then they waited for his return from the viceroy, and Hasan, who was their prisoner, kept saying to himself, "I wonder what they found in the conserve of pomegranate grains to do this to me!"

When the vizier returned from the viceroy, who had given him official permission to take his debtor and depart with him, he called for the cook. His servants brought him with his arms tied by his turban, and when Badar al-Din Hasan saw his uncle, he began to weep and said, "My lord, what have I done to offend you?"

"Are you the man who prepared the conserve of pomegranate grains?" asked the vizier.

"Yes," Hasan answered. "Did you find something in it that calls for the cutting off of my head?"

"You deserve even worse!" replied the vizier.

"Then tell me what my crime is, and what's wrong with the pomegranate grains!"

"Soon," responded the vizier, and he called aloud to his servants and said, "Bring the camels here."

So they pulled up the tents, and the vizier gave orders to his servants to put Badar al-Din Hassan in a chest, which they padlocked, and to place him on a camel. Then they departed and traveled until nightfall, when they halted and ate some food. Badar al-Din Hasan was allowed to come out of the chest to eat, but afterward he was locked up again. Then they set out once more and traveled until they reached Kimrah, where they took him out of the chest and brought him before the vizier, who asked, "Are you the one who prepared that conserve of pomegranate grains?"

"Yes, my lord," he answered.

And the vizier said, "Tie him up!"

And they tied him up and returned him to the chest and journeyed until they reached Cairo, where they stopped in the quarter called Al-Raydaniyah. Then the vizier gave orders to have Badar al-Din taken out of the chest, sent for a carpenter, and said to him, "Make me a cross of wood for this fellow!"

"And what will you do with it?" cried Badar al-Din Hasan.

And the vizier replied, "I intend to crucify you on it.

I'm going to have you nailed to the cross and paraded all about the city!"

"Why? Why are you punishing me like this?"

"Because of your vile cooking! How could you prepare conserved pomegranate grains without pepper and sell it to me that way?"

"Just because it lacked pepper you're doing all this to me! Wasn't it enough that you destroyed my shop, locked me in a chest, and fed me but once a day?"

"Too little pepper! Too little pepper! This is a crime that can only be expiated on the cross!"

Badar al-Din Hasan was astounded and began to mourn for his life. Thereupon the vizier asked him, "What are you thinking about now?"

"About dunceheads like you!" responded Hasan. "If you had just an ounce of any sense, you wouldn't be treating me like this!"

"It's our duty to punish you like this," said the vizier, "so that you'll never do it again."

"Your least punishment was already too much punishment for what I did!" Hasan replied. "May Allah damn all conserves of pomegranate grains and curse the hour when I cooked it! I wish I had died before this!"

But the vizier responded, "Nothing can help you. I must crucify a man who sells pomegranate grains that lack pepper."

All this time the carpenter was shaping the wood, and Badar al-Din looked on. At nightfall, his uncle had him locked up in the chest again and said, "Tomorrow the thing shall be done!" Then he waited until he was sure that Badar al-Din was asleep, whereupon he mounted his horse, entered the city, and had the chest brought to his own house. Then he entered his mansion and said to his daughter, Sitt al-Husan, "Praise be to Allah, who has reunited you with your husband! Get up now and arrange the house as if it were your bridal night!"

So the servants arose and lit the candles, and the vizier took out his plan of the nuptial chamber and told them what to do until they had put everything in its proper place so that whoever saw the chamber would have believed that it was exactly the same as it was on the very night of the marriage. Then he ordered them to put Badar al-Din Hasan's turban beneath the bed with his bag trousers and the purse. After this he told his daughter to undress herself and go to bed in the private chamber as on her wedding night, and he added, "When your uncle's son comes into the room, you're to say to him, 'You've certainly dallied in the privy a long time!' Then call him and have him lie by your side and talk to him until daybreak, when we will explain the whole matter to him."

Then he had Badar al-Din Hasan taken out of the chest. After untying the rope from his feet and arms, he had everything stripped off him except the fine shirt of blue silk in which he had slept on his wedding night so that he was practically naked. All this was done while he was utterly unconscious. Soon thereafter, as if decreed by destiny, Badar al-Din Hasan turned over and awoke, and finding himself in a vestibule bright with lights, he said to himself, "Surely I'm in the middle of some dream." So he arose and explored his surroundings until he came to an inner door and looked in. To his surprise he saw he was in the very chamber in which the bride had been displayed to him, and he saw the bridal alcove and the turban and all his clothes. He was so bewildered by what he saw that he kept advancing and retreating and said to himself, "Am I asleep or awake?" And he began rubbing his forehead and saying, "By Allah, this is definitely the chamber of the bride who was displayed to me! Where am I then? Moments ago I was in a chest!" While he was talking to himself, Sitt al-Husan suddenly lifted the corner of the chamber curtain and said, "Oh lord, don't you want to come in? Indeed, you've dallied a long time in the privy."

When he heard her words and saw her face, he burst out laughing and said, "Indeed, this is a very nightmare among dreams!" Then he sighed and went in, pondering what had happened, and he was perplexed by all that was happening. Everything became even more mysterious when he saw his turban and trousers and found the purse containing the thousand gold pieces. So he muttered, "By Allah, I'm surely having some sort of wild daydream!"

Then the Lady of Beauty said to him, "You look so puzzled and perplexed. What's the matter with you? You were a very different man at the beginning of the night."

He laughed and asked her, "How long have I been away from you?"

And she answered, "By Allah, you've only been gone an hour and have just returned. Have you gone clean out of your head?"

When Badar al-Din Hasan heard this, he laughed and said, "You're right, but when I left you, I became distracted in the privy and dreamed that I was a cook in Damascus and lived there ten years. And I met a boy who was the son of a great noble, and he was with a eunuch." As he was talking, he passed his hand over his forehead and, feeling the scar, he cried out, "By Allah, oh my lady! It must have been true, for he struck my forehead with a stone and cut it open from eyebrow to eyebrow. And here is the mark. So it must have happened." Then he added, "But perhaps I dreamed it when we fell asleep, you and I, in each other's arms. Yet, it seems to me that I traveled to Damascus without tarbush and trousers and worked as a cook." Then he was confused and thought awhile. "By Allah, I also imagined that I had prepared a conserve of pomegranates and put too little pepper in it. I must have slept in the privy and have seen all of this in a dream. But that dream was certainly long!"

"And what else did you see?" asked Sitt al-Husan.

So he told her everything and soon said, "By Allah, if I hadn't wakened, they would have nailed me to a cross of wood!"

"What for?" she asked.

"For putting too little pepper in the conserve of pomegranate grains," he replied. "And it seemed to me that they demolished my shop, destroyed all my equipment, and put me in a chest. Then they sent for a carpenter to make a cross for me, and they would have crucified me on it. Thanks to Allah, this happened to me in a dream, and not while I was awake!"

Sitt al-Husan laughed and clasped him to her bosom, and he embraced her. Then he thought again and said, "By Allah, it couldn't have happened while I was awake. Truly I don't know what to think of it all."

Then he lay down, and throughout the night he kept wondering about what had happened, sometimes saying, "I must have been dreaming," and then saying, "I was awake." When morning arrived, his uncle, Shams al-Din, came to him and greeted him. When Badar al-Din Hasan saw him, he said, "By Allah, aren't you the man who ordered that my hands be tied behind me and that my shop be smashed? Weren't you going to nail me to a cross because my dish of pomegranates lacked a sufficient amount of pepper?"

Thereupon the vizier said to him, "I must tell you, my son, that the truth has won out! All that was hidden has been revealed. You are the son of my brother, and I did all this to you to make sure that you were indeed the young man who slept with my daughter the night of her wedding. I couldn't be certain of this until I saw that you knew the chamber and the turban, trousers, and gold, for I had never seen you before, and I couldn't recognize you. With regard to your mother, I have prevailed upon her to come with me from Bassorah." After saying all this, he threw himself on his nephew's breast and wept for joy. After hearing these words from his uncle, Badar al-Din Hassan was astonished and also shed tears of delight. Then the vizier said to him, "All of this happened, my son, because your father and I once had a major quarrel." And he told him why they had separated, and why his father had journeyed to Bassorah. Finally, the vizier sent for Ajib, and when Badar saw him, he cried, "This is the one who struck me with the stone!"

"This is your son!" said the vizier.

And Badar al-Din Hasan embraced him and was extremely happy to be with his son. Just then his mother entered and threw herself into his arms. Then she wept and told him what had happened to her since his departure, while he related to her what he had suffered, and they thanked Allah Almighty for their reunion.

Two days after his arrival, the Vizier Shams al-Din went to see the sultan, and after kissing the ground, he greeted him in a manner suited for kings. The sultan rejoiced at his return, and after placing the vizier by his side, he asked him to tell him all that he had seen during his journey and all that had happened to him. So the vizier told him all that had occurred from first to last, and the sultan said, "Thanks be to Allah for your triumph, your reunion with your children, and your safe return to

your people! And now I want to see your brother's son.
So bring him to the audience hall tomorrow."

Shams al-Din replied, "He will stand in your presence
tomorrow, if it be God's will."

Then the vizier saluted him and returned to his own
house, where he informed his nephew of the sultan's
desire to see him, whereupon Hasan consented. So the
next day he accompanied his uncle to the divan, and after
saluting the sultan, he showed him his respect with a
courtly verse. The sultan smiled and signaled him to sit
down. After Hasan took a seat close to his uncle, Shams
al-Din, the sultan asked him his name.

"Your lowliest of slaves," said Badar al-Din Hasan, "is
known as Hasan the Bassorite, who prays for you day
and night."

The sultan was pleased by these words and began
testing his learning and good breeding, and Hasan rose to
the occasion with witty and polite verses.

"Hasan," said the sultan, "you've spoken extremely
well and have proved yourself accomplished in every
way. Now explain to me how many meanings there are in
the Arabic language for the word *khál* or mole."

"May Allah keep the king," replied Hasan, "there are
fifty-seven, but some say according to tradition that there
are only fifty."

"You're correct," said the sultan. "Do you have any
knowledge as to the points of excellence in beauty?"

"Yes," answered Badar al-Din Hasan. "Beauty con-
sists in brightness of face, clearness of complexion, shape-
liness of nose, gentleness of eyes, sweetness of mouth,
cleverness of speech, slenderness of shape, and seemli-
ness of all attributes. But the acme of beauty is in the
hair."

The sultan was so captivated by the way Hasan spoke
that he regarded him as a friend and asked, "What's the
meaning of the saying 'Shurayh is foxier than the fox'?"

And Hasan answered, "Oh sultan, you must know that
the lawyer Shurayh was accustomed to making visits to
Al-Najaf during the days of the plague, and whenever he
stood up to pray, a fox would come and plant himself in
front of him. Then, by mimicking his movements, the fox
would distract him from his devotions. Now, one day,
when this became tiresome to him, he doffed his shirt

and set it upon a cane and shook out the sleeves. Then, placing his turban on the top and making a belt with a shawl around the middle, he stuck it up in the place where he used to pray. Soon the fox trotted up as he was accustomed to do and stood across from the figure. Then Shurayh came from behind and grabbed the fox. Hence the saying 'Shurayh is foxier than the fox.' "

When the sultan heard Badar al-Din Hasan's explanation, he said to his uncle, Shams al-Din, "Truly, your brother's son is perfect in courtly breeding, and I'm convinced that there's no one like him anywhere in Cairo."

Upon hearing this, Hasan arose and kissed the ground before him and sat down again as a mameluke should sit before his master. When the sultan had thus assured himself of his courtly breeding and bearing and his knowledge of the liberal arts and belles lettres, he rejoiced and invested him with a splendid robe of honor and promoted him to an office that would help him advance his career. Then Badar al-Din Hasan arose and requested the king's permission to retire with his uncle. The sultan consented, and the two returned home, where food was set before them, and they ate what Allah had given them. After finishing his meal, Hasan went to the sitting chamber of his wife, the Lady of Beauty, and told her what had happened between him and the sultan, whereupon she said, "I'm sure that he will make you a boon companion and bestow favors on you. In this way, the rays of your perfection will spread on shore and on sea thanks to Allah's blessing."

"I propose to write a kasidah, an ode, in the sultan's praise," he said, "and perhaps his affection for me may increase."

"That's a good idea," she answered. "Weigh your words carefully, and I'm sure that the sultan will look upon your work with favor."

So Hasan shut himself up in his chamber and composed a remarkable poem. When he had finished transcribing the lines, he had one of his uncle's slaves carry them to the sultan, who read the poem and was very pleased by it. In fact, he read the ode to all those present, and they praised it with the highest praise. Thereupon, the sultan sent for the writer, and when Hasan entered his sitting chamber, he said, "From this day on you will be my boon companion, and I'm granting you a monthly salary of ten thousand dirhams over and above what I granted you before."

So Hasan arose and, after kissing the ground before the sultan several times, prayed for the king's glory, greatness, and long life. Thus Badar al-Din continued to gain great honor, and his fame spread to many regions. He lived in comfort and took great delight in life with his uncle and his own people until death overtook him.

After the Caliph Harun al-Rashid heard this story from the lips of his vizier, Ja'afar the Barmecide, he was extremely astounded and said, "These stories deserve to be written down in liquid gold." Then he granted the slave his freedom and endowed the young man who had slain his wife with a monthly stipend that would suffice to make his life easy. He also gave him a concubine from among his own slave girls, and the young man became one of his boon companions.

"Yet, this story," continued Scheherazade, "is in no way stranger than the tale of the hunchback."

"And what happened to him?" asked the king.

"Have patience," Scherherazade said, and she asked his permission to tell her tale the following night, and the king was most happy to grant her wish.

PENGUIN POPULAR CLASSICS

Published or forthcoming